TWO FACES OF OEDIPUS

ALSO TRANSLATED BY FREDERICK AHL

Virgil, *Aeneid*
Seneca, *Trojan Women*
Seneca, *Phaedra*
Seneca, *Medea*

TWO FACES OF OEDIPUS

SOPHOCLES' *OEDIPUS TYRANNUS*

AND SENECA'S *OEDIPUS*

TRANSLATED AND WITH

AN INTRODUCTION BY

FREDERICK AHL

Cornell University Press

ITHACA AND LONDON

First published 2008 by Cornell University Press
First printing, Cornell Paperbacks, 2008

Printed in the United States of America

Library of Congress Cataloging-in-Publication Data

Two faces of Oedipus : Sophocles' Oedipus Tyrannus and Seneca's Oedipus / translated and with an introduction by Frederick Ahl.
  p. cm.
  Translator attributes second work to either Seneca the Younger (ca. 4 B.C.–65 A.D.) or to Seneca the Elder (ca. 55 B.C.–ca. 39 A.D.).
  Includes bibliographical references and index.
  ISBN 978-0-8014-4635-1 (cloth : alk. paper)—ISBN 978-0-8014-7397-5 (pbk. : alk.paper)
  I. Ahl, Frederick, 1941– II. Seneca, Lucius Annaeus, ca. 55 B.C.–ca. 39 A.D. III. Sophocles. Oedipus Rex. English. IV. Seneca, Lucius Annaeus, ca. 4 B.C.–65 A.D. Oedipus. English. V. Title: 2 faces of Oedipus. VI. Title.

  PA4414.O7A35 2007
  882'.01—dc22

                              2007029239

Cloth printing   10 9 8 7 6 5 4 3 2 1
Paperback printing   10 9 8 7 6 5 4 3 2 1

For Pietro Pucci
And in memory of
Alan Ansen and
Gordon Kirkwood

Contents

Acknowledgments

Many people have contributed to the production of this long overdue book. Most of all I thank Max Brecher of Amsterdam, whose interest and enthusiasm kept me going when I felt like giving up, and who offered not only encouragement but much sound advice on many aspects of Sophocles' *Oedipus* as a work of philosophy and theater and whose forthcoming novel about Oedipus will make exciting reading. I also thank those who have helped me test the translations in several public performances and less formal readings in Athens and in Ithaca (New York): Lee Carole Owen, Sandor Goodheart, Cole Long, Brian Rose, Brad Wilson, and above all my colleague of many years, Pietro Pucci, who has read through both translations for me. He and I have vastly different views about the meaning of Sophocles' *Oedipus* and he took upon himself the task of making sure that my translation did not violate, as it were, the neutrality of the Greek text, which we both share. He and Gordon Kirkwood, between them, made central New York a place where Sophoclean studies flourished.

I am grateful also to the National Endowment for the Humanities, which granted me a Translation Fellowship in 1991. This is a down payment on a debt still partially due, since I was not fortunate enough to be awarded a leave from teaching to take up the grant.

I also thank my colleagues, Jeff Rusten and Iannis Tsiogas; Brett de Bary and the Society for the Humanities at Cornell University; Kimon Iokarinis and Steve Diamant of College Year in Athens, and Rosemary Donnelly, John Zervos, and Sally Tong of the Athens Centre; and Bernhard Kendler, Teresa Jesionowski, and Roger Haydon of Cornell University Press, without whose support the project would never have been finished, and Herman Rapaport of Wake Forest University, who offered many useful suggestions and criticisms. My greatest debt, however, is to Nicola Minott-Ahl who offered many suggestions about wording, phrasing, and costuming, and assisted me through countless hours of rehearsing performances.

F.A.

TWO FACES OF OEDIPUS

Facing the entrance hall, just past the gate, in the gullet of Orcus,
Sorrows have set up their quarters, and Heartaches crying for vengeance.
Here pale Diseases reside, grim Senility, Terror, and Hunger
Powering evil and crime, and Poverty, vile and degrading,
Shapes terrifying the eyes that behold. Then there's Death and Hard Labour.
Next lurks listless Sleep, Death's blood-relation, and nearby
Evil Pleasures of Mind and, across, in the opposite threshhold,
War, who is bearer of Death, steeled bedrooms of Family Vengeance,
Mad Civil Strife, viper hair interlaced by her gore-clotted ribbons.
Centrally set: a dark elm with extending branches, its forearms,
Centuries old, peopled strangely. It's here that what men deem elusive
Dreams wreathe nests, it is said, clinging tightly beneath all its foliage.
Many additional monsters lurk here, bestial hybrids:
Centaurs have stables adjoining the gates, as do Scyllas—part human,
Part beast—Briareus, too, with his hundred arms, and the Hydra
Hissing out terror; Chimaera, whose weapons are flames; then the Gorgons,
Harpies, and Cerberus' shape with its three-bodied shadow.

Virgil, *Aeneid* 6.273–89

Two Faces of Oedipus
An Introductory Essay

As Sophocles' tragedy *Oedipus* opens, Oedipus faces a crisis. He is expected to be able to handle it because he resolved a major crisis at some point in the past by solving the riddle of the Sphinx. That's why he, an outsider, is now the tyrant of Thebes. How many years previously he solved the riddle we never learn. For the Sphinx belongs to the once-upon-a-time mythic past as, to a large extent, does Oedipus himself. And myth collapses time. The Sphinx, conventionally represented in Greek art as a fantastical winged and taloned quadruped, with the body of a lion and the head of a woman, appears to have predicated her existence on the assumption that no one could solve her verbal puzzle, the traditional form of which is, at least in later antiquity, this: What moves first on four feet, then on two feet, then on three? We can't be sure this formulation represents either the riddle as Sophocles envisaged it or the Sphinx as he envisaged her. No one in *Oedipus* says what the riddle was or details what the Sphinx looked like.

If Sophocles did so envisage the riddle and the Sphinx, then Oedipus, in grasping that the answer is man, acknowledges a definition of human-ity in terms of feet. At best, he has done what Plato's Socrates did when he described man as a wingless biped, a description the Cynic philosopher Diogenes later mocked when he produced a plucked chicken and declared that this was Plato's man.

Why there should have been a national crisis in Thebes because no one, not even the expert on prodigies, Teiresias, could solve a kind of children's riddle posed by an improbable winged female quadruped is never explained

1

in the play.[1] As we will see later, there were several different explanations current in antiquity for what the Sphinx was, almost all more plausible than the one familiar from Greek poetry and pottery, and almost all more obviously menacing to Thebes. But, whatever the riddle and the Sphinx were in Sophocles' mind, Oedipus is proud that he has used his intellect to render them harmless.

Unfortunately, as the play opens, the problem he faces is a plague. And plagues are not as amenable as are folk-tales, riddles, or philosophical abstractions to verbal solutions. Sphinxes are like the monsters lurking under the leaves on Virgil's elm, the tree of punishment in the underworld, creatures of myth. They are imaginary. Plagues are real. The mythic Oedipus, as he steps into the world of stage reality before an audience of living people who have experienced a plague, is challenged to deploy his mythic expertise on a real-world problem.

When asked by the Priest of Zeus to take action, Oedipus declares he has done the best thing he could think of doing. He has sent his brother-in-law Creon to consult the Delphic oracle. Oedipus has thus delegated authority to a man whose name suggests that he should be occupying the position Oedipus holds because "Creon" means "Ruler" in Greek. Creon would, logically, have served as interim ruler of Thebes between the death of the previous tyrant, Laius, and Oedipus' accession to power. But Sophocles does not have his characters clarify this issue; both Oedipus and Creon avoid discussing it.

Oedipus re-empowers traditional religion not only by turning to an oracular source but also by summoning the same expert on prodigies whose authority has been hurt in the past by his inability to solve the Sphinx's riddle. He expects, though he expresses a hint of reluctance, that Teiresias may help with a crisis he cannot deal with himself. Mythic Thebes and, for that matter, historical Athens of the fifth century BC, have default substructures of traditional beliefs. Religious leaders and popular spokesmen learn how to adapt to changing conditions and are able to resume power as soon as the intellectuals, who on occasion displace them, begin to tire and flag, unable to provide the kind of instant answers to social problems that had initially swept them into power. In that sense, the story of Oedipus, as framed by Sophocles, is as

---

[1] I use the more familiar Greek spelling Teiresias instead of the Latin Tiresias in both plays, and the Romanized Greek spelling Polyneices instead of the Latin Polynices throughout this introductory essay.

political as it is psychological or philosophical, and as modern as it is ancient. It could as easily serve as a model for the collective experience of a society as for that of a particular individual.

Our traditional way of reading Sophocles' *Oedipus* validates Oedipus' behavior in a very unsettling way. For the testimony on which Oedipus bases his arguments and conclusions is extraordinarily flimsy and contradictory. We never even learn the exact words of the response Creon receives at Delphi, since Sophocles gives us only Creon's summary and interpretation of it. But, presuming that Creon is reporting and interpreting the oracle correctly, the gist of it is that the plague is caused by the unsolved murder of the former tyrant Laius.

Most of us understand that diseases are not caused by unsolved murders in the distant past and cured by verbal magic or acts of contrition. So did the ancient Athenians, as Thucydides makes clear in his *History* (2.47). But there are always those, in the modern as well as in the ancient world, who are ready to believe that God or the gods punish communities for the crime of an individual. Many readers suppose that Sophocles was such a believer himself and interpret the play on the basis of this supposition.

This book explores the myth of Oedipus not just through Sophocles' *Oedipus* but also through Seneca's. It differs from other studies in that, among its contents, are translations of the two plays, not just arguments about them. The views expressed in this introductory essay, however, are the by-product of the translation process, rather than the precursors or shapers of the translations. They could as easily be read after as before reading the translations. They are intended to raise questions rather than to dictate answers. I did my first draft of both translations long before I wrote anything about either play.

The academic world treats translation with a certain disdain, as if it were distinct from "real" scholarship, an improvised vehicle for conveying to those who cannot read the original languages a general sense of what the original says or ought to be saying. As a result, translations tend to be either by-products (rather than primary products) of scholarly activity or products of a specialized craft whose practitioners are not necessarily otherwise involved in the critical investigation of the authors they translate. The result is that translations of the two *Oedipus* tragedies are often fuzzy, where Sophocles is precise, or prosaic, where Seneca is poetic, but in either case simplified versions of their originals.

The first play, that of Sophocles, composed in Greek some two thousand five hundred years ago, is today the most famous of all ancient tragedies and, by general consensus, a literary masterpiece. The second, composed in Latin some two thousand years ago, is today among the least commonly read of ancient tragedies, largely because the scholarly world regards it as a dull and vastly inferior work.

I began my translation of the Senecan play to see if I could convey my feeling that Seneca had been misjudged. I wanted to transpose his Latin into an English form that retained his poetic power without straying too far from the "literal" meaning of the Latin. No word or nuance was to be glossed over, and I tried hard not to paraphrase. Any work of literature, of course, takes on a different appearance once you have gone over it syllable by syllable and reassembled it in another language. And the Senecan tragedies are particularly difficult to render into English because the original Latin is so compressed that our grammar and syntax need at least twice as many words as Seneca needs to convey the full force of his poetry. But Seneca's *Oedipus* proved to be a far more interesting work of poetry than I had imagined. And when I staged it, I was delighted at what good theater it was. There is a kind of power in Senecan thought and language that has few rivals.

I translated Sophocles' *Oedipus* because I had always had problems teaching it in translation. Translators are so confident that they know what the play is about that they cut corners and, in their attempts to smooth out conflicting statements, make a complex text far too simple. I also wanted to come to terms with that disquieting feeling almost everyone has when transposing Greek into English: that one cannot easily do so without somehow Latinizing it and Christianizing it. While my dictionaries assured me, for instance, that Greek *physis* meant "nature," as does Latin *natura,* decades of reading and teaching ancient Greek texts made me unhappy with treating *physis* as an image of birthing, as *natura* is (from *nasci,* "to be born"), rather than as an image of "begetting" or "sprouting." So I spent time going over some of Sophocles' most frequently used words, in particular, those whose "roots" were felt, rightly or wrongly, to be semantically related by Greek authors. *Alétheia* and *léthe,* for example, are normally translated by words with different roots in English: "truth" and "forgetfulness, oblivion," respectively. I worked to retain something of the Greek "root-sense relationship" without distorting the English. For Sophocles' *Oedipus* is, more than any other ancient tragedy, a play about shifts in language, naming, and definition.

4

1. The Life of Sophocles: A Brief Sketch

Sophocles, son of Sophillos, was born in 497 or 496 BC and died in 406–405. He was a prominent citizen of Athens during the heyday of Athenian imperial democracy and held the (annually) elected office of *stratēgós*, "leader of the armed forces," "general," though in practice, "admiral," since Athens' main military arm was her fleet. Each year Athens elected ten *stratēgoí*, who were the highest political and military officials in the state. During his ninety years of life, Sophocles saw Athens occupied and destroyed by invading Persians in 480 BC and saw the Persians defeated in 480 and 479. He saw Athens' era of expansion and warfare. And he saw Athens' gradual collapse during the Peloponnesian War (431–404 BC) against a league of Greek city-states, including Corinth and Thebes, led by Sparta, which had the strongest and essentially the only professional army in Greece. But he did not live to see Athens' defeat and surrender in 404.

During one major crisis (413–411), after Athens had lost an entire army in Sicily, Sophocles was probably appointed to a board of commissioners (*próbouloi*) to manage the city under conditions approximating limited martial law. There remains, however, some confusion about the nature and extent of his political and military career, because he had a namesake: Sophocles son of Sostratides, an important Athenian military commander in the early years of Peloponnesian War.[2]

What we know of Sophocles' life suggests that he may have been associated with those, such as Socrates and certain of his students, like Critias and Theramenes, who, to varying degrees, wanted to reform, limit, or even overthrow democracy.[3] That does not mean Sophocles favored disenfranchisement of the people, but rather that he favored the placement of some checks on popular power. Democracy in Athens, if one bears in mind that

---

[2] Donald Kagan in his popular and influential *The Peloponnesian War* (New York and London, 2004) does not distinguish the two at all in his text and lists just one Sophocles in his index, which the incautious reader is bound to suppose is the tragedian since Sophocles' poetic activities are mentioned on pages xxiii and 328–29.

[3] For more on Sophocles' political career, see Victor Ehrenberg, *The People of Aristophanes* (Oxford, 1951), 353; cf. 146 and 355–57 and his long discussion in *Sophocles and Pericles* (Oxford, 1954), 75–105. P. Karavites, "Tradition, Skepticism, and Sophocles' Political Career," *Klio* 58 (1976): 359–65; M. H. Jameson, "Sophocles and the Four Hundred," *Historia* 20 (1971): 541–68; Martin Ostwald, *From Popular Sovereignty to the Sovereignty of Law: Law, Society, and Politics in Fifth-Century Athens* (Berkeley and Los Angeles, 1986), 340–41. For a different view, see Harry Avery, "Sophocles' Political Career," *Historia* 22 (1973): 509–14.

women have never been full citizens in any country until the last century or so, pretty well meant what the word says, "people-rule." Each male citizen had the right to speak in the Assembly and to vote on *all* issues, and to submit his name for appointment to public office, by lottery, or, in the case of the office of *strategós*, by election. No elected official, however, was empowered to declare war. Only the people declared war. What we call "democracy," Athenians would have regarded as a mixed system of oligarchy, plutocracy, and limited term monarchy in which the people speak and vote on national issues in the Assembly, through the intermediacy of *prostátai*, "champions" or "spokesmen," elected from among candidates chosen by oligarchic clubs. The people itself has no direct political control between elections. Among the male population of Athens only foreigners or slaves needed to speak through a *prostátes*. All Athenian women, however, needed *prostátai*.

The Athenian democracy was capable, as are all governments, of behaving criminally and irresponsibly. Around the time *Oedipus* was produced, the Athenians voted to condemn to death the entire male population of one of their allies, the city Mytilene, because it had revolted from the alliance; all the women and children were to be sold into slavery. The people were prompted to this action, the historian Thucydides says (3.36), by Cleon, an orator who wielded immense persuasive power in the Assembly and was the most famous *prostátes* of the disenfranchised in Athenian history. A warship was dispatched to carry out the sentence. But the next day (and here we see a better side of democracy) an otherwise unknown citizen argued that it was not in Athens' interests to behave in this way. His motion won approval and another warship was dispatched to countermand the orders given to Paches, the commander of the first trireme. In an exciting narrative, Thucydides (3.49.2) describes the arrival of the second warship in the harbor of Mytilene just as Paches was preparing to carry out his orders. The atrocity was prevented.

The Athenian democracy could change its mind in a flash, as Oedipus does in Sophocles' *Oedipus,* where, in less than fifty lines, he first declares he will have Creon put to death and then frees him altogether, thanks to the intervention of his wife. In 416 BC, however, long after *Oedipus* was produced, the Athenians condemned the population of Melos to precisely the same doom and carried out the sentence.

After the massacre on Melos, Athens overextended itself in war, and in 405 BC stood on the brink of defeat by the forces of Sparta, Corinth, and Thebes. Its three greatest tragic poets, part of whose function was to educate adults, were dead. Aeschylus had died a half-century earlier. But Sophocles and Euripides had died just a year before. In 405, the comic poet, Aristophanes, presented a comedy, *Frogs,* in which Dionysus, the god of wine and of drama, goes to the underworld to bring back the ghost of Euripides to help Athens at this critical time. The god's choice is surprising, since Athens' Spartan foes often made it clear that they would be readier to negotiate if Athens agreed to replace democracy with a more oligarchic form of government. Yet Dionysus is off in quest of Euripides, the quintessentially democratic poet.

When Dionysus arrives, he finds himself judge of a poetic contest between the ghosts of Euripides and Aeschylus and alters his plans. He decides that he will bring the winner back to life. That the winner proves to be Aeschylus seems, at first glance, as much the product of wishful thinking (that Athens could be back in her glory days) as anything else, since the ghostly Aeschylus knows nothing about the last half-century. But lurking amidst Aeschylus' comic banter is a very strangely undemocratic allegory: that although one should not nurture the cub of a lion, king of beasts, in the city, one should humor him if one does. It is a statement that, however tentatively, validates the option of suspending democracy as it appears to have been suspended during the days of the Persian invasion in 480 BC.

More curiously still, Sophocles' ghost does not put himself forward as a competitor. This is odd for a dramatist who had not only won more first prizes than either of his rivals, but had also, alone among the three great tragedians, served as a general in wartime. Aeschylus had fought in the ranks, not as a leader, at the famous victory over the Persians at Marathon in 490 BC. Aristophanes probably calculated that Sophocles would not be a good name to suggest to the people overtly, since Athens was living under the threat of a coup d'état orchestrated by Socrates' student Critias, who was planning to replace democracy with an oligarchy. Critias, along with the more moderate Theramenes, had earlier been associated with the suspension of democracy in 411.[4] And Sophocles may have been linked with them in 411 when he served on the board of commissioners.

Sophocles probably had a too arguably nondemocratic profile to be a viable choice for resurrection. And Aristophanes' large and rowdy audience might have concluded that Aristophanes was himself advocating a suspension

---

[4] Aeschines 1.173. See also J. Roisman, *The Rhetoric of Conspiracy in Ancient Athens* (Berkeley and Los Angeles, 2006), 72, 79, and the sources cited.

of democracy if he had gone in quest of him, rather than Euripides. So Aristophanes politely bypasses Sophocles and allows Aeschylus, the "common soldier" poet, long dead and free of entanglements in the politics of the day, to drop the covert hint that democracy might need to be compromised to secure peace with the Spartans.

In staging *Frogs* on several occasions, I noticed that Aristophanes could still have had Dionysus bring Euripides back instead of Aeschylus by changing just a few lines, since he defers the decision until the end of the play. Because his presentation of the two dramatists invites audience response, Aristophanes could, in fact, have had two endings ready to go, depending on audience reaction. After all, he was presenting *Frogs* in a competition and wanted to win the prize. If Aristophanes took his cue from the audience in deciding the outcome, instead of just hoping he had guessed correctly, then both audience and playwright would have been satisfied. In such a case Aeschylus would emerge as the *audience's* choice, rather than that of Dionysus or of Aristophanes himself. And all parties concerned could have read in this response a tacit willingness to accept, if not an active desire for, a more limited democracy.

All this is not to say that Sophocles (or Aristophanes) was a kind of rightwing conservative. Lenin also recognized the need for some system of checks and balances in the state, as did the founders of the American republic. And the critics of Athenian democracy were a varied group. When Critias overthrew the democracy the next year, 404, he went farther than many had expected and conducted a purge of his more moderate associates. One of his first victims was Theramenes, who was executed by being compelled to drink hemlock. Plato's Socrates argues in the *Apology* that, although he was not killed by Critias (as Theramenes was), he did not collaborate with Critias in his reign of terror. Yet I suspect that the trial and execution of Socrates (also by hemlock poisoning), carried out under the restored democracy in 399, was prompted as much by a popular desire to exact retribution for the political activities of those perceived as members of Socrates' circle of students and friends as by anything Socrates himself had ever thought, said, or done.

I mention these points because there is still a tendency to represent Sophocles as a kind of piously religious conservative and to read that perception of him into his tragedies. Sophocles appears, for instance, to have been among those responsible for introducing the cult of Asclepius, god of healing, to Athens, which is often taken as an indication of his religious conservatism. But Hippocrates, father of Greek medicine, was also in Athens at the time, founding his medical school, which he linked, symbolically, with the cult of Asclepius. And Hippocrates' *Epidemics* makes it plain that he was no naïve religious enthusiast. The serpents of Asclepius that he adopted as his symbols remain the symbols of the medical profession even today. In Sophocles' *Oedipus* 960, in fact, when a Corinthian stranger uses the word *rhopé*, "the tipping of the balance of the scales" in normal usage, to answer Oedipus' question as to the cause of Polybus' death, Oedipus takes it to mean that there was some sudden change in his medical condition, the way Hippocrates uses it in *Epidemics* 1.26.[5] As N. Collinge observes about Sophocles and medicine: "Sophocles is more truly medical, more seriously a devotee of the craft, than any other literary figure of the fifth and fourth centuries except (if we can call him literary) Aristotle."[6]

It is, I think, wiser to view Sophocles' scanty biographical information in the light of his tragedies than vice versa. And even there we have only around five percent of his output to go on.

Sophocles wrote at least a hundred and twenty-three plays (more than three times as many as Shakespeare), of which only seven survive. Their dates of production are not at all sure: *Ajax* (early, perhaps around 455), *Women of Trachis* (early, perhaps around 450), *Antigone* (between 444 and 441), *Oedipus* (probably between 429 and 425); *Electra* (around 420); *Philoctetes* (409), and *Oedipus at Colonus* (after 409; produced posthumously in 401). There are quotations here and there in ancient authors from numerous others tragedies. The "fragments" of these lost works are most accessible in Dana Sutton's *The Lost Sophocles*.[7] Sophocles won a phenomenal twenty-four first prizes at the festivals; *Oedipus*, however, was not among his successes.[8] He lost to the now forgotten Philocles. *Oedipus'* present popularity contrasts sharply with its less enthusiastic reception by the original judges.

The principal, but not the only, reason for dating *Oedipus* to the period between 429 and 425 is that Sophocles is the first writer to set the myth of Oedipus against the backdrop of a plague; and Athens experienced such a

---

[5] Aristotle, *Prob.* 1.861a uses the same expression as Sophocles' messenger in reference to the aged: *mikrà…rhopé*; cf. Aretaeus 3.12: "Old men…need only a short turn [*bracheías rhopês*] for the sleep of death." See also Bernard Knox, *Oedipus at Thebes* (New Haven, 1957), 184, and Thomas Gould, *Oedipus the King: A Translation with Commentary* (Englewood Cliffs, N.J., 1976), 63.

[6] N. Collinge, "Medical Terms and Clinical Attitudes in the Tragedians," *Bulletin of the Institute of Classical Studies* (1962): 47.

[7] D. Sutton, *The Lost Sophocles* (Lanham, Md., 1984). For the Greek texts see, H. Lloyd-Jones, *Sophocles Fragments* (Cambridge, Mass., 2003).

[8] See Stephen Radt, *Sophocles,* vol. 4 of *Tragicorum Graecorum Fragmenta* (Göttingen, 1977), 50.

plague, which we now know (if recent DNA tests on remains are correct) was typhoid fever, in 430–429 BC, with a recurrence in 427. It has been assumed by many that Sophocles' *Oedipus* was written and performed around this time, though surely not while the plague was at its height. And this may have been when he brought the cult of Asclepius, god of medicine, to Athens.[9] No one, to the best of my knowledge, has dated *Oedipus* earlier than 430 BC or later than 425 BC, even though there is no external evidence for any date at all. Some scholars, particularly those who want to see tragedy in isolation from contemporary events, or to bring Sophocles' three House of Oedipus tragedies closer together in time and construe them as if they were a trilogy, which they are not, prefer to be as vague as possible about performance dates. But there are quite plausible reasons for noting references to the politician Cleon in *Oedipus,* as we shall see. And Cleon does not become a major force in Athenian politics until around 430 BC, and dies in 422. His rise to power and tenure of power coincide with the plague and its aftermath.

The only other surviving tragedy generally dated to this period (429–425) is Euripides' *Hippolytus,* which shows some striking similarities with *Oedipus,* not only because it involves a father-son conflict and a stepmother's incestuous love for her illegitimate stepson, with disastrous consequences all round, but because both Hippolytus ("Destroyed by horses") in Euripides and Creon ("Ruler") in Sophocles, when accused of attempting to usurp power, argue that it is not in their natures to desire supreme power. Such similarities suggest that one play influenced the other. There is a great deal of such "intertextuality" in surviving tragedy. But who influenced whom is not always clear.

It seems to me most probable that *Oedipus* was produced either before the disease became epidemic, or, as lines 161–166 suggest, between the two outbreaks. The play gains some topical relevance if its *composition* is placed before the death of the great popular leader Pericles rather than after it, and that would mean 430 BC. If, by some mischance, composition preceded Pericles' death, but production occurred after Pericles' death in 429 BC, we may even have an explanation as to why *Oedipus* did not win the prize, as Sophocles' tragedies usually did. Whether Sophocles intended it or not, there were surely those who would have seen a parallel between the events

---

[9] Thucydides 2.47–51 and 3.87; *Etymologicum Magnum* 256.6. See J. S. Rusten, ed., *Thucydides: The Peloponnesian War* (Cambride, 1989), 179–192 and sources cited.

of the play and those of contemporary Athenian politics, where the influence of Pericles was beginning to crumble, and the rising star was a politician named Cleon.

2. The Life of Seneca: Some Tentative Sketches

While most Sophoclean scholars, whether they opt for an early date for the production of *Oedipus* or a later one, agree that the tragedy must be dated close to the great plague at Athens, Senecan scholars do not apply similar arguments to date Seneca's *Oedipus* close to the occurrence of any plague at Rome, for reasons, which, I hope, will soon become apparent.

The tragedies attributed to Seneca are the sole surviving examples of Roman tragedy. They have come down to us in a manuscript tradition that distinguishes "Seneca the Tragic Poet" from a composite "Seneca the Philosopher" and preserves their works separately.[10] But the two Senecas that modern scholars distinguish are the "Elder Seneca," the Rhetorician, and the "Younger Seneca," the Philosopher. They were father and son. Both lived in an era of imperial monarchy, not during a period of democracy, as did Sophocles. So the world of power they reflect is very different.

Seneca the Elder (circa 55 BC–AD 37) was born in Cordoba, Spain. He was a Roman citizen of equestrian rank (the second highest economic and social order of the Roman world). Unlike his more famous son (who probably edited some of his works), he was neither a senator nor a major figure in Roman political life. He was an expert on oratory, a man noted for, and proud of, his prodigious memory. He was also a subtle critic of both poetic and prose style, familiar with many of the important authors of the late Republic and early Imperial periods. His discussions of Ovid, in particular, show how close the worlds of rhetorical declamation and poetry were. His surviving works are the *Controversiae* and *Suasoriae*. And there are "echoes" of his attitudes to people and ideas in both the Younger Seneca and Lucan, author of one of the major works of Latin epic, the *Pharsalia* or *Civil War*. Further, in his *Controversiae* 2 (preface 3–4), the Elder Seneca praises his young son Mela's intellect as superior to that of his brothers and encourages him

---

[10] See R. J. Tarrant, "Greek and Roman in Seneca's Tragedies," *Harvard Studies in Classical Philology*, vol. 97, *Greece in Rome: Influence, Integration, Resistance* (1995), 215–230, and A. J. Boyle, *Roman Tragedy* (London and New York, 2006), for the best recent overview of Seneca and Roman tragedy. See also Janet Fairweather, *Seneca the Elder* (Cambridge, 1981).

to pursue his instinct to stay out of the political life that his brothers avidly pursue. Mela took that advice, but Mela's own son Lucan did not. Neither did the Younger Seneca.

Lucius Annaeus Seneca the Younger was also born in Cordoba, Spain, about 4 BC.[11] Like Sophocles, he lived at a major turning point in Western history. His younger brother, Annaeus Mela, was, as noted, the father of the poet Lucan, and his other brother, Lucius Iunius Novatus Gallio (so named because he was adopted by his father's friend, Iunius Gallio), is identified in Acts of the Apostles 18.12–18 as the proconsular governor of Achaea in Greece who refused to hear the Jewish case against Saint Paul. Early Christian writers were conscious of the contemporaneity of the founders of Christianity and the famous philosophical and political family of Seneca. Tertullian (*On the Soul* 20) describes Seneca as "often one of us." There even survives a collection of forged letters between Seneca and Saint Paul, full of mutual praise in rather awkward Latin.[12] People found it hard to believe that the world of the Annaei and that of the Christian missionary, which touched in so many ways, should not have yielded literary contact, especially since Paul and Seneca both fell victim to the emperor Nero. Paul and, traditionally, other disciples were put to death by Nero during his purge of Christians in the aftermath of the great fire at Rome and the ensuing plague (AD 64–65). Similarly Seneca and members of his family—Gallio and the apolitical Mela—were all suspected of involvement in a conspiracy to kill Nero. This plot began about the time of the fire (AD 64) and clearly involved Seneca's nephew, Lucan. The plot was discovered at the time of the plague (AD 65) and led to the forced suicides of Seneca and most of his male family members in AD 65.

The Younger Seneca spent most of his life in Rome under the Julio-Claudian imperial dynasty. He was born in Augustus' reign, held his first major political office under Tiberius (AD 33) and was a famous orator by the time Caligula succeeded to the throne (AD 37). Although his success

[11] See William Calder III, "Seneca, Tragedian of Imperial Rome," *Classical Journal* 72 (1976–77): 1–11. For bibliography see A. Balbo, I. Lana, and E. Malaspina, *Bibliographia Senecana del XX Secolo* (Bologna, 2005); also Anna Lydia Motto, *Seneca: A Critical Bibliography, 1900–1980* (Amsterdam, 1989); A. J. Boyle, *Roman Tragedy* and *Seneca Tragicus: Ramus Essays on Senecan Drama* (Berwick, Victoria, 1983), C. P. Segal, *Language and Desire in Seneca's Phaedra* (Princeton, 1984), and Thomas G. Rosenmeyer, *Senecan Drama and Stoic Cosmology* (Berkeley and Los Angeles, 1989).

[12] C. W. Barlow, *Epistolae Senecae ad Paulum et Pauli ad Senecam (Quae Vocantur)* (New York, 1938). Despite the forbidding title, the text is given both in Latin and in English translation.

apparently excited Caligula's jealousy, it was not until the first year of Claudius' reign (AD 41) that Seneca experienced the force of imperial displeasure. Claudius' wife, Messalina, arranged his banishment to the island of Corsica for eight years. He was recalled after Messalina's execution, when Claudius' ambitious fourth wife, Agrippina, arranged for him to be tutor to her twelve-year-old son Nero.

The Younger Seneca is notable not only as a politician but as a philosopher.[13] His major philosophical works, the *Epistles to Lucilius,* the *Moral Essays,* the *On Clemency* and *On Anger,* among others, mark him as one of the most important writers of the Stoic school. In very brief terms, the Stoics held that the universe was a finite, but infinitely divisible, material continuum, permeated by reason and presided over by a beneficent Divine Providence. All events follow a predetermined plan, since everything is bound together in a nexus of causality.

Seneca's Stoicism, however, is not doctrinaire. He frequently draws on ideas from other philosophical schools, notably the Epicureans, whose view of the universe was almost diametrically opposed to that of the Stoics. Epicureans held that the universe was made up of an infinite number of finite particles falling through an infinite void, but which formed temporary clusters, thanks to the spiraling force of a kind of cosmic wind and their own ability to swerve of their own will toward other neighboring atoms.

Seneca's famous treatise *On Anger,* often regarded as a quintessentially "Stoic" work, has much in common with Plutarch's *On Anger.*[14] Plutarch, however, had no patience with Stoicism, and wrote two stinging essays, along with extensive negative comments elsewhere, attacking what he considered to be the absurdities of Stoic philosophy: *On Stoic Self-Contradictions* and *Against the Stoics on Common Conceptions.*

The controlling force in the Stoic universe was fate (Greek *heimarméne* and Latin *fatum*); the controlling forces in the Epicurean universe were chance (Greek *tyche* and Latin *casus*) and free will. In neither the Stoic nor the Epicurean worlds are the gods malevolent; nor do they intervene to direct or redirect human behavior. And neither of these schools of philosophy came into existence until a century after the death of Sophocles.

[13] See Miriam Griffin, *Seneca: A Philosopher in Politics* (Oxford, 1992).

[14] For both the similarities and differences, see L. van Hoof, "Strategic Differences: Seneca and Plutarch on Controlling Anger," *Mnemosyne* 60 (2007): 59–68, and his extensive bibliography.

With Seneca's recall from exile in AD 49 began the period of his greatest political influence. He moved from being Nero's tutor to being his major adviser when Nero became emperor in AD 54, and his ascendancy lasted until at least AD 59, and, in a more limited way, until AD 62. Thereafter Nero became increasingly suspicious of him. Distrust came to a head with disclosure of the plot against Nero (AD 65) that culminated in Seneca's compelled suicide in AD 65.

The tragedies attributed to Seneca vary so widely in the subtlety of their thought, the intricacy of their poetry, and the power of their dramatic impact that one might sometimes think them an anthology of works by different hands. *Agamemnon,* for example, often echoes the phrasing and thought of *Trojan Women,* but somehow less effectively and pertinently. And the *Thyestes* is so brilliant that it might even be the lost and lamented tragedy of Varius.[15] The overwhelming consensus of scholars, however, is that all but one or possibly two of the collection were written by the Younger Seneca. And the remaining eight are widely interpreted as if they were the work of a Stoic philosopher writing tragedies about fate.[16]

I have included a biography of the Younger Seneca's father because that consensus of identification is modern and hangs on a very slender thread. While there is ample external testimony that the Greek *Oedipus* was written by Sophocles, there is only one piece of external testimony that connects *any* of the ten "Senecan" plays to someone named Seneca.

In *Instructing the Orator* 9.2.8, Quintilian cites *Medea* 354, which he attributes to a writer named Seneca. But, in the context of Quintilian's discussion of rhetoric, the reference could more reasonably be to the Elder Seneca, as it clearly is later in the same section (9.2.42), where he talks about Seneca's *Controversiae,* which survive and are unquestionably the work of the *Elder* Seneca. There is no indication that Quintilian is referring to a different Seneca in the second passage. The only reason for attributing the tragedies to the Younger rather than to the Elder Seneca is that, among the collection is an intruder from a different genre: a Roman historical drama, *Octavia.* In it the Younger Seneca and Nero are characters, and therefore the play could not have been written by the Elder Seneca, unless he was alive and writing at the age of over 120.

---

[15] See Tarrant, "Greek and Roman in Seneca's Tragedies," especially 216–17, and P. J. Davis' excellent *Seneca: Thyestes* (London, 2003).

[16] D. Henry and Walker, "The Oedipus of Seneca: An Imperial Tragedy," in *Seneca Tragicus,* ed. A. J. Boyle (Berwick, Vic., 1983).

14

Almost no one now believes that Seneca the Younger wrote *Octavia;* and substantial doubts have been raised about another play, among the ten that survive, *Hercules on Oeta.* The eight remaining plays are: *Hercules in His Madness, Medea, Trojan Women, Phoenician Women, Phaedra, Oedipus, Agamemnon,* and *Thyestes.* With *Octavia* removed from the Senecan *corpus,* the main reason to assume the writer of *Medea,* and perhaps other plays, was the Younger rather than the Elder Seneca is that to do otherwise we would have to re-think our scholarly models. The political environment and conditions affecting the public performance of drama changed substantially between the final decades BC, when Octavian (Augustus) controlled the Roman world, and the reigns of the emperors Caligula, Claudius, and Nero a half century or so later. There is no question that tragedies were performed publicly in the age of Augustus, but there are serious doubts about their public performance under subsequent emperors.

Although the Senecan *Oedipus,* like Sophocles', is set against the backdrop of a plague, scholars do not try to date his tragedy in proximity to any epidemic at Rome. Plagues or major famines are known to have occurred in Rome within the lifetimes of both the Elder and Younger Seneca: in 22 BC, AD 6, and AD 65. The first two dates are ruled out if one accepts the scholarly consensus, which attributes the tragedies to Seneca the Younger (4 BC–AD 65), since they are too far removed in time to be of immediate dramatic relevance. And 65 is too close to Seneca the Younger's own suicide to be appealing to most critics. So scholars assume that Seneca's *Oedipus* was not written with a contemporary plague in mind, but simply in imitation of Sophocles. If so, it is odd that the descriptions of the plague in Seneca are much longer and more medically precise than those in the medically minded Sophocles, who supplies little clinical detail. Indeed, they refer not only to a plague, even an enforced quarantine, but to an accompanying drought and thus, possibly, a famine.

I will return to the plague and the question of authorship later because I am intrigued by the possibility that there could be echoes of either Augustan or Neronian Rome in Seneca's *Oedipus,* as there are almost certainly echoes of (post-)Periclean Athens in Sophocles. Let me leave this topic now with one concluding paragraph.

One of the consequences of assuming that the author of the tragedies is the Younger Seneca is that it provides the kind of theoretical framework scholars like to have when interpreting literature. The Younger Seneca was a Stoic; therefore, some reason, these are "Stoic" tragedies. But not all determinism is Stoic. And though characters in Senecan tragedy often use the vocabulary of determinism, the dark universe they envisage, a universe in which there is no sense of a beneficent Providence or of any force capable of controlling the wickedness of humanity, does not fit well into the brighter Stoic slipper. It can be made to fit only if we compress the foot and stretch the slipper.[17] A tragedy is, after all, not a sermon. Even if viewed as in essence philosophical, it is a kind of Platonic dialogue of differing rather than identical voices and ideas which do not always arrive at an agreed conclusion. Different people see the world in different ways in drama, as in life.

3. Poetic Myth

Oedipus is the most familiar of all ancient Greek names in the modern world and Sophocles' *Oedipus* is now "perhaps *the* preeminent classical text in the Western tradition."[18] It has achieved this privileged position not only because Oedipus is the main character in a theatrical masterpiece by Sophocles, but also because Sigmund Freud used Oedipus to symbolize what he saw as the repressed desire of the son to kill his father and have sexual intercourse with his mother.[19] I say "used," because Freud does not explain Sophocles' *Oedipus* itself in such universal terms. He describes it, rather, as the drama of a particular legendary person who discovers that he actually did kill his father and marry his mother *without ever having wished to do so,* and who punishes himself for these acts as the god prescribes. In many ways it would, then, be truer to say that the German Romantics' reading of Sophocles' *Oedipus,* modified by Freud, rather than the play itself has become the privileged text.

Sophocles and the other Greek tragedians are poets: makers, and re-makers of myth, not anthropologists recording myth. They retold traditional stories

---

[17] For problems with the Stoic reading of Seneca, see Henry and Walker, *The Oedipus of Seneca,* 136 ff.; Denis Henry and Elizabeth Henry, *The Mask of Power: Seneca's Tragedies and Imperial Rome* (Chicago, 1985); also A. J. Boyle, *Roman Tragedy,* chapter 7, and "Senecan Tragedy: Twelve Propositions," *Ramus* 16 (1987): 78–101, and *Tragic Seneca: An Essay in the Theatrical Tradition* (London, 1997); cf. my own comments in *Seneca: Three Tragedies* (Ithaca and London, 1986). See Thomas G. Rosenmeyer, *Senecan Drama and Stoic Cosmology;* Anna Lydia Motto, *Seneca* (New York, 1973); Norman Pratt, *Seneca's Dramas* (Chapel Hill, 1983), and R. Mayer, "Personata Stoa: Neostoicism and Senecan Tragedy," *Journal of the Warburg and Courtauld Institutes* 57 (1994): 151–74, for the "Stoic" view.

[18] Peter Rudnytsky, *Freud and Oedipus* (New York, 1987), 337.

[19] See R. Caldwell, "The Blindness of Oedipus," *International Review of Psycho-Analysis* 1 (1974): 207–218, and David Konstan, "Oedipus and His Parents: The Biological Family from Sophocles to Dryden," *Scholia* 3 (1994): 3–23.

in contemporary settings in countless ways, outdoing one another with ever more surprising new twists of plot and detail. In doing so, they created characters assembled from prior literary tradition and local lore, endowed them with contemporary modes of thinking and behavior, and brought them to the stage where they were given an illusory sense of reality to their audiences and to "themselves." Tragedians made no attempt to re-create authentic scenarios of a "fixed" past, as historians do. With two exceptions, Greek tragedies do not take historical incidents and what we would call "real" people as their subject matter.[20]

What most distinguishes poetic myth from prose history is that tragic poets are usually presenting stories already familiar to audiences in unfamiliar ways. They are deconstructing and re-fashioning their audiences' sense of what they know. Historians are more often either creating a narrative of persons and events less familiar, even totally unfamiliar to their audiences, or trying to preserve the memory of a particular series of events that might otherwise be lost or assimilated to already existing traditions.

Understandably, once historical modes of thinking became established, and myths were transposed from poetry into prose, many readers, from ancient times on, began to approach Greek myth as if it were a kind of history colored by the fantastical. That is probably why, when referring to the actions of mythic characters, we tend to use the past tense, as if we were talking of historical personages, rather than the present tense, which we use when talking of personages in a novel: "Caesar became ruler of Rome" and "Creon became ruler of Thebes," but "Edmund Dantes *becomes* the Count of Monte Cristo." As a result, we sometimes assume that, lurking beneath, say, the mythic Creon is a real person whose biography can be set, at least in outline, rather than a generically named "Ruler" whose name (and whose mask) would to some degree declare its wearer's role and status relative to others in the drama.

The very idea of history, as we understand the term, does not really take shape until after the middle of the fifth century in the writings of Herodotus, Sophocles' contemporary. Herodotus is also the first extant writer of

---

[20] The only exceptions are the now lost tragedy by Phrynichus, *The Capture of Miletus,* who told of the fall of the Greek city of Miletus to the Persians in 492 BC, and was fined for reminding the Athenians of their own misfortunes, and Aeschylus' *Persians,* the earliest surviving tragedy, which gives us the earliest account of the battle of Salamis in 480 BC, and in which all the characters are Persian.

Greek prose. And the only prose writer listed among the Greek sources Herodotus cites in his *Histories* is Hecataeus of Miletus, of whose work some fragments survive. Before Hecataeus and Herodotus the evidence for the use of prose in Greek is more or less confined to data inscribed on stone. The Athenian public learned about its culture through poetic myth and local folklore, which did not yield just one Oedipus, as Freud implies, and a single, unified myth centered on Oedipus, but numerous variants.

4. What Are the Oedipus Tragedies About?

Oedipus was a character in several epics and in a number of tragedies in addition to those of Sophocles and Seneca. Aeschylus, Euripides, and Meletus (one of Socrates' accusers at his trial in 399 BC) all wrote Oedipus tragedies. Sadly, they, like most of the alternate Greek poetic versions, are lost. Oedipus was also noted as a personage by antiquarians, travelers, and historians. The two tragedies in this volume, then, are the only survivors from antiquity that tell us the most famous part of the story of Oedipus. In both, Oedipus concludes (a) that he has killed Laius, his predecessor on the Theban throne, (b) that Laius is his father, and (c) that his wife, Laius' widow, is also his mother. He then blinds himself and prepares to go into exile. Both plays are also set against the backdrop of a plague. So the questions that I now pose may seem to have self-evident answers. What are these two tragedies about? And are these two tragedies about the same thing?

Sophocles' *Oedipus* tells not one story, but several interwoven stories, each of which has its own dynamic. The synopsis I gave in the previous paragraph is the only one, however, to which we pay serious attention. If you are an actor, you will know that *Oedipus* tells other stories too.

There is a longish story about a powerful man, named Creon, "Ruler," whom the tyrant of Thebes accuses of planning a coup d'état. Creon declares he has no tyrannical ambitions, but is nonetheless threatened with execution. He survives, thanks to the intervention of the chorus and his sister, the tyrant's wife, and thanks to the tyrant's own willingness to defer to the opinions of others; by the end of the play, Creon has become ruler of Thebes without any opposition from either the chorus or his predecessor.

This second story, then, is about a change in the rulership in the city, made possible by the tyrant's self-indictment and self-punishment. It is *Oedipus* from Creon's point of view: the story of a ruler's rise, set in counterpoint to the story of Oedipus' fall. And it is as crucial to our understanding of the play as is the story of Oedipus himself.

There is a shorter story about a famous blind expert on prodigies whose most humiliating professional failure was his inability to solve the riddle of the Sphinx, which was instead solved by a mere amateur with no special training, whose success earned him the throne as his prize. But in the interim, the expert on prodigies has acquired formidable rhetorical skills, like those of the great Dominican and Jesuit preachers, and is now hailed by the chorus as the master of *élenchos,* "cross-examination" (it was tempting to use the word "inquisitor" in the translation here). He is given another chance to prove his abilities because the ruler cannot repeat, in dealing with the plague, the kind of triumph he enjoyed over the Sphinx. And the expert succeeds. He annihilates Oedipus rhetorically.

There is a long story about the people of a city who desperately want someone to find an end to the plague besetting them, and who are distressed that their leaders are quarreling among themselves and ignoring the problems of the city as a whole. They are, however, reluctant to choose sides in what they seem to regard as a struggle for power. Whether they obtain the desired end to the plague we never learn.

There is also a story about a widowed queen who is married to a man obsessed for years with the fear that he will kill his father and marry his mother, and who, she observes, believes anything frightening that anyone tells him. She has to move decisively to stop him from executing or banishing her brother, but then has to watch powerlessly as she sees him persuaded of things about his past that will clearly lead him to the conclusion that he is her child. Her life is ruined, regardless of whether she thinks he is right or wrong in drawing this conclusion. She is reported dead by a messenger shortly after her final exit, though her body is never brought on stage.

There is also a shorter story about a man from Corinth who rushes to Thebes, hoping to be rewarded for being the first to bring news that Oedipus' father Polybus is dead and that the throne of Corinth is therefore available, but who faces the unexpected dilemma that Oedipus does not want to go back to his home city. His hopes of a reward are ruined unless he can persuade Oedipus that there is no reason to be afraid of returning home.

There is an even briefer story of an old slave who is reputed (a) to be the houseboy, who, according to Creon and Jocasta, is the sole surviving witness to the killing of Laius, Oedipus' predecessor on the Theban throne, and (b) to be the herdsman who, instead of leaving Laius' unwanted child to die on the mountains, gave it to a shepherd from Corinth. This old man, being a slave, can give evidence only under torture according to the laws of Athens and of most Greek cities. He knows he must tell Oedipus what he suspects Oedipus wants him to say, if he is to evade protracted pain and possible death.

Sophocles' *Oedipus* is surely all of these stories. And even they do not constitute the whole picture. For Sophocles is telling them all more or less simultaneously to an audience that has itself just suffered through such a plague, or is currently suffering through it, and has either just lost its longtime popular leader, or is about to lose him; and that popular leader has a successor waiting in the wings.

In Seneca's *Oedipus* the focus is more tightly on Oedipus' self-examination from beginning to end. Although Seneca needs four actors to put his *Oedipus* on stage, one more than the three Sophocles uses, he could get by with two in most of the play. His *Oedipus* reads more like an early tragedy by Aeschylus than a tragedy by Sophocles. For the development of subplots demands careful use of the third actor.

Seneca's strategy here must be deliberate. In other plays, he deploys three actors to better dramatic effect than he deploys four here. In *Trojan Women,* for instance, three speaking characters are combined with two nonspeaking characters to create the most action-packed scene in either Greek or Roman tragedy. So unless we postulate that *Trojan Women* is by a different poet, there is no reason to assume that the author of the Latin *Oedipus* was incapable of crafting a complex scene if he had wanted to.[21]

Seneca also shapes in *Oedipus* an incipient story about the ruler's brother-in-law Creon, whose name in Latin, *Creo,* if it has any special significance, means "I create." Creon does indeed create some of the most elaborate verbal illusions in the play and is very different from Sophocles' Creon. He is in some ways more candid. He actually cites, in oracular hexameters, the Delphic oracle's response, whereas Sophocles' Creon gives Oedipus instead his own summary and interpretation of the oracle, not the response itself. He even tries to persuade Oedipus to abdicate. Seneca's Oedipus, however, assumes Creon is plotting a coup and throws him into a dungeon from which he does not re-emerge. The city has no ruler at all at the end of the Senecan tragedy. Oedipus thinks he is taking the plague with him as he leaves Thebes and expresses no interest in making any provision for a successor.

---

[21] The chorus in *Trojan Women* has a decidedly Epicurean outlook at several points, most notably in 371–408 and 1009–1055, the second of which echoes a famous passage of Lucretius (2.1–6).

Seneca's expert on prodigies consults the entrails and organs of oxen with the help of Manto, his daughter, who first appears in Euripides' *Phoenician Women* (though she is not named there). But Teiresias is uncertain about the meaning of the omens observed and never gets into a confrontation with Oedipus, as does Sophocles' Teiresias, even though Oedipus comes to suspect Teiresias is somehow in league with Creon. In his use of Teiresias Seneca differs profoundly from Sophocles. When Seneca's Teiresias takes omens, he discloses what will happen as the result of Oedipus' self-condemnation: the bull and heifer sacrificed clearly symbolize Oedipus and Jocasta, and the viscera predict future civil wars. Sophocles' Teiresias, in contrast, never looks beyond Oedipus in the play, takes no omens, and is more a master of dialectic than a seer. Oedipus, however, in both plays, is interested primarily in the past.

There is also, in Seneca, a story about a messenger from Corinth who brings Oedipus news of his father's death and his appointment as king of Corinth. And though he tries to dissuade Oedipus, if we follow the manuscripts' attribution of these lines to him, from enquiring into the details of his own past, he finally tells Oedipus a dubious tale of past events that leads Oedipus to conclude that he has killed his father and married his mother.

Another strikingly different element of the Senecan *Oedipus* is the chorus, which situates the story of Oedipus in a much larger mythical and geographical context than Sophocles' play does, and foregrounds the god Dionysus' relationship to Thebes, the city of his birth. The Senecan chorus transports us to an earlier generation, when Dionysus takes vengeance on the house of Cadmus, founder of Thebes, for the impiety of his grandson Pentheus, and even to Cadmus himself. In punishment for his arrogance, Pentheus is torn limb from limb by his mother Agave, his sister Ino, and other women of Thebes while they are under the spell of the god's magic. The tale is most famously told by Euripides in his tragedy *The Bacchae.* The chorus also takes us beyond the Greek world to Britain and to India and yet makes no mention of Italy. It is the geography of the Roman world, but without Rome.

Whether Seneca's *Oedipus* has any more specific frame of reference to the author's contemporary environment is largely unexplored, because the date of its composition is unknown and the identity of its author hangs on a single thread. There are a few clues, though they have not been followed with any success. But we should not assume that, because the subject matter is Greek myth, the core of its meaning is not Roman. In a famous passage from Tacitus' *Dialogus* (3.3), a Roman dramatist named Maternus, whose friends worried that he was attacking the tyranny of the Caesars too openly in his historical play about Cato (the Roman ideological opponent of Julius Caesar) replied that he would add what he had *omitted* in *Cato* in his forthcoming (and mythically Greek) *Thyestes*. The allegory of Greek myth afforded more freedom of expression than the presentation of a Roman historical personage. And this is what is so often saddening about Roman imperial literature. Its protests are cries of pain from residents of a huge and often luxuriously appointed intellectual prison more often than calls by the destitute for revolution. Roman writers cannot themselves lift the weight of tyranny that stands huge upon their tongues, but they want so desperately to be able to describe it.

I leave readers to piece together the remaining stories from Seneca, since, I think, the general pattern of Seneca's divergence from Sophocles is established. There is little doubt that Seneca's tragedy is about an Oedipus who is called a king, Latin *rex*. But *rex* is, in Roman political terms, a bad word, not a glamorous or "noble" word as it is in English. Rumors that he wanted to be king cost Julius Caesar his life. The cynical way Seneca's Oedipus expresses himself to, and handles, Creon is exactly what we would expect of a brutal autocrat and what Romans would expect of a *rex*. Sophocles' *Oedipus* is about an Oedipus, who, though called a tyrant (Greek *tyrannos*), behaves more like an elected or appointed official conscious of his need to defer to the people. That is why it is also a play about other people as well as Oedipus. And that is why Sophocles' tragedy is more dynamic as theater. It has a cast of arguing individuals performing before an audience empowered as individuals. In the top-heavy autocratic world of Seneca's *Oedipus,* the only persons the king has to listen to are those he chooses to listen to and himself. To oppose him is to invite and often get summary retaliation. And the audience, if there is one, is aware that it too is being watched by those who thrive, as informers, on regal paranoia. The strength of the Senecan *Oedipus* is the concentrated power of its frustrated political and moral energy compressed into poetry.

5. Freud and the Senecan Oedipus

Seneca was well known to the western European world from the Renaissance until the end of the eighteenth century; and, in the history of the European theater, his influence predates that of Sophocles by several centuries. By the time Sophocles was reintroduced to the literate public of London, Paris, and Vienna, Seneca had already shaped perceptions of tragedy. We must therefore be prepared to consider the paradox that while

Sophocles influenced Seneca, Seneca has himself influenced our understanding of Sophocles. The Oxford Classical Texts of Sophocles and Seneca frame the paradox perfectly: *Sophoclis Fabulae* and *Senecae Tragoediae: The (Roman) Plays* of Sophocles and *The Tragedies* of Seneca. The habit of calling Sophocles' tragedy by the Latin title *Oedipus Rex* further privileges the Roman perspective on the more famous Greek play.

Firsthand knowledge of the Greek language and of Greek literature was largely lost in western Europe from the capture of Rome by Alaric and the Goths in AD 410 until the fall of the "Eastern Rome," Constantinople, to the Ottomans over a thousand years later, in 1453. During that period, Christianity, the official religion of the Roman Empire from about a century before Alaric sacked Rome, had followed such different paths in the Latin west and the Greek east that a great rift had opened between (Greek) Orthodox Christianity in the eastern Roman empire and (Roman) Catholic Christianity in the western empire, a rift which was, and arguably still is, the most fundamental divide in mainstream Christian ritual and theology.

While knowledge of Greek disappeared in western Europe, the Latin language, in contrast, remained the fundamental idiom of learned discourse for over a thousand years after the fall of Rome's western empire, and even longer in some regions, such as Poland and Hungary, and in certain academic disciplines such as botany and zoology. But its vocabulary and its pre-Christian literature were accommodated to, and interpreted in the light of, Catholic Christian thought. Indeed, by the sixteenth century, there were those who began wondering whether the Renaissance had not officially re-paganized Catholic Christianity.

When Luther and Calvin broke with Catholicism and created Protestantism, they were as much in revolt against the Roman as against the Catholic. And with the fall of Constantinople to the Ottomans (who had little use for Christianity of any variety, or Greek poetry) and the invention of the printing press, a language and literature of greater antiquity than Latin—and untainted by Catholicism—became available and spread quickly. Virgil and Ovid gave way to Homer, Seneca to the Greek tragedians, and the Bible was translated from Greek into most vernaculars. Protestant Europe was busy re-inventing its past and building what it thought was a direct route between Germanic Europe and Greece, by-passing the catholicized Romans.

But one very Roman element remained. The new Protestantism was deterministic. God had a fixed plan for everyone and everything. Catholicism, in contrast, held the very non-Stoic view that while God was indeed omniscient, man was free to make his own decisions. Calvinist scholars "read" their determinism into their understanding of Greek literature, as the over-whelming surge of German scholarship came to dominate the interpretation of both Greek and Latin literature in the nineteenth and early twentieth centuries. It even swept away those who, like Freud and Nietzsche, were not themselves believers in Christianity. Freud and Nietzsche both went much further in the direction of a precisely fixed destiny than the Protestant Milton did two centuries earlier in *Paradise Lost*. In England, where the Anglican Church retained much of its Catholic heritage, the influence of Calvinistic determinism in mainstream thought was much more muted and the schol-arly environment much less anti-Roman.

Bearing this in mind, let us consider Freud's summary of Sophocles' *Oedipus*, which remains the starting point for many discussions today. In "The Development of the Libido and the Sexual Organizations," Freud writes,

> You all know the Greek legend of King Oedipus, who was *destined by fate* to kill his father and take his mother to wife, who did everything possible to escape the oracle's *decree* and punished himself by blinding when he learned that he had none the less unwittingly committed both these crimes. I hope many of you may yourselves have felt the shattering effect of the tragedy in which Sophocles has treated the story. The work of the Athenian dramatist exhibits the way in which the long-past deed of Oedipus is gradually brought to light by an investigation ingeniously protracted and fanned into life by ever fresh relays of evidence.[22]

Freud gives the impression that he is making Sophocles' character Oedipus the single exception to the universal validity of his Oedipus complex. He had little alternative but to do so, because the play touches on subjects that would have outraged, unless set forth with particular care, pious readers in much of the twentieth century: patricide and incest. Had he tried to argue that Sophocles' Oedipus was himself an exemplar of the Oedipus complex, he would have embroiled himself in a battle with classical scholars, who worked hard to demonstrate that Sophocles was a very pious man, and *Oedipus* a very pious play—thereby ensuring its acceptability as a school text.

---

[22] Sigmund Freud, *Introductory Lectures on Psychoanalysis,* trans. and ed. James Strachey (New York and London, 1966), 330. See below, p. 53, for a discussion of Freud's "fresh relays of evidence."

Since Freud is himself advancing a theory of primal urges innate to the human condition, his use of the language of fate in his summary of Sophocles' tragedy, cited above, is quite understandable, and, in a way, supportive of his own thesis. But before discussing the words I have italicized, let us look at a chorus from *Oedipus* which comments, just after Oedipus has blinded himself, on the human condition:

> Destiny herds us on.
> Do not fight destiny.   980
> Anxiety and fretfulness
> cannot alter the spun threads
> by which we hang.
> All we endure,
> we humans marked for death,
> all that we do
> comes from above.
> Lachesis keeps guard
> on her spindle's
> downward spinning law
> which no hand can rewind.
> Everything moves down
> a preset path:
> the last day is determined
> by the first.
> Our individual thread
> runs its straight path
> woven in its causal tapestry.   990
> No god can make it swerve,
> no prayer can shift
> what has been planned
> for each of us.
> Many, indeed, are ruined
> by their fear.
> Many achieve their destiny
> while and because
> they fear
> what destiny may have in store.

25

These lines, which seem to validate Freud's synopsis, are from Seneca's *Oedipus,* not from Sophocles'. That is why I have italicized certain words in the citation from Freud. They show Freud's Stoic and very Latin notion of "fate," which, by his day, had been subsumed into and intensified not only by Calvinistic Protestant theologians, but by mechanistic positivists in their notions of causal determinism. Calvin had placed the individual in a much more rigidly preordained world order than had Plato, in his *Republic,* or the Stoics, by whom he was much influenced. It is a rare Stoic who does not see the virtues of rival philosophical schools; for Stoicism, despite monotheist tendencies, gives at least lip service to the plurality of the divine. And determinism is more readily expressed in monotheistic terms than in terms of the quarrelsome gods of Greek epic and tragedy.

Sophocles' *Oedipus,* however, precedes the birth of Stoicism by a century. Stoicism comes to life in a world where the city-state has been disempowered and absorbed into the large international empires created by Alexander the Great and his successors. In the more "local," pre-Stoic world of the fifth-century BC city-states, Greek notions of the divine and other forces governing men's lives are not well represented in deterministic terms. Greek oracles predict; they do not decree. In Sophocles' *Oedipus* there is no Greek word that can properly be translated as "fate" or "destiny." The closest approximation is *moira,* which has more the sense of an assigned portion or lot. That's what it means in *Oedipus* 712–714, where the chorus prays that its *moira,* its "portion" or "lot" in life, may be "reverent purity in all I say and do." Yet, in the same passage (in 882–896), the chorus wishes a bad *moira* on those who behave insolently, and says that there is no point in dancing for god if god does not punish the arrogant. Here the sense is something akin to "doom" in the sense of "death." It is the visitation of divine justice *in response* to human misbehavior. And I have used the word "doom" to translate the few remaining instances of *moira* in Sophocles' play (lines 376, 713, 1302). It is, in general, the *moira* of all mortals to die. That is one's lot as a human being. But Sophocles does not use *moira* as an indicator of an entire nexus of causality.

Tyche, "coincidence," "chance," occurs twice as often as *moira* in Sophocles' *Oedipus.*[23] Richmond Lattimore is overly restrictive when he observes that it "does not mean 'fate,' 'chance,' or 'fortune,' so strictly as it means 'contact,' or, say, 'coincidence,' the way things are put together."[24] Clearly it

---

[23] See lines 52, 80, 102, 263, 442, 680, 776, 997, 1036, and 1080.

[24] Richmond Lattimore, "Oedipus Tyrannus," in *Twentieth-Century Interpretations of Oedipus Rex,* ed. M. J. O'Brien (Englewood Cliffs, N.J., 1968), 45.

does not mean "fate." But its range of meaning does extend into what we would describe in English as "luck," when good, and "misfortune," when bad. And, like "Lady Luck," it often has a sense of divinity about it. Indeed *tyche* is called a god in Sophocles fragment 314, line 79.

The Romans tended to distinguish "chance" from "Luck" more clearly than the Greeks. To the Romans *casus* was "chance" and *fortuna* "luck." Roman Stoics often used *fortuna*, "fortune," to symbolize what we would probably describe as "the pressure of transient events" which it was, paradoxically, the duty of the wise man to resist in his effort to follow the larger plan of "fate." But in Stoic and in Calvinist thought there was no such thing as chance in the sense of coincidence or luck as it is most often used in Sophocles' *Oedipus*. For the Stoics, chance was, rather, a kind of shorthand for non-evident causality. Their operative word was, in Greek, *heimarméne* ("the spun thread of destiny"), not found in Sophocles, and, in Latin, *fatum*, from which our word "fate" derives. Fate (or destiny) is a part of Seneca's vocabulary, not of Sophocles'. And *fatum*, in Latin, is less forceful than fate is in English. It derives from the verb *fari*, "to speak." It has, then, a similar force to the biblical formula "it is written." *Fatum* is, in essence, the spoken word of Jupiter. But in the traditional pagan pantheon, Jupiter's word is often disputed by other gods.

It is therefore both wrong and unfair to Seneca to observe, as one critic has done, that

> Until approximately the 1790s, admiration for Sophocles' *Oedipus the King* was almost always contaminated by extraneous features, above all the baleful example of Seneca. Only when German Romantic writers and philosophers, following the lead of Lessing, were able to clear away neoclassical and Senecan excrescences, and behold Sophocles' drama afresh as a tragedy of self-knowledge, do we enter the "age of Oedipus" that reaches its apogee in Freud.[25]

The vehemence with which Seneca is demeaned at the same time as Sophocles' *Oedipus* is read in terms of deterministic Roman Stoicism never

---

[25] Rudnytsky, *Freud and Oedipus*, 97; cf. 108–9. For the influence of Senecan drama in the Renaissance, see Gordon Braden, *Renaissance Tragedy and the Senecan Tradition: Anger's Privilege* (New Haven, 1985). See also his earlier study, *The Classics and English Renaissance Poetry: Three Case Studies* (New Haven, 1978).

fails to astonish me. An influential classical scholar, E. R. Dodds, went so far as to declare that we have no business considering whether Oedipus could have "escaped his doom if he had been more careful," since "we are not entitled to ask questions that the dramatist did not intend us to ask."[26] This pronouncement is designed to intimidate the reader, to maintain orthodoxy, and to defend the faith of the young against subversion by heretics by limiting their choices of interpretation. "Heresy" is, after all, merely the Greek word *haíresis*, "choosing (for oneself)."

Such prohibitions, are, as often, so phrased to divert attention from the really central issue. And that issue, as M. S. Silk and J. P. Stern observe, is not, "Could Oedipus have escaped his doom?" but "Is there a specific doom for Oedipus to escape?" Oedipus is "hardly the protestant hero that Schelling makes out. It is not external fate, but rather his own determination to seek out the truth, that brings about his defeat."[27] They rightly see that a Calvinistic sense of determinism subtends Schelling's reading of *Oedipus*, which, in turn, subtends Freud's representation of Sophocles, even though Freud himself was no Calvinist.

To get a preliminary sense of the differences between what Sophocles' and Seneca's characters say on the issue of destiny and prophecy, let us now look at what Sophocles' chorus says after the expert on prodigies, Teiresias, has denounced Oedipus as the killer of Laius and husband to his own mother.

> Now the wise legislator of omens
> adds fearsome charges,
> fearsome confusion.
> I cannot believe them or reject them.   485
> I'm at a loss for words, fluttering
> amid various hopes, seeing neither what's in front of me
> nor what lurks behind.
> I for one have not learned
> what basis for dispute

[26] E. R. Dodds, "On Misunderstanding the *Oedipus Rex*," *Greece and Rome* 13 (1966): 37–49.

[27] M. S. Silk and J. P. Stern, *Nietzsche on Tragedy* (Cambridge, 1981), 309. For Friedrich von Schelling, see his *Samtliche Werke,* 14 vols. (Stuttgart, 1856–61), 5:693–94 and his *Werke,* ed. H. Buchner et al., 3 vols. (Stuttgart, 1976), 1:3, 106–7. For an opposing view, see Rudnytsky, *Freud and Oedipus,* 105–10.

existed ever in the past
or up to today,
on the Labdacid side,
on Polybus' son's side,   490
to serve me as touchstone of worth,
to justify assault on the public good name
of Oedipus,
to make me avenger
of Labdacus' house   495
in deaths with no clues.
Still, Zeus and Apollo
both understand,
both know what mortals do and did.
But when it comes down to men:
Does a seer fare better than *I* do?   500
There is no unelusive way to judge.
One man could surpass another's wisdom with his own.
Never would I, at least,
declare charges proven
before I saw straight talk.   505
There are clear factors on his side:
the wingèd maiden
who once came to us here.
We saw his wisdom:
He tested as gold, as joy to the city.
So then, for my part, he will never stand accused,   510
in my mind or my heart, of evilness.

The Sophoclean chorus talks of divine knowledge, not of destiny, and surmises that what it has heard indicates some hitherto unknown dispute between the house of Labdacus, that is to say, Creon and his people, and Oedipus.

In declaring this, the chorus concedes one major point, at least, to Oedipus: that Teiresias' statements are probably not independent of Creon's influence. Unlike those modern readers who feel sure, once Teiresias has spoken (he is, after all, a prophet), that Oedipus is doomed by god, Sophocles' chorus wants some facts and some evidence before passing judgment, and expresses much *less* certainty than it did before Teiresias spoke that this prophet really has a grasp of elusive *alétheia*, the Greek word we routinely translate as "truth."

My point is simply this: the intellectual framework in terms of which Freud and Dodds present Sophocles' *Oedipus* is much closer to that expressed by the Senecan chorus than to that expressed by Sophocles' chorus. The model of tragedy devised by the Enlightenment was not free from but more influenced than its proponents imagined by Seneca and Stoicized Christianity.

6. Canonical and Non-canonical Texts

The canonical synopsis of Sophocles' *Oedipus* remains more or less as Freud described it: Oedipus discovers that he actually did kill his father and marry his mother without ever having wished to do so, and punishes himself for these acts as the god prescribes. It is a pity that so rich a text has been so long corseted into a single shape. For the canonical reading is not the only interpretation advanced or possible. While no one, I think, would dispute that Oedipus concludes he has killed his father and married his mother, certain other matters are much debated among scholars. The principal issues explored are (a) whether, and, if so, to what extent, Sophocles' *Oedipus* is also a political play, and one which refracts the poet's contemporary political and social milieu; (b) whether or not Sophocles' hero is himself portrayed as driven by an unconscious desire to kill his father and marry his mother; (c) whether the testimony offered in the play is sufficient to justify the conclusions Oedipus draws.

There is little a translator can do, as translator, to help with (a), since full exploration of the "political" Sophocles demands that readers be familiar with the environment in which the poet wrote, and most are not and don't want to be. Indeed, there is always the fear that if one construes Sophocles' *Oedipus* in terms of its contemporary politics one moves it irrevocably from the universal to the particular, makes it less accessible and, like Aristophanic comedy, more difficult for the modern reader to understand. Victor Ehrenberg made a strong case for a political reading of Sophoclean drama half a century ago, and such a reading casts an altogether different light on several major scenes in the play. I have tried to "flag" some possible political issues so that those interested can detect where they are and evaluate them for themselves. Greek and Roman mythic texts routinely operate at several levels simultaneously, like the musical score of a symphony. One can read *Oedipus* as a commentary both on fifth-century Athens and on the human condition.

As far as (b) is concerned, I have done my best to avoid, in the translation, any words and phrases whose normal modern resonance is psychological, such as "regression," and "repression." To use them would be to imply that Sophocles' characters express themselves in self-consciously psychological terms, which they do not. It isn't that the ancients didn't grasp the general idea of what we call psychology, but that the surviving ancient texts deal primarily with its use for rhetorical purposes. As Aristotle notes in *Rhetoric* 1.7 (1365a), understanding how a particular individual thinks is the key to persuading him: the persuasive is that which persuades the person you intend to persuade. The boundaries of ancient rhetoric and modern psychology often overlap in Sophocles, but not nearly to the extent that they do in Seneca.

Not until Roman times do we find literary characters analyzing themselves in what approaches a psychological manner. In Virgil's *Aeneid,* for example, Aeneas describes (or invents) a dream in which he saw a vision of his dead cousin Hector, all scarred with wounds after Achilles had mutilated him.[28] Aeneas says that his dreaming mind failed to grasp that Hector was dead and substituted for his death a long, unaccountable absence, but could not explain the wounds at all. Consequently the news the ghostly Hector brings to his dreaming mind, that Troy is doomed, makes no sense at all to his unconscious, and frustrates the dream vision which tries to deliver its message anyway. It is all, of course, a rhetorical construct, in the sense that Aeneas is trying to make clear to his audience, particularly his host, Dido, queen of Carthage, that he was in no way responsible for the fall of Troy, and that his innocence extended so deeply into his unconscious that he had not even accepted Hector's death, much less the impending destruction of his city.

It is precisely this Virgilian self-analysis, further developed by Ovid, that distinguishes Seneca's *Oedipus* most clearly from Sophocles' *Oedipus*. Seneca's Oedipus admits us to his thoughts and his fears in his monologues almost as if he were disclosing his inner self to a psychiatrist. Whereas we observe Sophocles' Oedipus mostly from without, we are drawn *into* Seneca's Oedipus. Further, Latin poets, particularly Virgil and Ovid, often view

---

[28] *Aeneid* 2.268–97 and my notes on this passage in *Virgil: Aeneid,* trans. and notes by Frederick Ahl, with an Introduction by Elaine Fantham (Oxford, 2007).

aggression in clearly sexual terms.[29] I have found little trace of such a view in Sophocles, but have not tried either to erase it or highlight it where I have seen it.

The most problematic area is (c), the testimony on which Oedipus and commentators base their conclusions. Here classical scholars are sometimes imprecise in two critical areas. First, it is commonly assumed that because Sophocles wrote the whole play, we can detect his authorial opinion wherever we choose among statements made by his characters. The second is an extension of the first, namely, that what, in any other environment, would be critical differences in details of testimony are routinely dismissed as being of no significance in Sophocles' *Oedipus*.

Let me cite a single example of what I mean. In connection with Oedipus' concern at line 845 as to whether it was one or many people who killed Laius, Roger Dawe observes: "It is not for nothing that, at 290, Sophocles describes the point at issue as *kophà kaì palaì' épe* [silly talk of times past, long ago]."[30] Dawe writes as if the issue really did not matter and as if the words cited expressed the author's affirmation of their unimportance. In Greek tragedy, however, the authorial voice does not intrude itself, as it does in epic and sometimes in comedy. Nor does the audience know, as early as line 290, how critical it will be in Oedipus' mind that Laius should have been killed by many assailants rather than by one, though the audience may notice that Oedipus oscillates curiously between referring to a singular killer and plural killers. Much of the dramatic tension in Sophocles' *Oedipus* relies precisely on the fact that we are only gradually made privy to the memories that stir Oedipus' anxieties from early on.

In fact, it is *the chorus* that is talking at line 290 about its own recollection of events, not Sophocles speaking authorially and editorially. And the chorus is in the process of telling Oedipus that Laius was killed by *travelers*, not *robbers*, as Creon has claimed at line 122. Their collective voice is indicating, as inoffensively as possible, that Creon's report of what an alleged eyewitness said about the death of Laius is not the only version it has heard. They are

---

[29] See my discussion of *Aeneid* 11 in *Virgil: Aeneid*, 432–34.

[30] Roger Dawe, *Sophocles' Oedipus Rex* Cambridge, (2006), 7. We find this same lack of distinction between authorial voice and inner voice in other comments: "There is one prime piece of evidence, which even if it comes from a later play, does at least come from the author himself, writing about the same hero. It cannot be left unheard (*Oed. Col.* 962ff.): '(The killing and the marriage and all my misfortunes) were things I had to endure, alas against my will...'" Dawe is quoting not some editorial statement made by Sophocles, but words Sophocles attributes to Oedipus.

not preparing to say the same thing Creon has just said. But they must move warily since their account contradicts Creon, a powerful man in the state, on at least this one issue.

Line 290, then, is not Sophocles' "blurring the prehistory of the play." It is his Oedipus who causes the blurring. It is Oedipus who reacts as if *the chorus* were really making, as it said, trivial distinctions about the alleged witness's report. This is a powerful dramatic moment. Oedipus has just spent around a hundred lines trying to coax the members of the chorus to speak. Now, when they finally pluck up the courage to do so, he dismisses them sarcastically before he has heard anything other than their opening phrase. Indeed, many of Oedipus' problems stem from his failure to pay attention to small, conflicting details in testimony.

There are over a dozen critical moments in the play when the characters or chorus don't say quite what they ought to be saying, if the canonical reading is correct, and which scholars therefore prefer to see as trivial details or "inconsistencies"—"flaws" in Sophocles' presentation as opposed to problems resulting from the critics' own presuppositions. Hence I have attempted to provide a translation that enables readers to see almost all the "inconsistencies" the original offers. I say "almost all," because some of the figured usage in Sophocles' Greek defies translation into another language without, say, radically renaming some characters so that the word-plays based on their names can have English counterparts. No one would be happy with that.

7. Problems of the Divine

M. S. Silk and J. P. Stern, though seeing the problems in making "fate" the force governing Sophocles' *Oedipus,* nonetheless assume that what Oedipus seeks and finds is "the truth." "Truth" is a very positive concept in English, related by origin and semantics to "trust," and attainable in Christian culture by faith: by belief, rather than by knowledge. To many ancient Greek philosophers, however, *dóxa,* "belief," "the way things are assumed to be," was, along with *pseudés,* "false," an antonym of *alétheia,* the Greek word we translate as "truth." *Alétheia,* for the fifth-century writer, falls within the compass of knowledge rather than of belief. It was seen as the negation of an already negative term *léthe,* "elusiveness, forgetfulness": it is that which does not elude us, that which is not forgotten.

The Greeks assumed that we live in a world that normally does elude us and trip us. They talk of "non-elusiveness," *alétheia,* and *aspháleia,* "a state of not being tripped up," where we and, to some extent, the Romans, talk of truth and safety. But even a Roman, when feeling *securus,* was "non-anxious," rather than "secure" in our more comfortable sense. The Latin prefix *se-,* like the Greek prefix *a-,* is separative.

It *is,* admittedly, hard to think one's way out of a Judaeo-Christian reading of pre-Christian texts, especially in English, which has been, ever since its birth from Anglo-Saxon and Norman French, a Christian language and lacking in the pre-Christian undertones of other European languages. And polytheism is hard for almost all those acculturated in European societies to grasp. Late-night discussions about religion are framed in binary terms: of god or no-god, rather than of gods or no gods, even though Christianity was grafted onto Greek polytheism in eastern Europe and Roman polytheism in the West.

When a religion is introduced into a society it will reflect, to some degree, the structure and social realities of the host society. Orthodox and Catholic Christianity mirrored the Roman Empire within their hierarchical structures. Pontiffs, patriarchs, and prelates still dress much as they did in the fourth century AD. The cardinals constitute a *curia,* like the Roman senate, and popes follow the practice, begun by the founder of the Roman imperial monarchy, Octavian, of selecting a virtuous new name to suit their exalted station. Octavian used "Augustus"; they use "Pius," "Innocent," "Clement," and so forth. And there is much physical self-abasement in Catholic and Orthodox rituals that recalls the practices of autocratic monarchies: *proskýnesis,* getting down on one's hands and knees before the altar, genuflection, and bowing. Wine is even mixed with water at the Eucharist as it was at a Roman banquet.

The Anglican Church, born in Tudor days, restricts itself to courtly bows. The various Protestant sects, which had no use for monarchy, refused, in varying degrees, to bow before (or have) authority figures. They set up councils of elders, in the style of the Dutch republic, rather than cardinals and bishops. And the practice of asking priests or saints to intervene with God on their behalf was sternly rejected. Residual traces of polytheism were—and are—handled very gingerly. The devil and other immortals, angels or demons, are neither gods nor men. We generally don't confront the paradoxes of our tradition, or grasp the bizarre results when these paradoxes elude outsiders from a polytheistic culture. American visitors to Japan are occasionally amused or horrified to see a baby Santa in the Christmas crèche or an adult Santa on the cross in a shop window.[31]

For us, God remains one, male, and indivisible (though sometimes, like a shamrock, tripartite), and, above all, good. But from their earliest literature, the Greeks thought in terms of multiple gods, both male and female, embodying various natural energies and powers, or rivers and other geographical features, or cities. While Zeus is theoretically in command, other gods constantly subvert his and each other's authority in various ways. These gods suggest a far less authoritarian social and political order than we find in the imperial Roman world where Christianity was born and one in which so clearly defined a term as fate is hard to situate. And yet there is a puzzling element in ancient Greek religion that seems somehow anomalous. It is easiest to show what I mean with an example.

In Genesis 22, Abraham is required to offer up his firstborn child, Isaac, as a human sacrifice to secure God's goodwill. He is about to do so when God intervenes and instructs him to substitute a ram. If we leave aside the tale of Tantalus offering his son Pelops as sacrificial food for the gods, the best-known parallel in Greek tradition is Agamemnon's sacrifice of his firstborn, Iphigeneia, to Artemis, so that he can launch the Trojan War. True, there is also the tradition that the goddess herself substituted a deer at the last moment and carried Agamemnon's child away to safety.[32] But there is no surviving narrative that suggests Agamemnon was showing the ultimate in pious devotion in making the offering of his first-born, as we have in the case of Abraham. Even in the tradition that Iphigeneia is saved, it is the goddess who rescues Iphigeneia from death at Agamemnon's hands. The closest we get to a justification of Agamemnon's action is Iphigeneia's own defense of him to her mother in Euripides' *Iphigeneia at Aulis,* a defense based on the false assumption that her beloved father cannot be doing something wrong. As for Tantalus, he is one of the fixtures in the ancient pit of the damned, Tartarus.

In other words, it is hard to find traces of an archaic piety in the narratives of Greek human sacrifice, though such traditions must, presumably, have existed at some point.

The texts of Homer, as we have them, and the quarreling gods of Greek tragedy, are attributable, in some measure, to the initiatives of a single person,

[31] My colleague James-Henry Holland mentioned this point to me. On Athenian polytheism, see Robert Parker's excellent *Polytheism and Society in Ancient Athens* (Oxford, 2005).

[32] The fullest version of this tradition is in Euripides' *Iphigeneia in Aulis* and *Iphigeneia among the Taurians.*

Peisistratus, who seized power in Athens and held it, on and off, as tyrant, from 560 to 527 BC. Peisistratus was an innovator in many ways, not least in his introduction of tyranny to Athens. The words "tyrant" and "tyranny" are not used in Homer, and not of Greek origin. The first literary occurrence of "tyrant" in Greek is in Archilochus, *fragment* 22D, in reference to Gyges of Lydia. But Archilochus is more likely to be using the word as an insult than as a title. Herodotus, for instance, never calls Gyges or any other ruler of Lydia a tyrant. The earliest clear use of tyrant as a title appears to be in Corinth, around 655 BC, and the origins of tyranny could more plausibly be traced to Corinthian colonial and trading contacts with the Etruscan (Tyrrhenian) monarchies in Italy. During the seventh and early sixth centuries, Corinth was the most important trading city of Greece, and Peisistratus, like Athenian ceramic artists of the period, was much influenced by things Corinthian.

Not content with introducing a new form of government to Athens, Peisistratus also supervised an official edition of the Homeric poems, which was so successful that we no longer have any clear evidence for what they looked like in the poetic tradition before this so-called Peisistratean recension.[33] His program, in general, was to restructure Athens politically, economically, and culturally to make his city a real rival of Corinth in the Greek world. And among the surprising features of the Homeric poems as we have them, in particular the *Odyssey,* are the almost total absence of Corinth (called by its older name Ephyre in Homer), the omnipresence of Phoenicians as traders par excellence, and the close association of the hero Odysseus with the goddess Athena, specifically linked to Athens. In Peisistratus' day, Corinth dominated the Ionian Islands of which Odysseus' Ithaca was among the least significant.

Exactly what modifications Peisistratus made in the representation of the gods we don't know. But he certainly lived in an age when there were major disputes about mythic tradition and when major adjustments were made to it. Plutarch, for instance, tells us that Peisistratus altered the texts of Homer and Hesiod to make Theseus a more notable figure than he had been, and it has long been suspected that Telemachus' companion in *Odyssey* 3 and 4, a son of Nestor not mentioned in the *Iliad,* is a Peisistratean interpolation since his name too is Peisistratus.[34]

---

[33] For a concise general overview and bibliography, see P. Pucci, "Theology and Poetics in the *Iliad,*" *Arethusa* 35.1 (2002): 17–34.

[34] *Life of Theseus* 20. See also W. B. Tyrrell and F. S. Brown, *Athenian Myths and Institutions* (New York and Oxford, 1991), 161–65.

Epic poetry was only one of the media in which the battle for tradition was engaged. The early sixth century BC yields not only the elegiacs of Peisistratus' political rival Solon, the first Athenian poet some of whose works have survived, but some fragments of the poet Stesichorus, famous for his revisionist interpretations of mythology written in a kind of lyric epic. Another contemporary of Peisistratus is Sophilos, the first Athenian potter whose signature survives to us in full. On one piece he represents the funeral games for Patroclus, which are also described by Homer in *Iliad* 23.257–533, and labels them *Patroklous atla:* "Games for Patroclus," though his spelling, as scholars note, is not very accurate.[35] He also signs the piece as both potter and painter: the conventional verb with which the potter signs his work is *(e)poíesen,* "made." The conventional verb the painter uses of his painting is *égrapsen:* "wrote, inscribed, painted." Sophilos signs in full as a painter and appears to have signed as potter too (though a break in the pot leaves only the first two letters, "So—"). If we allow for Sophilos' eccentric spelling, it is possible that his own rather rare name was really Sophillos, identical with the name of the dramatist Sophocles' father. Given the tendency of Greek families to name children after grandfathers or great-grandfathers, there may have been some genealogical connection.

The potter, like the poet, is a *poietés,* a "maker." And Sophilos was not the only ceramic artist of the day who signed his work. Cleitias who decorated a large vessel made by the potter Ergotimus, which we now know as the François Vase, did so too.[36] Among the many motifs represented on the vase is the chariot race at the funeral games for Patroclus. But the participants listed are almost entirely different from those in *Iliad* 23; and Cleitias underscores his point by writing his preferred names for the competitors next to the painted figures. He also renames the muse of lyric Stesichore (instead of Terpsichore), as if either honoring or mocking Stesichorus, and shows the muse of epic, Calliope, as the only muse looking outward to face the viewing eye. Since Cleitias is clearly not following Homer, I suspect he is honoring rather than mocking Stesichorus and his muse.

---

[35] See J. M. Hurwit, *The Art and Culture of Early Greece* (Ithaca, N.Y., and London, 1985), 222–26.

[36] See my "Wordplay and Apparent Fiction in the *Odyssey,*" *Arethusa* 35.1 (2002): 117–32, especially 125–26; K. Friis Johansen, *The Iliad in Early Greek Art* (Copenhagen, 1967), 90–92, 266–67; M. S. Jensen, *The Oral Question and Oral Formulaic Theory* (Copenhagen, 1980), 104; T. H. Carpenter, *Art and Myth in Ancient Greece* (London, 1991), 13–21; G. Nagy, *Homeric Questions* (Austin, 1993), 107–8.

If there could be such large differences in heroic detail, there could as easily be large differences in detailing of the divine. But all we can safely say is that in the long-term battle for acceptance Peisistratus' Homer had most of the advantages. Writing, Socrates observes in an important passage in Plato's *Phaedrus* (274A–277), obliterates memory; and Peisistratus had "written" Homer. Further, by setting up dramatic contests at the festivals of Dionysus, Peisistratus was clearly developing what proved to be a very secular and democratic dimension to the gods and to religion. Greek gods are, inherently, much more morally neutral or ambivalent than the Christian god since they are equated with elemental forces such as rivers, weather, and sexuality rather than with ethical principles. When these forces are conceptualized anthropomorphically, and endowed with human emotions and intellect, their conduct invites a not necessarily sympathetic comparison with human conduct. When fully realized on stage, their inherently conflicted natures can become demonic.

Peisistratus empowered poets to put the gods on stage in publicly funded performances at religious festivals. And although the Athenians eventually got rid of Peisistratus' sons and established a democracy, they maintained the tragic competitions he had established and also set up state-funded competitions in comedy in which the gods were treated with an even heavier hand.

How the gods operate in Greek tragedy depends to a large extent on the particular myth that is staged and on the issues that are highlighted. It also depends on the playwright. Fundamental to the myth of Orestes, in Aeschylus and Euripides, for example, is that while Orestes is free not to kill his mother (and almost decides not to), he is exacting a punishment that Apollo authorizes him (but does not compel him) to exact: the avenging of kindred blood, the killing of his mother to avenge her murder of his father. Both Aeschylus and Euripides show us the social, legal, religious, and psychological scars that Orestes bears as a consequence of his action in their tragedies; they put Apollo himself on stage to confirm that, rightly or wrongly, Orestes kills Clytemnestra on his divine instructions.

Sophocles does nothing of the sort in his *Electra*. Orestes and Electra are motivated by hate and the strong inner conviction that they are right; Orestes kills so ruthlessly and remorselessly that it is hard to imagine him being susceptible to subsequent attacks of conscience. And Apollo never appears on stage in Sophocles' *Electra*.

Aeschylus puts Apollo and Athena on stage, and the Furies in the *orchestra*, the circular space in which the chorus danced, in his *Eumenides;* in *Prometheus Bound* (if it really is by Aeschylus) he gives us Hephaestus, Prometheus, and two divine personifications, "Rule" and "Violence." And Euripides has gods in abundance. Sophocles, however, rarely puts gods on stage in his plays.[37] There are none in his *Oedipus* and there are none in Seneca's. In Sophocles' earliest surviving tragedy, *Ajax,* Athena is in the prologue. Her ruthlessness shocks even Ajax's bitter rival Odysseus. Heracles, in *Women of Trachis,* is not yet deified as the play begins. In *Philoctetes,* Heracles, played by the actor who earlier played Odysseus, appears as a *deus ex machina,* claiming to be "the voice and the appearance of Heracles." Scholars disagree as to whether this character is Heracles or Odysseus in disguise.[38] In Sophocles' seven plays, then, the only undisputed divine stage presence is Athena in the *Ajax.*

Elsewhere, Sophocles presents characters who *claim* they are doing the will of the gods, such as Antigone, or speaking with divine authority, like Teiresias in *Antigone* and *Oedipus,* or reporting what they say an oracle has told them, like Creon in *Oedipus.* Sophocles leaves us to decide whether and to what extent we should believe them. He does not compel us to accept the stage "reality" of the gods, as Euripides does in *Orestes, Hippolytus,* or *Bacchae.* Rather, he allows us to view mythic horrors *without* blaming the gods for them, much as Euripides does in *Iphigeneia in Aulis.* If one postulates a scenario in which Oedipus commits crimes that the gods have predetermined, the gods and fate must arguably be held responsible for his actions, as Seneca's Oedipus points out (*Oedipus* 1042–46):

> Voice of destiny, who sits as god
> and arbiter of truth, I challenge you!
> My father's death alone settled my debt
> to destiny. Yet now I've also killed
> my mother. I am twice a parricide,
> more lethal and more guilty than I feared.
> My crime destroyed her.
>   Phoebus, how you lied!
> I have surpassed the immorality
> of destiny itself.

Seneca puts only one god on stage: Juno, in *Hercules in His Madness.* One of the sharpest contrasts between Euripides' *Hippolytus* and Seneca's *Phaedra,*

---

[37] See P. Pucci, "Gods' Intervention and Epiphany in Sophocles," *AJP* 115 (1994): 15–46. Pucci emphasizes the marginality of the divine epiphanies to the tragedies in which they occur.

[38] See Hanna M. Roisman, *Sophocles: Philoctetes* (London, 2005) 106–11.

based upon it, is Seneca's elimination of the goddesses Aphrodite and Artemis from the Euripidean cast. But Seneca does deploy the infernal demon Megaera in *Thyestes* and ghosts from the underworld in both *Thyestes* and *Agamemnon.* The powers of the underworld and of evil in Seneca, as in Statius' *Thebaid,* seem more capable of action than the Olympians.

If we do conclude that the (offstage) gods and divine destiny are responsible for Oedipus' dilemma in either Sophocles' or Seneca's *Oedipus,* that conclusion should be based on the extent to which the text gives credibility to what the characters say, not on an a priori assumption about the author's moral character, his alleged intentions, or a false sense that myth is either subtended by factual reality or fixed immutably in tradition.

Not everyone in ancient Athens was happy either about this secularization and democratization of the gods or about democracy itself. Plato's Socrates, in fact, suggests that poets should be banned from his ideal state until they agree to portray the gods as good. To illustrate his displeasure, he selects in *Republic* 2 (383A–C) not a passage from the notoriously god-maligning Euripides, but from Aeschylus, whom some modern scholars have almost turned into a theologian. Aeschylus earns Socrates' special wrath for having the goddess Thetis suggest that her fellow god Phoebus Apollo gave her a false prophecy of family happiness:

> Since Phoebus was a god I thought his mouth
> would not speak lies, that its prophetic skill
> would bring his words to promised flowering.
> He sang these songs himself, came to the feast
> in person. And that selfsame god who spoke:
> he killed my son.
>
> (Aeschylus *fragment* 350)[39]

If gods lie to each other, then what hope has man?

8. The Self-Destructive Hero

The Oedipus myth, as Sophocles tells it, differs from the Orestes myth in that there is absolutely no divine injunction on Oedipus to do violence to

---

[39] The Greek text is in S. Radt, *Aeschylus,* vol. 3 of *Tragicorum Graecorum Fragmenta* (Göttingen, 1985): *Incertarum Fabularum,* fragment 350.

his parents and that no case is made for the justice of his actions. Sophocles' Oedipus sets out on his quest, he tells Jocasta, because a drunk at a dinner party called him a bastard, not because of divine prophecies. What makes him so insecure is, at this point in the play, unclear. Even when, in his own account, Polybus and Merope, his Corinthian parents, reassure him that he is not illegitimate, he nonetheless visits Delphi to ask who his parents are. There he is told by the oracle that he will kill his father and marry his mother. The answer does not fit the question. But he decides not to return home; he acts, that is, as if the oracle had answered his question by saying "Polybus and Merope; and you will kill him and marry her."

His fears about his own legitimacy have not been dispelled, but, rather, overlaid with and augmented by new fears that he will kill Polybus and marry Merope. Indeed, the turning point in the play comes when a remark by Teiresias revitalizes the older fears. Oedipus' mind operates mythically rather than logically. The Neoplatonist Sallustius, talking of myth, stated the matter this way over a thousand years after Sophocles: "These things never were but always are. For the mind [*noûs*] sees everything at the same time, but reason [*lógos*] reasons as it speaks [*légei*] that some things are first, others second."[40]

Yet it is not only the formidable voices of Delphi, Creon, and Teiresias that prompt Oedipus to the devastating conclusion that he is the child of Laius and Jocasta. He is not robbed of his wits by a god, as is Ajax in Sophocles' *Ajax*. It is first an anonymous Corinthian and then later an anonymous slave whose words drive him to that conclusion. And what empowers them is precisely what empowers the anonymous drunk and whoever it was first teased him about his name: Oedipus' own fears. And fear, the ancient proverb runs, first created the gods, not vice versa.

Sophocles' characters are not only more self-motivated than those of his dramatic rivals, but also more self-destructive. The only death-wound delivered, arguably, on stage in extant Greek tragedy is that of Sophocles' Ajax. Seneca adds one in Roman tragedy, that of Jocasta in his *Oedipus*. And both Sophocles' Ajax and Seneca's Jocasta commit suicide. There are as many suicides in Sophocles' *Antigone* as in all nineteen plays attributed to Euripides; and there are no suicides at all among characters in Aeschylus' seven plays.

[40] Sallustius, *On the Gods and the Universe* 4.11. For further discussion of this passage, see my *Metaformations: Soundplay and Wordplay in Ovid and Other Classical Poets* (Ithaca, N.Y., and London, 1985), 284.

41

Self-destruction is not limited to acts of suicide. The science of rhetoric is based on the understanding that human beings can be manipulated if one channels their perceptions, if one understands what they are likely to believe and do. In that sense, it can operate, in literate societies, much as voodoo operates in nonliterate societies. Sophocles' Jocasta declares Oedipus is controlled by anyone who speaks to his fears—and is immediately proven right. Once Oedipus is convinced he has actually killed his father and married his mother, his self-blinding is a conscious act of self-punishment, suitably enacted to bring to fulfillment the most recent prophecy he has heard: the prediction of a seer whose own blindness Oedipus has insulted.

9. Questions and Answers

Sophocles' *Oedipus* is a product of the first era of widespread literacy, and of the only era of direct democracy, in human history. Thinkers, traders, and artists from all over the Greek-speaking world gathered in Athens, bringing with them new ideas and skills. Hippocrates was founding his medical school, philosophers and teachers of wisdom, the so-called sophists, were educating Athenians in new ways of thinking and speaking, as were the comic and tragic playwrights. Thanks to Plato's dialogues, written in the next century, it is also seen as the age of Socrates, who was at the peak of his influence in the mid 420s BC, cross-examining people in quest of the genuinely knowable and teachable. The influence of Socratic dialectic and its terminology is evident throughout Sophocles' *Oedipus,* not least in Oedipus himself, who, like Socrates, is reported to have been prompted to his most intensive interrogations by a response from the Delphic oracle to a close associate.

Athens had become a city of law courts, to which poor or aged citizens flocked to serve as paid members of juries. Rhetoric, the mastery of language and intricately subtle argument, was developed to a level of sophistication that was hardly surpassed even by the Romans, and which has never, since antiquity, reached comparable heights, despite the best efforts of Erasmus. And *Oedipus* is a masterpiece of rhetoric presented to an audience very familiar with the rhetoric and argumentation of the courts.

But the changes were coming so thick and fast that they left many far behind and very uncomfortable, as did the rapid acceleration of science and technology in the nineteenth century. Aristophanes, in his comedy *Clouds,* foresaw a day of reckoning when the gulf widened between revolutionary intellectuals like Socrates and the general public, which was still wary of this new order and the challenges it posed to conventional ways of thinking. This may be why Aristophanes offered his *Clouds* twice in public competition, first in 423, when it did not win the prize, and then in 413. In *Clouds,* the main characters are a wily but ignorant displaced farmer, Strepsiades, and Socrates himself. And when Strepsiades discovers he has lost more than he has gained by having his son trained in Socratic thinking, he attacks and destroys Socrates' "Thinkery." Such warnings of potentially violent reaction against Socrates, which probably seemed far-fetched in 423, before the Athenian disaster in Sicily, carried more punch a decade later, when everyone was looking for scapegoats.

Sophocles' *Oedipus* is a play of many questions asked, but only partly and incompletely answered. Bernard Knox comments: "The characteristic tone of Oedipus in the first two thirds of the play is that of an impatient, demanding questioner."[41] Knox reckons up the totals: Oedipus poses eleven questions to Creon in forty lines (89–129), some nineteen to Teiresias, and so forth. Yet Oedipus rarely digests the answers to one question before asking another. Unlike Plato, who presents Socrates' trial exclusively through Socrates' eyes, Sophocles gives us *all* testimony on which Oedipus bases his judgment. He lets us see the situation through various eyes, make our own assessment, and note what Oedipus does and does not take into account.

Oedipus deserves the same critical attention to detail we accord a Platonic dialogue, not least because there may be some elements of the mythical Oedipus in the perception of Socrates. But, like Freud, we privilege the template of our generalized sense of the myth over the specifics of Sophocles' text.[42] And if we are to pay attention to the details, we must have a text that permits us to see them. Many translators of Sophocles' *Oedipus* modify the text to remove "inconsistencies" in the original, mostly by altering the phrasing of crucial questions and answers. If, in a play of many questions and answers, we make answers fit questions, or vice versa, when they really do not, we are doing what Oedipus does when he decides not to go home after asking the oracle who his parents are and receiving the answer that he will kill his father and marry his mother. We are imposing a set of unproven assumptions

[41] Knox, *Oedipus at Thebes,* 121.

[42] Sigmund Freud, *The Interpretation of Dreams,* ed. and trans. James Strachey (New York, 1955). For a more detailed study of the problems of evidence and self-conviction in Sophocles' *Oedipus,* see my *Sophocles' Oedipus: Evidence and Self-Conviction* (Ithaca, N.Y., and London, 1991).

on a text whose complexity we have underestimated, and, of course, we are forcing our readers to do the same.

Let us examine how some popular translations handle questions and answers in *Oedipus* in a series of exchanges that occurs just after Jocasta has come on stage, and prayed, as follows, to the gods to help her deal with Oedipus (914–23):

> Oh, how I have begged him. I can do no more.
> For Oedipus lets his emotions run too high
> whenever stressed or pained. Unlike the thinking man,
> he doesn't assess the new from past experience.
> He's always owned by anyone who spells things out
> for him—provided that man spells out things he fears.
> To you, Apollo Lycaeus, since you're closest,
> I've come as suppliant, with these offerings, hoping
> you'll find there's some way out that leaves us undefiled.
> We all now cringe in horror as we see this man,
> this helmsman of our ship of state, so paralyzed.

As Jocasta finishes, a stranger enters and asks where he can find Oedipus. Much hinges on this stranger's words. He will soon be credentialed as a messenger by his questioner, Jocasta, Oedipus' wife; and he will persuade Oedipus of something we are taught to take for granted before we read the play: that Oedipus himself is not originally from Corinth, but from Thebes.

The chorus introduces Jocasta to the stranger as Oedipus' wife. Formalities over, she asks, in line 936, a question which is differently posed and differently answered in three popular translations:

1. Robert Fagles:
   Question: Who sent you? *Answer:* Corinth...[43]

2. Luci Berkowitz and Theodore Brunner:
   Question: Where do you come from? *Answer:* From Corinth...[44]

---

[43] *Sophocles: The Three Theban Plays,* trans. Robert Fagles, with introduction and notes by Bernard Knox (New York, 1982), 212.

[44] *Oedipus Tyrannus,* trans. and ed. Luci Berkowitz and Theodore F. Brunner (New York, 1970), 21.

3. Peter Arnott:
   Question: Who sent you here to us? *Answer:* I come from
   Corinth...[45]

The terse Greek text says:

Question: *Parà tínos d'* (from the presence of whom) *aphigménos*
(having arrived)? *Answer: ek tês Korínthou* (out of
              Corinth).

Sophocles' questioner is asking a stranger *who* he's come from; the stranger
replies with an answer that says *where* he's (come) from.

Two of the translations recast some part of either the question or the
answer because, in the original, the response does not answer the question
asked. Fagles sharpens "arrived from" into "sent" and ignores the emphatic
change of prepositions. He makes the answer fit the question. Berkowitz
and Brunner keep the idea of "arrived from" but dispel all sense that the
questioner is asking about a person, not a place. They make the question
fit the answer. Arnott also sharpens "arrived from" to "sent," but makes
no other adjustments. The first two versions don't allow us to see that the
Corinthian is evading the question. Fagles' modification, in fact, suggests
that the stranger is an official messenger from Corinth. In Berkowitz and
Brunner the issue of whether he is or is not a messenger does not arise. The
questioner asks only the visitor's point of origin and gets a brief and clear
response. In Arnott, the questioner assumes that the stranger is a messenger;
but the response raises doubts: he names the city he's from, not the person
who has sent him.

Two further responses that the Corinthian gives also show translators
adapting the text. The first is his reply to Jocasta's question about the nature
of his news—a question she really ought not to be asking, since the news is
for the head of state. Here are three versions:

1. Berkowitz and Brunner:
   Your husband now is ruler of the Isthmus![46]

---

[45] *Sophocles' Oedipus and Antigone,* trans. Peter Arnott (New York, 1960), 22.
[46] Berkowitz and Brunner, *Oedipus Tyrannus,* 21.

2. Kenneth Cavander:
   The people of Corinth—it was already announced there—will make
   Oedipus their king.[47]

3. Peter Arnott:
   The people living in the Isthmian land
   Will have him for their king; so goes the story.[48]

It is hard to believe all three are translating the same text. Berkowitz and
Brunner's Corinthian declares that Oedipus *is already* the ruler of Corinth,
even though Sophocles wrote a future tense: *stēsousin,* "will establish"; and
they omit much of the text altogether. Cavander's Corinthian reports an
announcement that the Corinthians *intend to choose* Oedipus as their king,
but does not claim he is the people's delegate to inform Oedipus of the move
officially. Arnott's Corinthian reports *a rumor* that the people will appoint
Oedipus their king, and thus distances himself from any official discussion or
decision-making, and from any standing as the official messenger of news.
The Greek phrase Berkowitz and Brunner omit, which Cavander renders
as "it was already announced," and which Arnott translates as "so goes the
story," is *hōs eudâto,* "so it was said."[49] Again, Arnott is closest to the Greek,
though he too translates *tyrannon,* "tyrant," with the gentler "king," which,
as we will see later, detaches the play from its Greek environment.

In Sophocles, then, the Corinthian does not begin with a claim that he
is an official messenger. In several of the translations cited, he is making
precisely such a claim.

Upon this detail a great deal depends. A translation that identifies the
stranger as a messenger at this point robs readers of all awareness that he is
passing on *hearsay,* not an official decision. An official messenger needs no
motive or reward for bringing news. That is his job. But if the stranger is
not an official messenger, what motivates him to travel to Thebes to report a
rumor to Oedipus? And why hasn't Sophocles given us, as Seneca does in his

---

[47] *Sophocles: Oedipus the King,* trans. Kenneth Cavander with an introduction by Tom Driver (San
Francisco, 1961), 29.

[48] Peter Arnott, *Sophocles' Oedipus and Antigone,* 24.

[49] Forms of the verb *audao* generally express the idea of not necessarily well-informed talk in the
Oedipus. In line 731, Jocasta comments on the report that Laius was killed at a place where three roads
meet and says, "This *eudato* and still is said," i.e., "such was the rumor." Similarly, in line 527 the chorus,
talking to Creon about accusations that he "set up" Teiresias to accuse Oedipus, comments, *eudâto mèn
táde, oîda d'ou gnómei tiní:* "It *was* said. What the thought or plan was, I don't know."

Oedipus, a messenger bearing an official offer, or a messenger with the usual messenger speech telling us how Polybus died?

Jocasta does not challenge the Corinthian's statement. If the throne of Corinth is available, its occupant must necessarily have been removed. And that's the issue she pursues: "How so?" Jocasta continues, "Is not the old man Polybus still in power?" "Not any more. For death now has him in the grave," he replies. The stranger, then, makes two related statements: first, the vague good news, that Oedipus may perhaps be able to return to Corinth as tyrant; and second, the definitely asserted bad news that subtends the good: that Oedipus' father is dead. If that second part is not true, the stranger's life will obviously be in jeopardy when Oedipus discovers, on his return, that Polybus is still alive. If the first part is as vague as it sounds, Oedipus' claim to power might be challenged. Polybus was a tyrant and tyranny does not convey automatic rights to succession. The Corinthian's rush to Thebes gives Oedipus a chance to move quickly if he wants to win power at home.

Jocasta sends for Oedipus. When Oedipus arrives, he asks *Jocasta,* not the Corinthian, about the news, thus allowing her to mediate and edit what the stranger has to say. Unlike Jocasta, however, he does not ask who sent the man. His question is: "Who on earth is this person? What's his news for me?" Jocasta replies with the same formula that the stranger himself used when he answered her: "Out of Corinth: *ek tês Korínthou.*" This time the answer is not obviously at odds with the question. Jocasta has separated the two parts of the Corinthian's news. She jettisons the rumor that Oedipus will be made tyrant of Corinth altogether and invests the second item, that Oedipus' father Polybus is dead, with all the authority of an official messenger's report. Here is her response, which I have rendered thus: "he will, officially, *announce* your father is no longer Polybus he's died." Her excited, run-on sentence does not result from a slip in proofreading. This Corinthian will, in due course, tell Oedipus that Polybus was not his father, not just that his father Polybus is no longer alive. That is why I have omitted the conventional semicolon after "Polybus," so Jocasta, in her excitement, can blurt out the whole line, as she does in the original, without our losing the double meaning.

Why Jocasta edits the report is a much more complicated matter that falls outside the scope of the act of translation, though the reader will probably suspect that she does not want Oedipus to go back to Corinth. The translator's job is to convey what the text says—and to make sure that the dramatic irony in Jocasta's words is discernible. Her use of the verb "to announce (as would a messenger)" has allowed the stranger to appropriate to himself what he did not claim before: the status of an official messenger. He does so immediately. When Oedipus asks the Corinthian to speak his news himself, the stranger accepts Jocasta's censorship, but hints that there is more to report: "If, as is clear, I must announce (*angeîlai*) the last part first. . . ." Jocasta, then, gives Oedipus the impression that the stranger is an official messenger, and the stranger seizes the opportunity to be fully "credentialed" in *Oedipus'* eyes.

Oedipus does not pursue the stranger's hint about the first part of his news. Indeed, a reader might even suppose that the Corinthian now leaves the stage, as messengers in tragedy usually do when they have said their say. But the Corinthian has not left. He is waiting and listening. If we have been reading Sophocles or Arnott, we know he has an agenda, which depends on the rumor that Oedipus has a chance to become tyrant in Corinth, a rumor Jocasta has suppressed, probably because she does not want him to go. The Corinthian grasps, as he eavesdrops, that what he thought was bad news is good news and that there is something upsetting about his good news. When Oedipus says he cannot return to Corinth through fear of "the woman still alive," he has his clue. And the last word Oedipus utters before the stranger re-enters the dialogue is "fear" (*phóbos*).

"Who is this woman that you both so greatly fear?" the stranger asks. I have introduced "both" to underscore the stranger's perceptive use of the plural "you" form, which we cannot distinguish from the singular in English: he has concluded that Jocasta is also afraid (hence her suppression of the first part of his report). For most messengers in Greek tragedy, the grand moment is their "messenger speech." Sophocles' Corinthian has no "messenger speech" at all. His grand moment comes as an interrogator. And his first question, though including Jocasta, in effect silences her. She cannot answer without revealing in public the nature of Oedipus' fears. But the audience will also recall that she has told the chorus immediately before the stranger's entrance that Oedipus is "always owned by anyone who spells things out for him—provided that man spells out things he fears." This man, if Jocasta's assessment of Oedipus is correct, has just begun a process of interrogation that will establish what Oedipus fears and thus empower him to "own" Oedipus by spelling out the "things he fears," much as Teiresias does earlier in the play.

"Fear" is the key word in this segment of the play. Between lines 917 and 1013 occur some twenty percent of all words indicating "fear" in the seven surviving plays of Sophocles. All are focused on Oedipus' fears. The Corinthian, now credentialed as a messenger, has the chance to reverse the magnetic poles of Oedipus' fears and get him to leave Thebes and try for the throne of Corinth—an undertaking that would leave Oedipus much indebted to the man who first alerted him to the opportunity to gain power in his hometown. And that, the stranger says, is why he came: for the reward.

The distance, then, between Arnott and the other translators cited is vast. There is a great deal more drama in the details of these interchanges than the others allow us to see. The Corinthian is not merely a purveyor of information in a play with just one character, Oedipus, surrounded by unfailingly truthful informants any more than is Aeschylus' Agamemnon or Shakespeare's Othello. Creon, Teiresias, Jocasta, the Corinthian, the Courtier, the Slave, the Priest, are all carefully crafted personages in their own right in a play written by a great master of rhetoric. And one of the features that almost all tragedies have in common is the prominent part played by deception and self-deception.

Translators who have edited Sophocles' words are delivering us not Sophocles' but Seneca's Corinthian, who comes in and says (*Oedipus*, 784–85):

> Corinth's people call you to the throne
> your father held. For Polybus has found
> eternal peace.

But Seneca's Corinthian, direct and blunt as he is, should not delude us into thinking that he hasn't got surprises in store for us too.

My last example is the exchange between Oedipus and the Corinthian, which follows the Corinthian's later claims (a) that he used to be a shepherd who grazed his flocks on Mount Cithaeron near Thebes (some hundred miles from Corinth and across the administrative boundaries of other Greek city-states) and (b) that, while there, he found Oedipus, who was then a baby, brought him back to Corinth and gave him to Polybus, tyrant of Corinth. Even characters in "foundling" comedies react more skeptically to such claims than Oedipus does here. The credibility of these claims rests on the accuracy of proof adduced and on the reliability of the reporter, who, in this case is a total stranger. But Oedipus, with all his fears about his legitimacy, accepts these claims without question. He simply asks how this hitherto unknown and forever anonymous Corinthian obtained the child. Here are five versions.

1. Storr:

   Question: *A foundling* or a purchased slave, this child?
   Answer: *I found* thee in Cithaeron's wooded glens.[50]

2. Cavander:

   Question: So you gave me to... Had you bought me for
                your slave
                Where did you find me?
   Answer: ***You were lying*** beneath the trees
                In a glade upon Cithaeron.[51]

3. Fitts and Fitzgerald:

   Question: What of you? Did you buy me? ***Did you find me***
                by chance?
   Answer: *I came upon you* in the crooked pass of Kithairon.[52]

4. Fagles:

   Question: And you, ***did you*** ... buy me? ***find me*** by accident?
   Answer: *I stumbled on you*, down by the woody flanks of
                Mount Cithaeron.[53]

5. Watling:

   Question: ***Was I... found?*** Or bought?
   Answer: ***Found***, in a wooded hollow of Cithaeron.[54]

Only Storr makes the stranger claim that he found the child personally. The other four place "find" or "found" as a prompt in Oedipus' question, and give the stranger a less definitive expression in response: "you were lying beneath," "I came upon," and "I stumbled on," or "found" by persons unnamed. The Greek word in the question, translated "Did you find?" or "Was I found?" in the last four, is *tychón* ("you, having chanced upon"). The Greek word in the answer is *heurón* ("I, having found"). Sophocles' Oedipus is absolutely *not* asking whether the stranger found the child himself, but

---

[50] F. Storr, *Sophocles* (London and New York, 1919), 1:94.

[51] Cavander, *Sophocles: Oedipus the King*, 31.

[52] *Sophocles: The Oedipus Cycle,* trans. Dudley Fitts and Robert Fitzgerald (New York, 1965), 50.

[53] *Sophocles,* trans. Fagles, 219.

[54] *Sophocles: The Theban Plays,* trans. E. F. Watling (Harmondsworth, 1947), 54.

whether the child came into the stranger's possession accidentally (by chance) or deliberately (by purchase). It's important to keep "chance," since Oedipus will conclude at the end of this scene that he is the child of chance (*tyche*). And *tyche* is the most often cited causal force in the play.

The displacement of the verb "find" from the stranger's answer to Oedipus' question lessens our alertness to a crucial change in the stranger's testimony a few lines later. When questioned about whom the child belonged to, the Corinthian says he does not know, but that the person who *gave* him the child will know. So he did not, by his own later admission, *find* the child at all. If he was not lying then, he's lying now, or vice-versa, and possibly lying on both occasions, as Jocasta later attempts to suggest. At line 1057 she declares that the stranger has spoken *máten,* "falsely," "nonsensically," a word used under rather similar circumstances by Ion to Creusa in Euripides, *Ion* 275: "Is this account made genuinely [*alethés*] or falsely (nonsensically) [*máten*]?"[55]

By transposing the word "find" from the question to the answer, translators are tampering with the testimony of a witness and encouraging us to rationalize the lie as a slip caused by a careless response to a leading question that *they* make Oedipus ask, but that Sophocles' Oedipus never asks at all. Watling's manipulation is the most subtle, since he provides "found" in both the question and the answer, but suppresses the person of the finder.

Why? Because it is critical to the canonical interpretation of Sophocles' *Oedipus* that the Corinthian should be telling Oedipus the truth, however improbable that truth may be. Once caught in a lie, his whole testimony should become, at the very least, suspect.

But, one may argue, what about Oedipus' feet? Doesn't their swollen condition prove that the Corinthian is correct in his identification of Oedipus as the foundling child? In Sophocles' *Oedipus* there is nothing to suggest that Oedipus actually has swollen feet *now.* That supposition rests on the mistranslation of the Greek word *óneidos,* which some editors gloss as "disfigurement," but which in every other instance in the Greek language means verbal, not physical, abuse and is arbitrarily assigned the meaning of "disfigurement" in this one example out of the hundreds attested in Greek

---

[55] Ion, child of Creusa as the result of her rape by Apollo, does not know who his parents are and is finally passed off on Xuthus, who is eager to have a child, as his own child by his mother Creusa, with the connivance of Apollo. The technical term for such a child was *plastòs patrí* (a child "faked" for the father). And this is exactly what the drunk called Oedipus (Sophocles, *Oedipus* 781–83).

to give the Corinthian the evidence that the text does not otherwise supply. Sophocles' Oedipus asks the Corinthian not why he is alluding to a fearsome disfigurement to his body in times past, but why he is alluding to *the abuse* he received because of his name in times past. We will return to this matter later.

The scholarly tradition subtending this manipulation of the Corinthian can be traced back to a mistake by Aristotle. In *Poetics* 1452a, to illustrate his notion of tragic reversal (*peripéteia*), Aristotle cites the arrival of the Corinthian whom he designates a "messenger" in Sophocles' *Oedipus.* He comes "to cheer Oedipus up and release him from his fear about his mother." Two centuries ago, before there was a canonical interpretation, Thomas Tyrwhitt summed matters up: "It is just as well we have the tragedy still surviving, for otherwise we would be bound to believe on the basis of Aristotle's statement that the messenger came for the express purpose of releasing Oedipus from fear about his mother."[56]

More recently, Roger Dawe has observed that "the role of the Corinthian messenger is curiously garbled by Aristotle.... What the messenger actually comes to do is to offer Oedipus the throne of Corinth now that Polybus is dead." But "garbled" is too kind a word. Aristotle is wrong, as he is when he says that Oedipus identifies himself as the son of Polybus in the prologue of the play. Dawe adds, correctly, that the messenger "is not an official representative," but then misses his own self-contradiction: if the man is not an official representative, he has no authorization to offer the throne of Corinth to anyone.[57]

Problems of adjusted translations are not restricted to this character and this passage, much less to these particular exchanges within the passage. The evidence upon which Oedipus bases his judgment against himself in this play is his own testimony for or against himself and unsupported, often conflicting, hearsay. So the reader needs to be alert for any details, however small, of conflict in testimony. Indeed, one would surely *expect* there to be conflict of testimony in any investigation.

Athenians were more familiar with legal procedures than most of us are, not only because their laws were less complex than ours, but also because many of them served regularly on juries. On the matter of testimony against oneself, Athenian law was clear: "a litigant could not be his own

---

[56] Thomas Tyrwhitt, *De Poetica Liber* (Oxford, 1794) on *Poetics* 1452a25.
[57] Dawe, *Oedipus Rex,* 190, 192.

witness."[58] Further, hearsay was inadmissible as evidence in Athenian courts (in contrast with Roman courts where it was sometimes admissible). The only exception allowed was in the case of "what a dead man was alleged to have said."[59] Demosthenes, in *Euboulides* 4, notes: "Nor do the laws allow hearsay as evidence, not even on the most serious charges"; and, in *On the Crown* 2.7: "they do not permit hearsay evidence from a living witness, only (a deposition) from one now dead."[60] Accepted forms of evidence were "laws," "witnesses," "agreements," "evidence under torture," and "oaths," but neither hearsay nor *oracles.*[61] What Freud describes as the "ever fresh relays of evidence" which reveal Oedipus' guilt are fresh relays of hearsay.[62]

J.-P. Vernant, citing Louis Gernet, observes: "The tragic writers' use of a technical legal vocabulary underlines the affinities between the most favored tragic themes and certain cases which fell within the competence of the courts.... [T]he tragic poets make use of this legal vocabulary, deliberately exploiting its ambiguities, its fluctuations and its incompleteness."[63] In Sophocles' *Oedipus* there is a search for evidence, cross-examination of witnesses (and the threat, at least, of cross-examination under torture of a slave), passing of judgment, and sentencing of the accused. There is also an inner audience, the chorus, before which all procedures occur, and to whose opinion those involved both refer and defer. And the man who plays prosecutor, judge, and agent of punishment comes to regard himself as the accused.

The problem is that myth is all based on hearsay and folklore. And details vary from one mythic version to another. Sophocles is showing us an interesting process in *Oedipus.* A cast of mythic characters is presenting and examining a mythic tradition of which they are part as if they were trained (some better than others) in the rhetoric of fifth-century Athens. Yet they are still creatures of myth in one important dimension: they have maddeningly little regard for time and sequences in time. When did this happen? "Years deeply layered could be measured back," and so forth. Further, each conflicting piece of folkloric hearsay adduced can be substantiated

[58] D. MacDowell, *The Law in Classical Athens* (Ithaca, N.Y., and London, 1978), 243.

[59] A. R. W. Harrison, *The Law of Athens: Procedure* (Oxford, 1971), 133–54.

[60] R. J. Bonner, *Evidence in Athenian Courts* (Chicago, 1905), 20 ff.; Aristotle *Rhetoric* 1375a24 ff.; cf. D. MacDowell, *The Law in Classical Athens* (Ithaca, N.Y., and London, 1978), 243.

[61] Harrison, *The Law of Athens,* 133.

[62] Freud, *Introductory Lectures on Psychoanalysis,* 330.

[63] J.-P. Vernant, P. Vidal-Naquet, *Tragedy and Myth in Ancient Greece,* trans. Janet Lloyd (Brighton, 1981), 3.

somewhere in different versions of the Oedipus myth outside Sophocles. A child was found, a child was given. Laius was killed by one assailant; he was killed by many. If Oedipus is a mythic being rather than a real person, he doesn't have a fixed biography. All actions attributed to him are equally valid and invalid. He is defined by each person who narrates him, however differently that person may narrate him, like myth itself, and owned by whatever narrative has him in the grip of fear at any given moment.

Sophocles has given us, in Oedipus, a mythic character with a special difference. Oedipus abandons the dramatic role he is being asked to play, that of finding a solution to the problem of a plague afflicting Thebes, and tries to construct a narrative of himself out of all the bits and pieces of conflicting testimony that tradition provides. He is myth trying to define itself in nonmythic terms. And those bits and pieces are presented to him by characters who are also trying to narrate themselves. So when these conflicting elements are juxtaposed in a fixed and logical environment, like a play, they become conflicts which do not allow us to draw the conventional conclusion. They cannot all be correct logically and dramatically, even though, in a mythic sense, they are all perfectly justifiable.

Ultimately, as Jocasta notes, and Oedipus concedes, Oedipus' fears overwhelm his logic. His insecurity, we learn from his exchanges with the Corinthian, began when people teased him about his name as a child. "Swell-foot," they called him, since the elements of his name Oidípous, in Greek, can yield that among other meanings. *Oideîn* means "to swell" and *poûs* means "foot." Then a drunk at a dinner party calls him a bastard, an illegitimate child passed off as legitimate on his unsuspecting father. Most people would not find this enough reason to call home and ask their parents if it were true, much less go to Delphi, after their parents have reassured them, in order to ask the same question of Apollo.

The "inconsistencies" in testimony, then, should be allowed to remain so readers can make up their own minds why they are there and what the results of their presence are. They should be not brushed away like troublesome wrinkles on the model in a fashion photo. The canonical "reading" *must* be able to withstand comparison with the text itself, not with the text as pre-adjusted to fit the interpretation. And the more recent the translation, the more likely it is to be pre-adjusted.

I have made my translation conform as closely as I could to the Greek text, pretty well line for line. It has three lines more than the original (marked 8a, 21a, and 917a) to allow a more expansive translation in places where the sense of a particular wordplay in Greek could not be conveyed without such expansion. In order to achieve this correspondence, I have used a version of the Greek iambic trimeter where the original has iambic trimeters rather than the more conventional English iambic pentameter that I have used for Seneca. Each Greek iamb equals two English iambs and looks like an English iambic hexameter, but yields a three-beat rather than a six-beat line and permits some non-iambic rhythms, usually in the first half of each measure.

10. Seneca and the Mythic Tradition

I noted above that many translators adjust the text of Sophocles to make it fit the canonical interpretation. This is not the same thing as failing to understand the grammar and syntax of the Greek and making an error. It is a deliberate reshaping of the original. In doing so, translators have inadvertently given us not Sophocles' Corinthian, but a version of Seneca's Corinthian, with overtones of "fate" rather than "chance."

Seneca's play is the only surviving work from the Greco-Roman world that covers exactly the same segment of Theban myth that Sophocles covers in *Oedipus.* Its author almost certainly had access to texts now lost to us, such as the *Oedipus* tragedies of Aeschylus and Euripides.[64] But because the Senecan *Oedipus* is in Latin and of a much later date, scholars of Greek literature pay it almost no attention and frequently dismiss it with a sneer. True, it lacks the dramatic power of rhetorical dialectic that we find in Sophocles; but, in my judgment at least, it contains some of the finest poetry in the Latin language and can, with a little imagination, be staged successfully even without resorting to the wholesale pruning that Ted Hughes applied in his otherwise admirable translation. But Seneca's Latin is much more densely compacted than Sophocles' Greek or anyone's English and cannot so easily be rendered line for line.

Seneca has been outside our canonical reading long enough for his rediscovery to be exciting and artistically stimulating. His drama is "other," malleable, the stuff of experiment and innovation in the theater. And that, Ted Hughes observed, is why Peter Brook wanted to produce Seneca's, not

---

[64] The best source of information on this subject is K. Töchterle, *Lucius Annaeus Seneca, Oedipus: Kommentar mit Einleitung, Text, und Übersetzung* (Heidelberg, 1994).

Sophocles', *Oedipus* in London at the Old Vic in 1968. The differences between Senecan and Athenian tragedy are often, as they were to the producers of Ted Hughes' adaptation of Seneca's *Oedipus,* precisely the strength and allure of the Latin dramas. Hughes wrote: "The Greek world saturates Sophocles too thoroughly: the evolution of his play seems complete, fully explored and, in spite of its blood-roots, fully civilized. The figures in Seneca's *Oedipus* are Greek only by convention: by nature they are more primitive than aboriginals. . . . Seneca hardly notices the intricate moral possibilities of his subject."[65] I thoroughly disagree with Hughes' assessment of both Senecan and Sophoclean drama and wince at how he expresses what he sees as the primitive nature of Senecan characters; but his other point is, I think, in essence, correct: Senecan tragedy is vastly and intriguingly different from Greek tragedy. Seneca is doing much more than rendering some extant or non-extant Greek original. As James Sanderson and Everett Zimmerman point out: "It is possible to become so concerned about the fact that Senecan drama is not Sophoclean drama that the intrinsic qualities of Senecan drama are completely ignored."[66]

It is also possible that we can learn things from Seneca that will help our understanding of Sophocles, and of Sophocles' *Oedipus* in particular. For Seneca offers us no less vexing problems of testimony than does Sophocles. These details, however, are not usually suppressed in translation, presumably because these days only a handful of people has any vested interest in what Seneca's *Oedipus* says. There *is* no fiercely maintained canonical reading that translators are obliged to support. Let me illustrate my point with the testimony about Laius' death from Seneca's *Oedipus* as it is translated in John Fitch's recent Loeb edition.[67] I have italicized certain key words and phrases.

When Oedipus asks why no inquiry was held about Laius' death, Creon responds: "It was prevented by the grim threat of the unspeakable riddle" (246), that is to say, by the Sphinx (whom we'll discuss in due course). And here is how Creon describes Laius' death:

> He *trod* a path hedged in by dense brush, where three roads branch out across open country. . . . Here, as he counted on peacetime, *a band of brigands* suddenly attacked him with *the sword* and performed the crime *unwitnessed.* (277–78; 286–87)

[65] *Seneca's Oedipus,* adapted by Ted Hughes (London, 1969), 8.
[66] J. Sanderson and E. Zimmerman, eds., *Oedipus: Myth and Dramatic Form* (Boston, 1968), 62.
[67] J. G. Fitch, *Seneca Tragedies II* (Cambridge, Mass., 2004).

Here is Oedipus' reaction on hearing Creon's report of what he alleges was said by the ghost of Laius, which accused Oedipus of being his killer:

Thebes mourned the loss of Laius *long before* I set foot on Boeotian soil. (665–66)

Here is what Oedipus tells Jocasta about his killing of an old man in the same area Creon mentions:

Yet a memory returns along a faint track, of someone felled by a blow from *my staff* when he blocked my way and sent to Dis—an *old man,* who first forced me arrogantly aside *with his chariot* when I was young—at a distance from Thebes, where the region of Phocis splits the road three ways. (768–72)

Finally, here is the exchange between Oedipus and Jocasta when he asks her to sort out some details for him:

Oedipus:	What span of life had Laius when he died? Did he fall when flourishing in his early prime, or in broken age?
Jocasta:	*Between old age and youth,* but closer to old age.
Oedipus:	Was there a large retinue surrounding the king?
Jocasta:	*Most* went astray, confused by the unclear path, but *a few stayed by his chariot* in loyal service.
Oedipus:	Did anyone fall beside the dying king?
Jocasta:	One loyal and courageous man shared his fate.
Oedipus:	I have the guilty man: the number and place match. And what of the time?
Jocasta:	Now is the tenth harvest.

(774–83)

Before venturing any comment, let me note that Fitch never suggests there is any reason to think Oedipus wrong in concluding that he is Laius' killer, even though he sets certain inconsistencies in much starker relief in his translation than I do in mine. First, Creon says that Laius, traveling on foot (and apparently unescorted) was killed with a sword by multiple bandits—and that the killing was unwitnessed. Creon is either reporting folklore or making the story up, unless, of course, he was involved in the action himself and thus did not count himself as a witness.

We can rationalize some of the details away by saying that the body, if discovered later, might have shown evidence of a sword-stroke, and that multiple footprints might have suggested multiple assailants who might have plundered the body and thus made it clear that they were bandits. But the more scrupulously we defend Creon's veracity here, the more likely we make it that Oedipus was not the killer, for we are postulating a careful crime-scene investigation.

Seneca's Oedipus, in contrast, seems quite confident that Laius was dead long before he himself first set foot in Theban territory. And he is definite that the old (not middle-aged) man he killed was in a chariot, not on foot, and that he killed him with his staff, not a sword. Yet, by the end of this play, he seems to have convinced himself that he *did* kill Laius with his sword. In Seneca's *Phoenician Women,* set at a later point in the myth, when Oedipus is exiled and blinded, Oedipus says that he killed Laius with a sword.

Jocasta's version (derived from what source we never learn) comes only in short responses to specific questions. We get a picture of Laius, in a chariot and accompanied by a considerable though disorganized retinue, of whom one man, and only one, died with Laius. The rest, presumably, survived and could, perhaps, bear witness. But no witnesses are called. How many were involved in the attack on Laius, Jocasta does not say, since Oedipus does not ask. He nonetheless feels he has enough evidence to decide at this point who is guilty, since the location and the number match. But what number is he thinking of: the multiple retainers of Laius, the total number of people killed? His own account gives no indication that Laius was escorted, nor has he mentioned killing anyone other than the arrogant old man. And who is the guilty killer? On balance it would seem to be Creon, if one is forced to make a snap judgment based on the testimony presented, since his report cannot possibly be correct. But Oedipus assumes that he himself is the guilty party.

Jocasta does, however, mention a number that specifies something no one else in either Sophocles' or Seneca's *Oedipus* ever specifies: exactly how long ago an event occurred. Since Romans counted inclusively, the tenth harvest indicates nine years ago. But why nine years? That sounds curiously recent, given both Oedipus' earlier confidence that Laius was long dead before he himself ever entered Theban territory and his recollection that he killed an old man at a crossroads in the dim past. Since we are given no other fixed points in time during the play, Jocasta's precision is more puzzling than everyone else's imprecision. We will return to this issue later.

There is no way to reconcile these various accounts. Further, no one has said anything from which Oedipus could conclude definitively that he, rather than, say, Creon, killed Laius, since none of the pieces of the puzzle really fit together properly. For everything Creon says is rendered suspect by his eyewitness-style account of a crime he declares went unobserved. The only weighty element in Oedipus' self-condemnation is his memory of killing an arrogant old man at a crossroads.

Has Seneca lost control of his narrative? Or are we facing the same sort of dilemma we face in Sophocles' *Oedipus,* that of a mythic character trying to do historical research into his own past? The main difference is that when Seneca's characters contradict themselves or others, we are more often left to notice the contradictions for ourselves. Perhaps it is an essential element of the myth of Oedipus that he is in quest of the unknowable, and that there is no single definitive answer. Myth is like the sea-god Proteus in Menelaus' account in *Odyssey* 4: the more you wrestle with it, the more it changes shape. When we think our Protean myth has ceased to move, it is really our own struggle, not the myth, that stops and yields the definition we choose to accept. In the quest for knowledge, when doubt ceases, it gives way to the certainty of belief. And with the certainty of belief comes blindness to other possibilities. That is why it is important not to approach either Sophocles' or Seneca's tragedy on the assumption that we already know the answers; for if we do, we begin where Oedipus ends, not where even he begins.

11. The Oedipus Myths

Greek myths were tales with many local variants, constantly in flux, appropriated and modified by successive narrators for their own purposes. It was only when they were written down and available to the reading public that popular versions began to become "standard," and, gradually, to displace their rivals. This process in Greece did not really start until the sixth century BC, when, as we have noted, the tyrant of Athens, Peisistratus, had an authoritative text of the Homeric poems produced: the texts of the *Iliad* and *Odyssey* more or less as we have them today. Peisistratus' Homer did not immediately sweep all rival versions away. But the authorized version triumphed over the centuries, as little by little, memory of, and interest in, the alternative versions faded away.

As early as the fourth century, a fragment of the comic writer Antiphanes, who began to write around 386 BC, some twenty years after Sophocles' death, made a parodic summary of how an Athenian of his day might view the Oedipus myth:[68]

> Tragedy is a blessed form of poetry in every way. First the stories are known by the audiences even before the dialogue begins. The poet only has to jog their memories. Say "Oedipus!" They know the rest: his father's name was Laius, his mother was Jocasta, these were his daughters, these his sons, this is what will happen to him, this is what he did.

What Antiphanes has summarized, from the dramatist's point of view, is precisely what makes the writing of a new "Oedipus" tragedy so difficult. Each poet usually made some radical inflection of what he perceived as the general outline of the myth in the public mind. A Greek tragic poet was competing for the prize at a dramatic contest and could not win simply by repeating what others had said and done before him. Successive poets outdid each other to make their versions definitive, since they were, after all, in constant competition with one another and were each other's best audience.

Of the two thousand or so Greek tragedies and their accompanying satyr plays whose titles we know or whose former existence we know about, only thirty-three survive. These thirty-three are written by the three writers whose texts the city of Athens maintained at public expense, and most of which were, in succeeding centuries, used as school texts: Aeschylus, Sophocles, and Euripides.

When one work is selected over another as a school text, there is usually some rationale behind it. We are painfully familiar nowadays with attempts by school boards to suppress works they regard as immoral, politically subversive, or politically "incorrect." What motivated the selection of particular tragic texts for pre-Christian Greek schools is less clear. While all the surviving plays of Aeschylus and Sophocles, and nine of Euripides', were used

---

[68] Fragment 191 in Edmonds, 1–8. Cited by Athenaeus in *Deipnosophists* 6.222A.

as school texts, it is clear from the comic poet Aristophanes that some of Euripides' most famous plays in his own day (*Telephus,* for example) are neither among those that became school texts nor among the ten that survived by chance and independently of the school curriculum.

Greek tragedies were offered for production in sets of three (called, technically, trilogies), with a satyr play (a comic and ribald spoof of themes that may or may not have been present in the preceding three) added at the end to make a fourth play, thus completing what we call a tetralogy. Among the surviving works we have one satyr play, Euripides' *Cyclops;* one intact trilogy: Aeschylus' *Agamemnon, Libation Bearers,* and *Eumenides,* known collectively as *The Oresteia;* and no tetralogies. But not all dramatists composed their tetralogies with such continuity of plot. None of Sophocles' surviving plays, for instance, seems to have been presented as part of a tetralogy in which a given story is developed from one play to the next.

The plays of Aeschylus' trilogy tell, in order: (1) the murder of Agamemnon and Cassandra, his captive, by Agamemnon's wife Clytemnestra; (2) the murder of Clytemnestra, in revenge, by her son Orestes, aided by his sister Electra and his friend Pylades; (3) the trial and acquittal of Orestes. This set of three nicely complements a reading of Homer, for Agamemnon features prominently as the commander-in-chief of the Greek forces in the *Iliad,* and the warning example of an incautious return home to Odysseus in the *Odyssey.* At the same time, the trilogy alerts the reader to changes Aeschylus has made in the Homeric version. In Homer, Agamemnon makes the disastrous mistake of leaving his wife under the supervision of a poet as he heads off for war. And poets tell stories as they please. In Homer it is Clytemnestra's lover who kills Agamemnon, abetted by Clytemnestra. But in Aeschylus the killer is Clytemnestra—a change that surely surprised his audience as much as it surprised his chorus. Aeschylus was displaying a woman acting decisively, politically, and murderously in a way no woman could have done in the Athens of his day.

The house of Agamemnon also yields the only subject about which the ancient selection of school texts left surviving plays by all three dramatists: the tale of the killing of Clytemnestra by her son Orestes in Aeschylus' *Libation Bearers,* and in the *Electras* of Sophocles and Euripides, not to mention Euripides' *Orestes.* Indeed Orestes is the most commonly occurring character in extant Greek tragedy.

The house of Oedipus is less well represented in surviving Greek literature, epic or tragic. There *were* epics about the royal house of Thebes and its conflicts, but they have not survived. The famous war from this epic tradition is between the sons of Oedipus, Eteocles and Polyneices, by his second wife, Euryganeia (whom he married after his first wife killed herself on discovering that she was his mother), according to the lost epic *Oedipodeia,* as reported by Pausanias, a writer of the second century AD (*Description of Greece* 9.5.10–11; cf. Apollodorus, Library 3.55). In this version, one brother, Polyneices (whose name means "Quarrelsome"), assisted by six famous warriors from other cities who, together, make up the famous "Seven against Thebes," attacks Thebes; the other, Eteocles ("Just Glory"), defends the city as these siblings compete for the throne after Oedipus is banished in disgrace. The brothers kill each other in a climactic duel, and their mother kills herself either just before the duel or over her sons' bodies.

After the deaths of Oedipus' sons, Oedipus' brother-in-law Creon takes control of the city. Creon is, in turn, driven from power and killed by the king of Athens, Theseus, as Euripides tells the tale in his *Suppliants.* The only surviving ancient epic on the subject is by the Roman poet Statius, who wrote his Latin *Thebaid* in the late first century AD. Wherever there is a conflict between the Greek epic and tragic traditions of Oedipus, Statius seems to give precedence to the versions found in Greek tragedy.

Our earliest references to Oedipus in texts that survive from antiquity are in the *Iliad* and *Odyssey.* In *Iliad* 23.679–80, there is a passing reference to someone who won a contest in Thebes at the funeral games for Oedipus; and in *Odyssey* 11.271–80, if the lines are not an interpolation, Odysseus claims he saw the ghost of Oedipus' mother among the dead:

> Epicaste, who, in ignorance, married her own son. And he married her after killing his father—though, as time passed, the gods made things clear. He ruled over Cadmus' people in beautiful Thebes and suffered grievously through the terrible will of the gods. She passed on to Hades with its strong gates after looping a noose high from the ceiling, obsessed by her own misery, leaving him a legacy of pain and all such things as a mother's avenging spirit can accomplish.

Epicaste, not Jocasta, is the name by which Oedipus' wife is known in Homer and in other now lost epics, the *Oidipodeia* and the (Greek) *Thebaid,* as quotations in later writers show. And Oedipus seems to have continued to rule Thebes after she died. When later writers talk of Epicaste as Oedipus' wife, they are probably drawing on these works that predate Greek tragedy.

Odysseus, in the passage cited above, is very vague about the consequences of Oedipus' actions. He does not preclude Oedipus' self-blinding, the civil wars between his sons and grandsons, or his expulsion from Thebes, but he equally certainly does not mention them.

In tragedy, the house of Oedipus is the topic of Aeschylus' *Seven against Thebes* and of Euripides' *Suppliants* and *Phoenician Women* (in which Oedipus himself is a character). But it is best known from three tragedies, all by Sophocles: *Antigone* (circa 442 BC), *Oedipus* (circa 429–425 BC), and *Oedipus at Colonus* (posthumously: 401 BC). These three Sophocles plays, however, were not written as, and do not constitute, a trilogy as Aeschylus' Theban plays did. Each is a self-contained dramatic entity. As is evident from their likely performance dates, *Antigone* is at least twelve years earlier and *Oedipus at Colonus* at least fifteen years later than *Oedipus*.

Each of Sophocles' Theban plays treats major elements in the myth rather differently. In *Oedipus*, for instance, Oedipus' daughters are taken from him by Creon. In *Oedipus at Colonus*, Antigone accompanies her father in his exile. Our awareness of the differences in characterization in the three Oedipus plays by Sophocles has been dulled by the practice, common among translators, of packaging them as if they were a trilogy, sometimes altering elements of their content to make them fit together.

Oedipus' son Eteocles is a character in Aeschylus' *The Seven against Thebes*, and both Eteocles and Oedipus' other son Polyneices are, along with their sisters Ismene and Antigone, Jocasta, and Oedipus himself, characters in Euripides' *Phoenician Women*. But Sophocles is the only classical Greek poet who gives us a full version of Oedipus' fall from power as tyrant of Thebes. So, given the summary of Antiphanes, cited earlier, it is all too easy to suppose that the myth of Oedipus was already in a fully standardized form by the time the great era of Greek tragedy ended with the deaths of Sophocles and Euripides in 406 BC, and that it had moved quite far away from what it was in the tantalizing scraps of the earlier epic tradition. But there are some indications to the contrary.

12. Aeschylus' Oedipus Trilogy

Aeschylus wrote a Theban trilogy as well as an *Oresteia* trilogy: *Laius, Oedipus, The Seven against Thebes,* and added the mandatory satyr play, *The Sphinx,* to round out the tetralogy. Only *The Seven against Thebes* has survived. We know of only one other full Theban tetralogy, written by, of all people, Meletus, the principal accuser of Socrates at his trial in 399 BC, according to the ancient commentator on Plato's *Apology.* So it is not entirely clear what ground Aeschylus covered and to what extent he was responsible for creating the definitive model for the story of Oedipus himself.

If we allow for the element of distortion that is always likely in comedy, a passage from Aristophanes' *Frogs,* mentioned earlier, may help. Aristophanes, we may recall, has the god of tragedy (and of wine), Dionysus, travel to the underworld to bring back the ghost of Euripides to help Athens in a moment of wartime crisis. But, in the poetic contest staged when Dionysus arrives, only two poets compete. The contest thus mirrors the practice at the lesser of the two feasts of Dionysus at which tragedies were performed. So Aristophanes is producing his own tragic competition, inside a comedy, at a festival of Dionysus where other "real" tragedies were being performed. It is hard to imagine a more devastating public indictment of the worth of those still living playwrights whose tragedies were being staged at the same festival.

In the course of the debate, Euripides attacks Aeschylus' tendency to repeat himself in his prologues. Then Aeschylus counterattacks:

Aeschylus: And how do *you* write your prologues?
Euripides: I'll cite you one,
           And if there's somewhere that I say [*pou dis eipo*] the same
              thing twice,
           or if you see superfluous bombast, spit on me!

                                                (Frogs 1177–79)

The fleeting presence of Oedipus in anagrammatic form is no accident. For here is the example Euripides' ghost selects:

Euripides: Oedipus was, at first, a man blessed by the gods…
Aeschylus: Oh no, by Zeus! He was cursed at conception by the gods!
               Before he was begotten, in fact, Apollo claimed
               he'd kill his father, yes even before he was ever born!
               So how was he then "at first, a man favored by Chance"?
Euripides: Then later he became most wretched of mankind.
Aeschylus: Oh no, by Zeus! He never stopped being precisely that!
               How so? The moment he was born they put him out,
           though it was winter, in a piece of pottery [*ostrákōi*]
           so he'd not grow up and become his father's killer.

Then off he went to Polybus, **with swollen feet [oidôn tō póde]**, and then, though he was young, he married an old crone who was his own mother as well, to top it off. And then he blinded himself.

(Frogs 1182–95)

I set some lines in bold because they both echo and contradict what Sophocles' Corinthian says when trying to get an old herdsman to recall how the two of them supposedly ran their flocks together on Mount Cithaeron during the *summer* until the rising of Arcturus in the autumn. Since shepherds don't normally run flocks on mountains in winter, Sophocles' Corinthian has presumably changed the season to make it possible for shepherds to pass on a child, but in doing so clearly breaks with some tradition that these events occurred during the winter.

Seneca's Corinthian, we should note, follows the ghostly Aeschylus on this point:

Oedipus:	You gave me
	to my parent? But who gave me to you?
Corinthian:	A herdsman on snow-covered Cithaeron.
Oedipus:	What brought you to Cithaeron? Just pure chance?
Corinthian:	I followed my horned flocks up to that peak.

(Oedipus 807 ff.)

The Corinthian's claim that he took his flocks about a hundred miles from Corinth into the hills of Cithaeron, near Thebes, is itself, as we have noted, improbable. We have faced that same improbability in the case of Sophocles' Corinthian. The details have been scrambled to adapt the story. So it is worth noting that, in the old Greek alphabet, which did not distinguish omicron from omega, Kithairon is an exact anagram of Korinthia; and Sophocles' Corinthian has, as we'll see later, a penchant for wordplay.

Seneca's Corinthian, however, claims that he made this trek to snow-covered Cithaeron, which implies that he went in the winter, not in the summer, as does Sophocles' Corinthian. So there is an exchange of improbabilities between the two versions. Sophocles' Corinthian is, in terms of Aeschylean precedent and good herdsmanship, on Cithaeron at the right time to meet the Theban shepherd, but at the wrong time to find the baby, and Seneca's Corinthian is on Cithaeron at the right time to find the baby, but at the wrong time to meet the other herdsman. For Seneca's herdsman, Phorbas, points out, quite sensibly (846–47):

> Cithaeron, always rich in grass to graze
> provides the *summer* pasture for our flocks.

The fact that Seneca exploits this contradiction in his play increases the likelihood that he had access to, and was using, in places, either the lost *Oedipus* of Aeschylus, or at least Aeschylus' lost *Laius*.

Another curious detail in the summary given by Aeschylus' ghost is the attribution to himself of a most uncharacteristic piece of wordplay: the etymologizing of Oedipus' name as "Swell-foot." The earliest occurrence of this etymology in surviving literature is in Sophocles' *Oedipus,* composed at least twenty years before Aristophanes wrote *Frogs.* But if the ghost of Aeschylus is actually quoting his own tragedy, then he, not Sophocles, first adduced this wordplay.

In Sophocles' *Oedipus,* Oedipus seems to have assumed that he was teased about being named "Swell-foot" because his name was susceptible of such an explanation rather than because he actually had swollen feet, much as a child nowadays with a surname such as Ramsbottom is likely to be teased among us, even though his posterior may bear no resemblance to a sheep's hindquarters, except in the slanderous graffiti on the school walls.

When Sophocles' Jocasta describes how her child by Laius was exposed, she says the following:

> His child did not survive birth even by three days.
> That man lashed his two feet by the ankles in one bond
> And cast him on pathless peaks—but using others' hands.

> (817–19)

Binding the feet for a short time would not leave any lasting marks.[69] But Sophocles' Corinthian, whose contradictions (to put it politely) we have noted, uses Aeschylus' explanation:

Corinthian: I saved your life at that moment in time, my child.
Oedipus: What pain threatened me as you took me in your hands?

---

[69] Fitton Brown noted this point in *Proceedings of the Cambridge Philological Society,* new series 12 (1966): 22, and was ridiculed by Dawe, *Oedipus the King,* in his note on *Oedipus* 1031, for making an

Corinthian:	The ankles of your feet should bear witness for that!
Oedipus:	Dear me, why give new life to this bad ancient tale
	[*ennépeis*]?
Corinthian:	I was the one who freed you when your feet were pinned.
Oedipus:	That coarse slander's been my scourge since infancy.
Corinthian:	Because you're named for your mischance. It's who you are!

(Oedipus 1030ff.)

Pinning of the feet might well leave marks that would last over the years. But notice that Oedipus still takes the remark to be a retelling of an old tale rather than a reference to any condition of his feet that he has ever noted. The verb he uses (*ennépeis*) is the same Homer uses in the first line of the *Odyssey* to ask the Muse to sing for him the tale of a man: *ándra moi énnepe, Moûsa*. Oedipus then continues to describe the name as slander (*óneidos*), not as a description of a physical deformity. Throughout this tragedy *óneidos* and its companion verb *oneidízein* are used to indicate verbal abuse. As noted earlier, they *never* indicate physical abuse anywhere in Greek, much less "disfigurement" as Dawe (on 1035) translates *óneidos* in his commentary. He is adjusting the meaning to fit the canonical interpretation.

Seneca seems to follow the Aeschylean model. His Oedipus is well aware that he has scarred ankles and tests the Corinthian to see if *he* knows this is so:

Oedipus:	I have marks on my body. What are they?
Corinthian:	Insteps pierced through with iron. Your swollen, piteously injured feet [*vitio pedum*] gave you your name.

(811–13)

The phrase *vitio pedum* is the closest Latin allows Seneca to approach encoding the name Oedipus in a Latin wordplay.

A final detail is worth noting. When Aeschylus cites Euripides' opening line back at him, he substitutes "chance" for "blessed by the gods." And "chance," *tyche,* is a word much used by Oedipus in Sophocles' *Oedipus.* To help readers locate it in the text, I have translated *tyche* by "chance,"

---

argument from "real life." But Dawe offers no justification at all for his own unsupported translation of *óneidos* as "disfigurement" on line 1035.

"mischance," or "luck," everywhere it occurs, and have not used these English words to render any Greek word not derived from the root *tych*.

We must, of course, be a little wary about taking the passage from Aristophanes, cited above, as clear evidence of what Aeschylus actually wrote, because Aristophanes is also having Aeschylus' ghost parody Aeschylus himself. Not only does "Aeschylus" continue to repeat himself, as Euripides insists he usually did, but he says that the child was exposed in a "piece of pottery," an *óstrakon*. This seems to be a jesting comparison of the practice of "exposing" children in an earthenware pot (*chytra*) to the Athenian reversed electoral process of ostracism (a means of getting rid of politically unwanted *adults* by inscribing their names on potsherd ballots). It could be that the practice of ostracism was designed as a kind of symbolic communal "chytrism" or exposure of adults. Since the ancient commentary on Aristophanes' *Wasps* 289 says that Aeschylus, in his lost *Laius,* told how someone, presumably Oedipus, was exposed in a pot, a *chytra,* the likelihood is increased that the ghostly Aeschylus is indeed citing his own works in our passage from *Frogs.*[70]

Aeschylus' surviving play from his Oedipus tetralogy, *The Seven against Thebes,* is particularly important for our understanding of Sophocles' (and Seneca's) *Oedipus.* For it tells about what we know was the epic core of the Theban tradition: the war between Eteocles and Polyneices who, in Aeschylus, are Oedipus' sons by Jocasta, not by his second wife, Euryganeia, as in the lost Greek epic tradition, and who were cursed by Oedipus for some reason not clearly explained. The most dramatic scene in the *Seven* is the one in which a messenger arrives to inform Eteocles that his brother Polyneices, along with six Argive captains, is attacking the seven gates of Thebes.

The messenger could have begun by stating first the gate at which Polyneices was fighting. But he does not. He goes, gate by gate, down the list, describing the shields that each attacking warrior bears, leaving Polyneices until last. And, one by one, Eteocles sends the six Theban captains, to whom he makes the seventh, out to oppose the seven attacking Argive captains, choosing each by reason of the motif on his shield. When the sixth Argive is announced, Eteocles must know that the seventh will be Polyneices. But still he sends someone else to fight the sixth Argive captain, thereby leaving himself no alternative but to face Polyneices personally. Then he reacts to

---

[70] Aeschylus, frag. 122 in S. Radt, *Aeschylus*, vol. 3 of *Tragicorum Graecorum Fragmenta* (Göttingen, 1985).

the announcement of Polyneices' presence at the seventh gate as if it were a surprise, the fulfillment of his father's curse, rather than the result of the messenger's order of presenting the Argives and of his own gradual elimination of all alternatives.

I have set out this portion of Aeschylus' *Seven against Thebes* in detail for several reasons. First, it shows Oedipus' son explaining his forthcoming and self-destructive duel with his brother as the fulfillment of a curse his father placed upon him, when it is quite clearly the result of choices made by the messenger and by himself. Just because a character in a tragedy sees a given outcome as the product of a curse or divine action does not mean that the author does too. Second, it shows the disastrous consequences of Oedipus' self-punishment. His sons have taken Thebes into that most destructive of all plagues, war, and a war with many features of civil war. Worse is to follow. Though Thebes survives the attack of "The Seven," it does not survive the attack of their sons, known to mythographers as the *Epigonoi,* "The Successors." Oedipus' self-destruction sets Thebes on a path toward civic self-destruction. What Pietro Pucci observes of Homer's gods might equally well be applied to any gods in literary texts:

> The gods therefore are not the masters of the heroes' destinies, but the servants of the heroes' poetic destiny.[71]

My third reason is the most troublesome: if you read Sophocles' *Oedipus* in isolation, you would never guess that Oedipus' sons would have (or cause) problems, much less that Oedipus had cursed them. On the contrary, Sophocles' Oedipus declares he is satisfied that his sons can manage for themselves and worries, rather, about his two daughters, whom Creon allows him to approach and touch. Oedipus does not distinguish the girls from each other, but collectivizes them by using not the plural number, but the much less common dual, whose distinctive forms emphasize that things referred to are to be thought of as a pair. In this context of blindness, the dual generates an implicit play on the double sense of the Greek *kóre* as "eye" and "girl." No other passage in any extant Greek text uses the dual so frequently and insistently as this, and I cannot re-create the force of this usage in English. When Creon quickly separates the two girls from Oedipus, he symbolically blinds Oedipus all over again.

---

[71] Pucci, "Theology and Poetics in the *Iliad,*" 34.

In Seneca's *Oedipus,* the four children are presented to the audience only in oblique allusions. Teiresias discerns their menace when he takes the omens, as does the more learned reader or listener. But neither Oedipus nor Jocasta, both preoccupied by the past, expresses any interest in or concern for their future. Part of the explanation may lie in the fact that neither Sophocles' nor Seneca's *Oedipus* plays are part of a trilogy, as Aeschylus' *Oedipus* was. They were obviously not written with an immediate sequel in mind. The problem with the Theban myth is not only the difficulty of deciding where to end, but, as Statius points out at the beginning of his *Thebaid*, where to begin. At the same time, ancient audiences would note the irony in Oedipus' words, at least in Sophocles, since they were very familiar with the sequels.

Finally, Sophocles has Creon take over the government of Thebes the instant Oedipus is incapacitated in his *Oedipus.* We might, with reason, suspect that Creon had been ruler of Thebes between Laius' death and Oedipus' accession too, though Creon carefully dodges that issue at *Oedipus* 126–27. But no one else has him assume power after Oedipus' self-blinding until the deaths of Eteocles and Polyneices. Such is the case everywhere else in the Greek and Roman tradition of Thebes (including not just Seneca, but also Sophocles' own earlier *Antigone*). In Seneca's *Oedipus,* Creon is imprisoned by Oedipus and does not re-emerge during the remainder of the play. When Seneca's Oedipus leaves the stage at the end of the play, there is no indication as to who, if anyone, will rule Thebes; for if Oedipus did kill Laius a mere nine years earlier, Eteocles and Polyneices are too young to lead armies and fight duels, unless they are children by an earlier marriage.

Fundamental to the differences between the *Oedipus* tragedies of Sophocles and Seneca, on the one hand, and Aeschylus' Theban trilogy, on the other, then, is that theirs were individual, self-contained plays, whereas Aeschylus' trilogy was a dramatic continuum extending over the three tragedies and into the satyr play. This is not to say that there is no intertextuality among the three House of Oedipus plays by Sophocles. On the contrary, the last play, *Oedipus at Colonus,* in which Oedipus and his daughters seek asylum in Athenian territory, seems devised to look back, in particular, on the earliest play, *Antigone.*

Since *Oedipus at Colonus* was produced posthumously, it may have been edited by other hands (possibly by Sophocles' son, himself a playwright) before it was staged in order to integrate it better with the earlier tragedies. In *Oedipus,* Oedipus begs Creon to exile him from the land. Whether Creon does so is unclear. But certainly Creon takes Oedipus' daughters from him. If he goes into exile, he goes alone. But in *Oedipus at Colonus* (599–601) Oedipus says he was driven into exile by his sons. And he also makes an emphatic statement that he was acting in self-defense when he killed the old man at the crossroads in a situation that he represents, rather, as "road-rage" in *Oedipus.*[72] Similarly, Jocasta (who is usually a part of the civil war scenario between Eteocles and Polyneices) is passed over in silence in *Oedipus at Colonus,* though Oedipus' references to her in the past tense imply that she is dead. And this again would fit better with the story as represented in *Oedipus.*

Oedipus at Colonus, further, adds the fresh element of a possibly ruinous conflict between Athens and Thebes to the story, appropriate enough in the dark days of the Peloponnesian War, as Athens comes closer to defeat. *Oedipus at Colonus* has something of the nature of a prayer about it: that Athens' mythic role as refuge for the exiled and forlorn will stand it in good stead in the current war as it did in myth, where the king of Athens, Theseus, defeats the bullying Creon. It did not. And the play is notably lacking in the traditional Sophoclean subtlety of language, wordplay, and argumentation that characterize his other surviving tragedies. The dialectician is displaced by the preacher.

It is precisely this subsequent "tailoring" of *Oedipus at Colonus* to fit with the earlier plays that threatens our understanding of both *Oedipus* and *Antigone.* It inclines us to "read back" Oedipus' self-proclaimed innocence from *Oedipus at Colonus* into *Oedipus,* and to read back Antigone's special concern for Polyneices from *Oedipus at Colonus* into *Antigone.* In short, it is likely that someone, whether Sophocles himself in advanced old age, or, as I suspect, a posthumous editor, tried to adjust the text of *Oedipus at Colonus* so that it could serve as a sequel to *Oedipus* and what filmmakers call a "prequel" to *Antigone,* which was composed at least thirty years earlier. While our understanding of *Oedipus at Colonus* is advanced by recognizing how it modifies themes from the earlier plays, it does not make good critical sense to assume that the earlier plays were composed in anticipation of *Oedipus at Colonus.* The results are damaging to a coherent understanding of both *Antigone* and *Oedipus.* Such packaging shifts a great deal of the focus from Oedipus to Creon, the only character in all three plays, with several

---

[72] In *Oedipus at Colonus* 546–48, Oedipus claims that if he had not killed his attackers they would have killed him, and that thus he was innocent of murder. His account in *Oedipus,* however, suggests that he was responding to the old man's arrogant attempt to get him out of his way rather than to an immediate threat to his life.

accompanying incongruities. The idea that the Creon of *Oedipus at Colonus* would ever have betrothed his son to Antigone is hard to contemplate.

It is in their treatment of the war between Eteocles and Polyneices that we see a gulf loom between Sophocles and Seneca. For Oedipus' Thebes was a powerful city and a foe of Athens in Sophocles' day, not ruins, like Agamemnon's Mycenae. Greek dramatists, in fact, routinely relocate the mythic tales of Agamemnon's house to Mycenae's more prosperous neighbor Argos, one of Athens' allies. But in Seneca's day the glory of Thebes was also a thing of the past. Less than a century after Sophocles produced *Oedipus,* Alexander the Great reduced the whole of Thebes, apart from the poet Pindar's house, to rubble. Thus Seneca's play about the later fortunes of the House of Oedipus, the incomplete (or abbreviated) *Phoenician Women,* lacks the direct connection between mythic Thebes and contemporary Thebes that energizes Sophocles' *Oedipus at Colonus.* And Seneca's *Phoenician Women* is a different kind of meditation on the struggle for power among rivals, suggesting a more Roman dynastic war.

In Seneca's *Phoenician Women,* Oedipus, accompanied by his daughter Antigone, is still alive and wandering as his sons prepare for civil war. But he is an embittered man. Antigone begs him to intervene and stop the war, but to no avail. Oedipus is ready to let Thebes go to ruin, not to offer himself up as a sacrifice as he does at the end of the Senecan *Oedipus.* On the contrary, he goes off into the wilds to overhear their conflict which he no longer has eyes to watch. Jocasta is very much alive, and she does attempt to intervene, but is resolutely rebuffed by Eteocles who utters the memorable final line: "Power is a bargain whatever price you pay" (*Phoenician Women* 664).

The Oedipus tradition that Seneca is building on in *Phoenician Women* is that of Euripides, not that of either Sophocles of Aeschylus.

13. Euripides' Oedipus

We know little about Euripides' *Oedipus.* But there is quite a lot in two surviving lines from it cited by an ancient commentator on Euripides, *Phoenician Women* 61:

> In [Euripides'] *Oedipus,* however, Laius' attendants blinded him:
> "But we threw the son of Polybus to the ground
> and gouged out his eyes and destroyed them."

We can see instantly that this play was a radical departure from anything else that survives. Oedipus presumably encounters Laius, tyrant of Thebes, kills him, and is then set upon by Laius' attendants and blinded. So when the ghost of Aeschylus summarizes the Oedipus tradition in the *Frogs*, he is very oddly ignoring Euripides' own variant version; and Euripides' ghost does not contest the issue with him. Antiphanes also ignores Euripides' version in the synopsis cited earlier. In Euripides there was no mystery about who killed Laius, as there is in Sophocles and Seneca and, if the passage from the *Frogs* is any guide, as there was in Aeschylus too. Oedipus' assailants clearly thought Oedipus the son of Polybus, ruler of Corinth, when they reported their attack, presumably to someone at Thebes. These lines not only imply that several of Laius' attendants survived, but that Oedipus was both blind and known to those attendants as Laius' killer before he married Jocasta and came to the throne of Thebes.

Yet in the very lines of Euripides' *Phoenician Women* that prompt the scholiast's comment, Jocasta says Oedipus blinded himself (60–61): "Oedipus, enduring all one can suffer, brutally killed his own eyesight." We don't know the date of Euripides' *Oedipus*, though it is almost certainly earlier than Sophocles' *Oedipus*. But Euripides' *Phoenician Women* was staged between 411 and 408 BC, seventeen to twenty years after Sophocles' *Oedipus*. By this point, then, Euripides has adopted Aeschylus' and Sophocles' account of Oedipus' self-inflicted blindness, while maintaining independence on another matter. In Sophocles' *Oedipus*, a messenger announces that Jocasta hanged herself before Oedipus blinded himself. In Euripides' *Phoenician Women*, Jocasta lives long after Oedipus destroys his eyesight.[73] But she, as always, eventually destroys herself.

In two different plays, then, Euripides offers two radically different versions of how Oedipus' blindness occurred. Myth is variable, and playwrights are not consistent in their use of the same myth from play to play. Sometimes Euripides is in accord with Sophocles' *Oedipus*, sometimes not, even in the same play. In Euripides' *Phoenician Women*, Jocasta is probably assimilated to the epic tradition's Euryganeia, Oedipus' second wife (who is now permanently eliminated from the literary tradition) and lives until the civil

---

[73] On the psychological implications of Oedipus' self-blinding, see Richard Caldwell, "The Blindness of Oedipus," *International Review of Psycho-Analysis* 1 (1974): 207–18.

war between Oedipus' sons.[74] In *Phoenician Women,* Euripides' Jocasta is, as in most ancient writers after the early epics, the mother of Oedipus' sons Eteocles and Polyneices and kills herself over their bodies after they perish in a duel (1349ff., 1455ff.). In Statius' *Thebaid,* Jocasta kills herself *before* the duel (*Thebaid* 12.634–47); and she dies not by hanging but by the sword, as in Seneca's *Oedipus* 1034–39.[75]

Euripides' Jocasta talks thus of Laius' exposure of Oedipus:

> He, having fathered a child, knowing
> the riddling words and oracle of god,
> gives the child to cowherds to expose
> on Hera's Meadow and the mountain ridge
> of Cithaeron, piercing his lower legs
> with iron spurs. Because of this all Greece
> named him Oedipus, "The Swollen Foot."
> Then Polybus' horse-tenders picked him up,
> and brought him home and placed him in the hands
> of their mistress.
>
> (*Phoenician Women* 22–30)

At first these words may suggest that Euripides is now more in accord with Sophocles' version. But this is not quite the case. In Euripides, the child is passed not to Polybus, but to Polybus' wife (usually named Merope). This statement, then, has two mutually contradictory parallels in Sophocles' *Oedipus.* Oedipus says a drunk at a dinner party once called him a *plastòs patrí,* "a child passed off on his father," a spurious child that a wife tricks her husband into thinking is his own. But Sophocles' Corinthian says he gave the infant Oedipus *to Polybus himself,* who happily acknowledged him because he had no children of his own. And Seneca's Corinthian says he gave the child to Oedipus' parent, without specifying which one.

---

[74] For detailed accounts of the variants in the Oedipus tradition, see Lowell Edmunds, *The Sphinx in the Oedipus Legend,* vol. 127 of Beiträge zur Klassischen Philologie (Königstein/Ts, 1981), and Carl Robert, *Oedipus: Geschichte eines Poetischen Stoffs im Griechischen Altertum,* 2 vols. (Berlin, 1915).

[75] There is even a variance about what sword Jocasta used to kill herself. In Euripides' *Phoenissae* 1455ff., she uses the swords belonging to her dead son, in Seneca's *Oedipus* and Statius' *Thebaid,* she uses the sword with which Oedipus killed Laius. See Paolo Venini's note on *Thebaid* 11.6 in *P. Papini Stati Thebaidos Liber Undecimus* (Florence, 1970).

14. The Sphinx

The riddle of the Sphinx lurks allusively somewhere in almost all traditions of Oedipus, though none of the tragedians says precisely what the riddle is. The word "sphinx" itself is Egyptian, as is its most famous representation, the archetypal Sphinx that stands guard before the pyramids of Giza, a hybrid creature—a gigantic lion with the face of a human whose construction by the Pharaoh Chephren predates even the earliest Greek traditions by well over a thousand years.[76] Other Egyptian sphinxes, represented with the features of the reigning pharaoh, were symbols of royal power; and, significantly, the Greeks associated the Sphinx with the royal house of Thebes, a city whose name is a double for the name by which the Greeks called the Egyptian city of Waset (Luxor). Immanuel Velikovsky sought to establish a connection between the Oedipus myth and the Egyptian pharaoh Amenhotep III in his *Oedipus and Akhnaton*.[77] What makes the Sphinx different from other Egyptian deities is that the body is animal and the head human. In other hybrid Egyptian gods the body is human and the head animal.

Greeks certainly had close connections with Egypt from at least as early as the mid-seventh century BC when Greek mercenaries enabled a dispossessed Egyptian prince Psamtik to gain control of his homeland. He, in gratitude, allowed Greeks to establish such colonies as Naucratis in Egyptian territory. And things Egyptian influenced many aspects of Greek life. Not only does the development of Greek pottery, masonry, and sculpture owe a great deal to Egyptian influence, but some Greeks even gave their children Egyptian names. The last tyrant of Corinth, Psammetichus, was named after Psamtik himself. The lyric poet Alcaeus traveled to Egypt, and Homer says Helen and Menelaus visited too (*Odyssey* 4), and even mentions an Egyptian named Polybus (*Odyssey* 4.126). There is also a tradition, best known from Euripides' *Helen,* that Helen never went to Troy at all, but spent the duration of the war in Egypt under the kindly guardianship of Proteus and the more menacing sponsorship of his successor, Theoclymenus, who wanted to marry her.

Several other Greek myths posit close and sometimes hostile interaction between Greeks and Egyptians, most notably the tale of the fifty sons of Aegyptus who forcibly marry the fifty daughters of Danaus, king of

---

[76] See the recent discussion in Martin Bernal, *Black Athena,* vol. 3: *The Linguistic Evidence* (New Brunswick, N.J., 2006), 465, 469–71, and the sources cited.

[77] Immanuel Velikovsky, *Oedipus and Akhnaton* (New York, 1960).

Argos—the theme of Aeschylus' *Suppliants*. The Argive princess Io was identified in various ways with the Egyptian goddess Isis. In more recent times, the Thebans had sided with Xerxes and the Persians against Athens and Sparta; and the navy that accompanied Xerxes included large numbers of Egyptian and Phoenician warships. Athenian troops had served in Egypt during Sophocles' lifetime, and Herodotus had devoted the second book of his *Histories* to Egypt.

The word "Sphinx" might well evoke thoughts of the Egyptian Sphinx in an Athenian tragic audience, ever alert to connections between dramatic myth and contemporary realities. But if there is anything in Sophocles' *Oedipus* that makes use of such an Egyptian "resonance," I've missed it. Indeed, the reason Sophocles says so little about the Sphinx (named only once in the play, by Creon at line 130) may be to minimize the chance that his audience's thoughts would stray to Egypt. In Seneca the Egyptian Sphinx may have a topical relevance, as we will see later. For his is the first mention, by name, of the Sphinx in Roman poetry between Plautus and Statius, a period of about three centuries. And Plautus' reference is in The *Little Carthaginian* 442–44, a remark made to someone from Phoenician Carthage.

There is a strong Greek tradition that the Thebes in Greece was founded by Cadmus, who arrived from Phoenicia (present-day Lebanon). And the Phoenician connection may be the reason why sphinxes in Greek are female and Egyptian sphinxes predominantly male. Not only were Phoenician (or Canaanite) sphinxes female, but there is a tradition that the Theban Sphinx was the first wife of Cadmus, founder of Greek Thebes.[78] Thus the Sphinx may be associated with the notion of (disliked) foreigners, as Wallis Budge says it was in Egypt.[79] In Aeschylus' *Seven against Thebes,* the Thebans are distinguished ethnically and linguistically from their Argive (Greek) opponents and called Cadmeans, even though there is no reason to suppose that, in Aeschylus' times, any language but the local dialect of Greek was spoken there.[80]

[78] See Bernal, *Black Athena,* 3:470.

[79] E. A. W. Budge, *The Gods of the Egyptians; or, Studies in Egyptian Mythology,* 2 vols. (London, 1904), 472.

[80] There is also another tradition of Thebes' foundation by the Greek twins Amphion and Zethus, which, I suspect, may be in some way linked with the mysterious Mycenaean (Bronze Age) fortification that lies below Thebes, but within sight of the Kadmeion, the citadel of upper Thebes. This lower site was built in connection with a huge Late Bronze Age engineering project to drain Lake Copais. The site was occupied for only about a century-and-a-half and is known nowadays by the non-Greek name of Gla.

Greek artistic representations of the Sphinx differ from the earliest Egyptian sphinxes in that they have wings and female heads, like those of the later Egyptian sphinxes from the fifteenth century BC onward. They thus share features in common with other hybrid female monsters such as the harpies (part woman and part bird) who are strongly associated with death. Although none of the Greek tragedians offers us a description of what the Sphinx looked like in any surviving work, it is hard to imagine that Aeschylus' satyr play, *The Sphinx,* did not. In both the surviving plays, and in the titles and fragments of plays that have not survived, Aeschylus shows a penchant for describing the monstrous and is satirized for doing so in Aristophanes' *Frogs.* So it is entirely possible that Seneca, who does give us Oedipus' description of the Sphinx, was drawing on Aeschylus as he appears to have drawn on him for other details:

> I faced her bloodstained jaws,
> this prophetess too hideous to describe,
> the soil beneath her white with scattered bones.
> On her cliff-top perch she flexed her wings,
> hovered above her prey, coiled her whiplash
> tail to goad her menacing fury,
> like a fierce lion. "Sing me your riddling song,"
> I said. Then, from above, her hideous scream,
> her evil jaws noisily grinding, claws
> tearing at rocks. She could not wait to rip
> into my vitals. But I did unlash
> the knot of her enigma's webbed deceit,
> the grimly riddling song of the winged beast.
>
> (92–102)

There are no references to the Sphinx in Homer. But sometimes what dropped from the literary tradition was maintained for centuries in local lore and cult. That is why observations in nonliterary sources are so important, most notably those of Pausanias, a Greek of the second century AD, who traveled throughout Greece and left an impressive record of the monuments he saw and local traditions he encountered. Pausanias offers this account of the Sphinx and her habitat (9.26, 2–4), which I have divided into numbered sections in order to isolate the different strands.

1. Farther along there is a mountain from which they say the Sphinx, singing a riddle, rushed out to destroy those she caught.

2. Others say she came ashore at Anthedon with a naval force, wandering around to waylay and plunder, that she seized the mountain and used it for plundering raids until Oedipus overpowered her with a large army, which he brought with him from Corinth.

3. It is also said she was the bastard daughter of Laius. Through fondness for her, he told her the oracle given to Cadmus by Delphi. Apart from kings, no one else knew the oracle. Whenever someone came to dispute with the Sphinx the right to rule—for Laius had sons by concubines, and the oracles from Delphi applied only to Epicaste and her children—the Sphinx tricked her brothers with words: if they really were Laius' children, they would know the oracle. When they couldn't answer, she put them to death as punishment, since they had unjustly claimed royal descent and the right to rule. Oedipus then arrived, having learned the oracle in a dream.

In the first segment the nature of the Sphinx is not specified: she could be either human or monster. This version is compatible with Oedipus' recollection that he was *traveling alone* when he first approached Thebes, as he implies that he is in both Sophocles' and Seneca's *Oedipus* tragedies, provided that we assume that Oedipus solved the riddle on the same journey into Boeotia during which he killed an old man and all those with him at a Forked Road.

In the second segment above, the Sphinx is a foreign invader who lands a naval expedition on the *east* coast of Boeotia in the general area where Athens, at war with Thebes and Corinth, sent its own invading army around the time Sophocles wrote *Oedipus*. This looks like a later strand of tradition, though it is supported by the scholiast on Hesiod's *Theogony* 326, who also describes the Sphinx as "a woman brigand." In this version, Oedipus is captain of an *army* from Corinth and is thus approaching Boeotia from the west. This tradition matches Sophocles' *Oedipus* 122, in which Creon says Laius was killed by brigands who waylaid him when the complex-riddle-singing Sphinx was at large (130), and with Oedipus' claim in Seneca's *Oedipus* that Thebes had been in mourning for Laius long before he arrived in Boeotia. In Seneca's version, Laius could himself have been a victim of the Sphinx. Thebes could have been saved from one foreign army by another foreign army, led by Oedipus. So, to be independent, Thebes would need to be rescued from the rule of the foreign man who had liberated the city from the foreign Sphinx.

In the third version above, the Sphinx is the daughter of Laius himself and, if not herself a female claimant to the Theban throne, a female arbiter of who could possess that throne. Laius, as mentioned, also has illegitimate sons by way of his concubines, sons who seek to establish their own claims on the throne of Thebes.[81] Thus the Sphinx and her riddle are the agents whereby any claimant can establish that he really is a son of Epicaste. By knowing the answer to the Sphinx's riddle, Oedipus proves he is Epicaste's son. The antiquity of this third version is borne out by Pausanias' use of Epicaste for Jocasta, as in Homer, and in references to the now lost Theban epics. In this third version Oedipus must prove he is Epicaste's son if he is to rule Thebes.

As a sort of monster, the Sphinx is more common in Greek art than in surviving Greek literature, and extremely rare in classical Roman poetry and art. This creates an additional riddle as to why the Sphinx, as monster, features more prominently in Seneca's *Oedipus* than in Sophocles'. In Sophocles, Oedipus himself refers to her as a "riddle-singing bitch [*kyon*]," a derogatory term that much as its English equivalent is more often applied to a woman than to a non-canine monster. But I suspect she first took literary form as we imagine her today in Aeschylus' *Sphinx*. And as she is an outsider, an alien presence dominating Thebes, so too is her destroyer Oedipus, who has come to the land of the Cadmeans from Greek Corinth.

15. The Death of Laius

There is much disagreement in ancient tradition about how many people were with Laius when he was killed but less disagreement about where he was killed—though even these differences can be troublesome. Sophocles' Jocasta and Pausanias situate the killing at the intersection between the

---

[81] M. L. West, *Hesiod, Works and Days* (Oxford, 1978). West's note on line 533 (alluding to the riddle) argues that the Sphinx is not pre-Hesiodic. In Hesiod's *Theogony* 326 she is called Phix, which, Plato notes in *Cratylus* 414C–D, is what the Boeotians call her (cf. M. L. West, *Hesiod, Theogony* [Oxford, 1966], on *Theogony*, 326). The Sphinx, or Phix, is part of Theban geography. Sphinx Mountain—also called *Phoinikion*, "Phoenician Mountain," according to Strabo 9.2.26 and Pausanias 9.26.1–5—went through a variety of spelling changes in various ancient and Byzantine sources before becoming Mt. Phagas, as it is today (as in the Hesiodic *Shield of Heracles* 33, where it is *Phikeion*). See Paul Wallace, *Strabo's Description of Boeotia*, vol. 65 of Bibliothek der Klassischen Altertumwissenschaften (Heidelberg, 1979), 108–9. The Sphinx and her mountain (or rock) remained a symbol of political banditry in Hellenistic times (Athenaeus *Deipnosophists* 6.253E–F). See, in general, Lowell Edmunds, *The Sphinx in the Oedipus Legend*, especially 1–29.

east-west road between Thebes and Delphi and the road north to Daulis. Pausanias describes the site as a three-way crossroad: a *Schistè Hodós* (Forked Road) (10.5.4). The merged branches of the Forked Road continue south past Thebes and Plataea through the mountains and constitute the main ancient route from central Greece to Corinth and Athens.

A speaker in the one surviving fragment of Aeschylus' *Oedipus,* however, situates the incident at a crossroads in Potniae, which is a few kilometers south of where the road from Thebes to Delphi intersects with the northern fork leading to Daulis. The distance is short, but the significance of that distance is considerable. For Potniae is where the road from Plataea intersects with the north-south road. If Laius encountered his killer even this far south of the road between Thebes and Delphi, Laius was not traveling from Thebes to Delphi and his killer was not traveling from Delphi to Thebes in the version given by this speaker in Aeschylus' *Oedipus.*[82]

Pausanias' account of the site of Laius' death, however, agrees with those of Jocasta in Sophocles' *Oedipus* and Creon in Seneca's *Oedipus,* but adds the following details:

> There are the memorials [*mnémata*] *both to Laius and to the houseboy* [*oikétes*] *who followed him.* They remain at the midpoint of the crossroads even now, and unfinished stones were piled on them. According to tradition it was Damasistratus, then king of Plataea, who came across the bodies and buried them. (10.5.4)

The tradition that the king of Plataea is said to have found and buried the remains, however, suggests that folklore is trying to accommodate both the Sophoclean and Aeschylean traditions, since a traveler from Plataea would have joined the main north-south highway at Potniae.

There is no way of knowing when the monument was actually built, of course, especially since the Thebans had destroyed Plataea, and Alexander the Great destroyed Thebes completely before the end of the fourth century BC. So the chances of a disruption of tradition are considerable. If such a monument existed in the fifth century, however, many Athenians would have known about it, since they would have passed it often in delegations to

---

[82] For a fuller discussion see Alister Cameron, *The Identity of Oedipus the King: Five Essays on Oedipus Tyrannus* (New York, 1968), 10.

Delphi and on their way to battle (a) with the Persians at Plataea in Aeschylus' day (479) or (b) with the Thebans on several occasions in Sophocles' day. At the very least, this monument commemorates a strong local tradition that only one man stayed at Laius' side and died with him. And that is what Jocasta says in Seneca's *Oedipus:*

Oedipus:	Did anyone, then, die at the king's side?	780
Jocasta:	Just one. His loyalty and valor kept him there.	

Euripides, in his *Oedipus,* assumed there were enough survivors of Laius' entourage to attack and blind Laius' killer.

But Creon, in a passage from Seneca's *Oedipus,* cited earlier, implies that there were no survivors at all, and Sophocles' Creon says that there was only one survivor, as does Sophocles' Jocasta, who identifies him as a houseboy: the lone casualty becomes the lone survivor. Creon and Jocasta, and, if they are reporting accurately, the houseboy are the sole voices in tradition that maintain that there was only one survivor. So Creon's insistence, early in Sophocles' play, on only one survivor, would have met with some resistance from those in Sophocles' audience who had traveled to Thebes.

Sophocles' Oedipus admits that he killed an old man and *all of his companions* at a crossroads at some unspecified time in the past. In his version of events there were *no survivors at all.* And while this appalling confession of a dimly remembered multiple homicide provoked by an old man's act of insolence (rather than intent to kill) might be used as defense against the charge that he killed Laius, it nonetheless establishes: (1) that Oedipus is, by his own admission, a murderer with blood on his hands, guilty not of one, but of at least five killings and (2) that he has never shown any interest in finding out whom he killed and in making any kind of atonement. His only anxiety is that one of them may prove to be his father. It is part of that same curious disposition that makes him glad to get news of Polybus' death, since that news means that he did not kill his father.

Why does Sophocles' Oedipus not challenge, as a good cross-questioner would, the claim that there was one survivor (or many, for that matter) if he remembers killing everyone? Probably because when Sophocles' Creon makes his claim, the location of the killing has not been mentioned. Oedipus is preoccupied by the alleged plurality of *assailants*. He knows (but the audience doesn't yet know) that he killed an old man and his entire company while traveling alone. Oedipus so focuses on identifying the killer(s) that he either does not notice or does not think it advantageous to challenge an allegedly universal consensus that there was a single survivor who insists that Laius was killed by a plurality of assailants. Creon's account leaves only one witness to interrogate. Oedipus' account of killing an old man leaves none.

But if Creon is wrong, or lying, many survived as silent witnesses. And Oedipus soon becomes suspicious that people know more than they are saying. Yet he shuts off his one real chance of finding out by dismissing the chorus' mention of a tradition that Laius was killed by travelers (Sophocles, *Oedipus* 290 ff.). And the chorus pointedly observes later in line 530: "I don't see what rulers do."

The postulation of a single survivor who supposedly claims that Laius was killed by plural assailants favors Oedipus' innocence of that one particular murder, but leaves five more unaccounted for. He could not have killed Laius, since he left no survivors and was traveling alone. The problem, from anyone else's perspective, is that we have only Oedipus' word that he was traveling alone; and some traditions suggest he was not alone. But if there were no survivors, and he was traveling alone, Oedipus could not produce any independent counter-testimony, should the alleged "survivor" change his story and gave a plausible reason for why he had lied previously. Our clue that Sophocles' Oedipus is anxious about the situation is his persistent reference to a single killer, even though Creon's report insists on the plurality of killers. And when he asks for the "survivor" to be brought to him, he declares his innocence will be proved, *provided the survivor does not change his story.* Yet when the survivor arrives, Oedipus never asks him about the death of Laius. He has already come to believe that he is Laius' killer without the benefit of any eyewitness testimony and though his own memory of events indicates that he could not be Laius' killer.

It is reassuring to note, as pointed out earlier, that Seneca also introduces conflicting and potentially false witnesses. That is why we should consider the possibility that such "inconsistencies" were a characteristic feature of *Oedipus* plays, as Aristophanes' parody implies they were. The poets understood something we keep forgetting: that there really wasn't a single, retrievable Oedipus at all. There were as many Oedipuses as there were mythic variants of his story and of the stories of other major figures, such as the Sphinx, with whom his stories intersect.

Absent from Aristophanes' parody of the Oedipus myth is any mention of Sophocles' *Oedipus*. Pausanias too draws on Euripides rather than Sophocles. His description of the piercing of Oedipus' feet (10.5.3) recalls almost *verbatim* Euripides' *Phoenician Women* 25–26—another reminder that not all Greeks privileged Sophocles' version as we do, even though the Greek schools preserved his tragedy, rather than Aeschylus' or Euripides'.

16. Tyranny, Tragedy, and Psychology

The first competition of tragedies at Athens in 534 BC predates Sophocles' birth by only some forty years. Among the changes Peisistratus made in divine festivals, not least was the first state-sponsored staging of Greek tragedy at the festivals of Dionysus. The net result was to empower the dramatists to put the gods on stage and to allow an openness of public discourse about religion that is hard to parallel in the Occident subsequently. What it also suggests, at least to me, is that Peisistratus was attempting to *break down from the inside* the hold that traditional religion had on the state, thereby also breaking the hold that the aristocracy, who were in charge of religion and his chief rivals for power, had on the public mind. He was well aware of popular gullibility in religious matters, and indeed, after a period of exile, engineered his own restoration to power with a theatrical performance. He is said to have entered Attica in a chariot accompanied by a tall woman wearing armor whom the population would assume to be Athena, the goddess of Athens herself. What he may not have foreseen is that the poets would soon break the tyrant's hold on the people. For the dialectical polytheism of tragedy is the religion of democracy.

Tragic poets were officially recognized as teachers of their actors and choruses and, by Aristophanes, as teacher of the public at large. The winners of the tragic competitions not only had their names inscribed on public monuments, but were noted as having "taught," not composed, a particular set of plays. This practice may well be reflected in what seems to us the odd use of the verb "teach" within the plays themselves. Although each play was usually performed only once, under official sponsorship, the audience would have numbered in the thousands. The voices of the dramatists were hugely influential in shaping public opinion, since they addressed the entire voting population, as well as others, at the festivals of Dionysus.

The philosopher Aristotle, writing over fifty years after the deaths of Sophocles and Euripides, contended that tragedy had nothing to do with Dionysus. But he would probably have changed his mind if he had seen the Roman world in operation. Long before the Caesars became masters of

Rome in the first century BC, the Roman elite had taken legal action to suppress the cult of this god of the vine, Dionysus (also called Bacchus), because it was linked with unruly behavior by ordinary citizens, and by women in particular. The Romans wanted their state cults to be austere and controllable, not orgiastic and wild. Dionysus is a kind of Lord of Misrule, an agent of civic chaos.

The Athenian dramatic competitions devised by Peisistratus had offered an alternative to Roman "Prohibition." The original attraction to the tyrants of tragic performance may well have had something to do with the manipulation and control of popular religious beliefs and hero cults. And their approach was much more effective than banning (and thus privileging) religion, as Lenin did. Indeed, it may have been because of Peisistratus' influence that the myths which form the texts for Attic tragedy most often pertain to cities other than Athens and would therefore not excite local religious passions.

The competitions were also a means of harnessing and controlling, as well as encouraging, the energy of poets. They served as a brilliant means of channeling much of the energy unleashed by the cult of the wine-god into something creative and educational, not disruptive. And perhaps that is what subtends the vexing term *kátharsis,* "purgation" or "cleansing" that Aristotle talks about. The Dionysiac energy which could have turned into riots was directed to the theater where it was refined and absorbed by the music, words, sights, and competitive nature of tragedy and (though this is not our topic) comedy. It became a tool of education, a means of de-programming the population and making it more enquiring and sophisticated.

The Roman Seneca certainly did not want Bacchus left out of his *Oedipus.* In the choruses of his *Oedipus,* he offers a substantial tribute to Bacchus (Dionysus), which has no counterpart in Sophocles' *Oedipus,* as if to compensate for the lack of a festival to honor the god properly at Rome. But the Roman emperors made the same fatal political mistake governments continue to make nowadays: they did not use their resources to sponsor entertainments that would sharpen the intellects of the population and educate citizens. They directed popular energy toward nonintellectual and often cruel and bloody public contests in their theaters, training people to be not citizens but passive consumers of spectacular violence.

Peisistratus was not the only Greek tyrant who manipulated religious practices. Cleisthenes, tyrant of Sicyon, near Corinth, also reorganized his city's major religious festivals. Curiously, this process involved, among other

84

things, the substitution of the cult of Melanippus for that of Adrastus. Now Adrastus was famous as the only survivor of the famous "Seven against Thebes," who set out from Argos, just inland from Sicyon, to overthrow Eteocles, son of Oedipus, and establish Polyneices, now married to Adrastus' daughter, on the Theban throne. Melanippus was the Theban who killed the most formidable warrior in Adrastus' army, Tydeus, son-in-law of Adrastus, and father of Diomedes in the *Iliad*. Further, the displaced Adrastus, according to Herodotus (5.67) and the scholiast on Pindar's *Nemean 9*, was the grandson of Polybus, ruler of Corinth and its territories, which included Sicyon.[83] Cleisthenes of Sicyon substitutes a Theban for an Argive. In poetic terms, Korinthia has been moved closer to Kithairon as the cultural patron of his city. For the Polybus referred to here is the same Polybus who was reputed to be Oedipus' father. Therefore, Polybus was not otherwise childless, as Sophocles' Corinthian claims, or Adrastus was himself the son of Oedipus in some traditions rather than just the father-in-law of Oedipus' child Polyneices.

This change of patron heroes at Sicyon was an extraordinary move, since Cleisthenes was in effect severing a cultural tie with neighboring Argos, Adrastus' hometown, and establishing a new tie with Thebes. In doing so, he rejected the patronage of one cultural "father" and substituted one of the displaced "father"'s enemies.

Cleisthenes of Sicyon married his daughter to an Athenian named Megacles. He, in turn, had a son, named Cleisthenes after his grandfather, whose chief claim to fame is that he expelled the tyrant Peisistratus' family from Athens and established democracy around a decade before Sophocles was born. Cleisthenes of Athens' motive for establishing democracy was, says Herodotus, to secure a power-base for himself among the people, since all other clusters of vested interests already had leaders. And among his first acts upon gaining power was to reorganize Athenian tribal government along lines similar to those used by his tyrannical ancestor in Sicyon. In other words, when the tyrant Peisistratus' family was deposed, it would probably be more accurate to describe the change as evolutionary rather than revolutionary. In Herodotus' view, democracy has a tyrannical pedigree.

---

[83] Apollodorus (1.9.13) gives a rather different account. For other connections between the Oedipus tradition and tyranny in Corinth, see J.-P. Vernant, "From Oedipus to Periander: Lameness, Tyranny, Incest in Legend and History," *Arethusa* 15 (1982): 19–38. On the theme of lameness, see also C. Lévi-Strauss, *Anthropologie structurale* (Paris, 1958), 227–35, and J.-P. Vernant and M. Detienne, *Les ruses de l'intelligence,* 2nd ed. (Paris, 1978), 257–60.

The transition between tyranny and democracy was not achieved without violence. But the most harrowing violence was inflicted not by civil war, but by two attacks launched from the heart of the Middle East by the Persians, first in 490 BC and, more seriously in 480. In 480, the Athenians were forced to evacuate Athens as Xerxes' Persian invaders swept down and destroyed the city. The Delphic oracle had advised the Greek cities to come to terms with the Persians. Some, like Thebes, did; others, like Athens, did not. And, accompanying Xerxes, was the exiled last member of the tyrant Peisistratus' family, Hippias, who expected to be installed as tyrant after the Persian victory, and who was encouraged by, among other things, a dream that he had slept with his mother. Hippias took this to be a good sign that meant he would return to rule in his fatherland (Herodotus 6.107).

In both Greek and Latin, the words for one's homeland mean "fatherland": *patrís* and *patria* respectively. Julius Caesar had a dream similar to Hippias': that he slept with his mother the night before he crossed the Rubicon to take possession of Rome and Italy (Plutarch *Caesar* 32.6). Comon, a man from Messenia, a land conquered long before by the Spartans, even had a dream that he slept with his *dead* mother and that she returned to life, thereby indicating the recovery of his long enslaved fatherland (Pausanias 2.26.3). What we see as essentially illicit sexual fantasies were seen by the less sexually repressed Greek and Roman cultures as a yearning for illegal, tyrannical power disguised as the much less harmful fantasy of incest. As Jocasta observes,

> And as to intercourse with mother, don't fear this!
> Many a mortal before you has, in his dreams,
> also slept with his mother. He who places no
> significance on this bears life most easily.
>
> (*Oedipus* 980–83)

So when Oedipus is told that his father Polybus is dead, but not told explicitly that his homeland is likely to be his for the taking, thanks to Jocasta's suppression of the Corinthian's "good news," he loses an opportunity to fulfill the oracle in a way no Greek would have had trouble acknowledging: his father died of longing for him, and the marriage with his mother meant that he would gain control of his homeland.

When the Persians were defeated and expelled in 479, the Athenians returned to a city in ruins. A new beginning was required. The final product of Cleisthenes' reforms began to settle in: a political system that empowered the people to choose their governing council and their leaders by processes of election and lottery. State sponsorship of drama at the festivals of Dionysus was continued and was given very strong backing from an increasingly wealthy treasury during much of the fifth century.

Athenians remained keenly aware of the close relationship between democracy and tyranny. Pericles, the man who symbolizes Athenian democracy at its zenith, was himself a descendant of both the tyrant Cleisthenes and the Cleisthenes who founded democracy, and he looked like Peisistratus (Plutarch, *Pericles* 3; 7). Of Pericles' long political ascendancy in the years after the invasion by Xerxes, the historian Thucydides wrote: "It was in theory a democracy, but in practice rule by the leading man."

Admirers called Pericles a *prostátes,* a "champion" or "spokesman" of Athens. Enemies called him a tyrant. Athenians were anxious about political coups throughout the fifth century and maintained strong anti-tyrannical legislation.[84] Their practice of ostracism, a kind of election in reverse, whereby a man who seemed too powerful could be voted into banishment outside the city's territory for ten years, even if he had committed no crime, was but one example of the measures taken to keep tyranny at bay. The process by which a popular champion moves from being a leading citizen to a tyrant preoccupied Plato who, in *Republic* 8 (565D–566B), has Socrates ask why and how such a transformation occurs:

> How does this process of turning him around from being champion of the people [*prostátou*] to tyrant begin? Or does it become obvious that the champion [*prostátes*] begins to do the same thing as the man in the myth told about the shrine of Lycaean Zeus in Arcadia... that anyone who has tasted human flesh, even though it is only a morsel sliced up along with all the others from the consecrated foods, must become a wolf?
>
> It is the same, then, with someone who, as champion of the people, gains a hold on the people whom he has persuaded and who now obey him. He does not keep away from the blood of his own folk.... Isn't the sequel to this inevitable and pre-set? He will either be destroyed by his enemies or rule tyrannically and change from man to

---

[84] See J. F. McGlew, *Tyranny and Political Culture in Ancient Greece* (Ithaca, N.Y., and London, 1993).

wolf.... This is the man who stirs up hostility against the propertied classes. If he is thrown out and comes back despite the hostility of those that hate him, doesn't he return as an absolute tyrant?... If they don't have the power to turn him out or kill him after they have turned on him verbally and publicly, they get together and plot to kill him secretly?

Socrates describes not a particular champion, *prostátes,* turned tyrant, but the *habitual* metamorphosis of democracy into despotism—a theme dominating *Republic* 526A–576B. Similarly, in *Laws* 10 (906C) Plato establishes an equation between "what we call in living bodies a disease and what we call a plague in the seasons of the years and what we call in cities and states...injustice." Earlier in *Laws* 4 (709A), he notes that plagues often lead to revolutions. They certainly do in Sophocles' *Oedipus.*

To Plato's Socrates, justice in the state is indissociable from justice within the individual. The theme of metamorphosis symbolizes both the political brutality of the tyrant and of tyranny and the division in the soul between rational and animal instincts. Man is brutalized by the dominance of tyrannic over rational elements in the soul that makes real the grotesque desires and fantasies of the dream:

Those that awaken when we sleep...when one part of our soul is at rest—the part that approaches things reasonably and verbally, with gentle clarity, the part that rules the other element of the soul. That other element is like a wild and ferocious animal, gorged on food and drink. It leaps up, pushes sleep away from it, and goes off on a lively search to satisfy the call of its particular nature. You know it is bold and stops at nothing at these times, for it is freed from—and unburdened by—morality and thought. *Its lust, people think, does not shrink at intercourse with its mother* or anything human, divine, or animal. It will kill anything and has no taboos against any kind of food. To put it in one succinct statement: it will stop at nothing we would regard as mindless or disgusting. (*Republic* 8 [571C–D])

What Plato's Socrates describes sounds very much like what Freud called the id. And the struggle between the rational and irrational in Sophocles' *Oedipus* shows traces, I think, that Oedipus recognizes this same divide.

In response to Jocasta's exhortation not to worry about the fear of incest, he responds:

> You'd be correct in all of what you say if she,
> who gave me birth, were not alive. But since she lives,
> I am compelled to shrink from this—
>
> though you're correct.
>
> (984–86)

This is a sad testament to what fear has done to Oedipus' reasoning skills. In the past, he had displaced the authority of traditional religious formulae for solving problems of state. He had gained power by finding a rational solution to the riddle of the Sphinx. But he had also, because of his fears, never quite escaped the power of the traditionalist in himself. In this area he is very conflicted, oscillating between trust in oracles and almost atheistic contempt for them. It should be clear by this point, I think, that the Greek *tyrannos* must be translated in Sophocles' *Oedipus* and elsewhere in Attic tragedy as "tyrant," not "king"—as is the general practice. For here is a tyrant afraid of his own tyrannical soul. He holds high office but has lost all capacity to be a leader; he does not control others by inspiring fear or admiration in them, but is controlled by those who can manipulate his fears. He epitomizes the *demos,* the people, rather than their ruler.

It is not just in later antiquity that "undisguised Oedipal dreams... were common," as we see in the second-century AD writer Artemidorus of Daldi's "Interpretation of Dreams," *Oneirocritica* (1.79). Robert White comments:

> Artemidorus' surprisingly detailed treatment of them could be taken to imply a less rigorous repression of incestuous longings than is usual in modern societies. But it seems more reasonable to assume that since the forbidden impulse was not disguised in the dream images themselves, this was subsequently and necessarily accomplished through an interpretation which attached an innocent symbolic meaning to it.[85]

---

[85] Robert J. White, *The Interpretation of Dreams: Oneirocritica by Artemidorus* (Park Ridge, N.J., 1975), 81.

Oedipal dreams in ancient literature are generally associated with people holding military and (or) political power—in other words with "tyrannical" types.

What distinguishes Sophocles' Oedipus from Peisistratus' son Hippias, or Caesar, is that he takes the fantasy literally, rather than allegorically and politically, as they do. He is afraid, whereas they on the whole are confident. He assumes the prophecy *must* have a negative literal force. His literal interpretation of the oracle marks his tale off from that of other mythic (or mythicized) figures confronted by oracles or prophetic dreams.[86]

17. Tragic Competition

If you wished to compete in one of the two festivals of Dionysus—whose timing roughly corresponds to Apokries or Carnival before Lent and Easter on both the Orthodox and Catholic calendars—you had to submit a tetralogy to one of the nine annually elected archons (chief administrative officers) of Athens. For the less prestigious festival of Dionysus Lenaeus, at the end of January when the weather was cold, the seas dangerous, and few traveled abroad, you submitted your manuscript to the king (archon), the *basileús,* who selected from among the entrants what he considered to be the best two sets of plays. For the "City Dionysia," the more important of the two feasts of Dionysus held at the end of March when the weather was better and travel by sea much safer and many foreign visitors were in the city, you submitted your manuscript to the Eponymous archon who gave his name to the year. And he selected what he considered the three best sets of plays submitted for performance.

Each tetralogy selected was sponsored by a *choregós,* a wealthy citizen, who, as a civic duty, was required to equip a *choros.* A chorus was a troupe of costumed, singing dancers, which, in the earliest days, was the major element of each play. Tragedy, in short, was a combination of music, song, and dance; it was, as W. S. Gilbert put it, in act 2 of *The Grand Duke,* "ballet-operatic."

Unfortunately we have no musical scores for tragedy—only a tantalizing fragment from Euripides' *Orestes* and a couple of scraps from Euripides'

---

[86] For a fuller discussion of Plato and the tyrant, see my earlier treatment in my *Metaformations,* especially chap. 1 and the sources cited there.

Iphigeneia at Aulis. We know little about the choreography. Yet the ancient Greek terms *tragoidía* and *choros* survive in modern Greek as *tragoúdhi,* "song," and *choros,* "dance." What is left of Greek tragedy is the libretti. We know absolutely nothing about such music as may have accompanied the surviving Roman tragedies.

Until the early fifth century, there was only one actor. Aeschylus, the earliest tragedian who wrote works which survive, added a second, thereby permitting dialogue without the chorus. But the chorus, once it had entered, stayed on stage for the rest of the play and heard everything said. And the first feature of Sophocles' *Oedipus* that differentiates it from most other trag-edies is that there is never a moment when the actors are alone on stage. In the opening lines Oedipus addresses a group of people who have accompa-nied the Priest on his visit to the tyrant's home and who appear to be priests themselves. And when that group leaves, the chorus enters.

Sophocles added a third actor. All three were male. As actors were added, the role of the chorus diminished and the number of *characters* increased, since each actor could assume several roles. But a given role in a tragedy was never played by more than one actor, though sometimes nonspeaking actors were used for montages, as in the final scene of Euripides' *Orestes,* to represent the physical presence of a character whose actor was playing another role at the time. Roman tragedians seem to have followed this con-vention to some extent in their writing, though Seneca seems to need four actors for his *Oedipus.* In Sophocles' *Oedipus,* it is generally held that the lead actor (the protagonist) plays Oedipus, the second actor (the deuterago-nist) plays the Priest, Jocasta, the Courtier, and the Slave, and the third (the tritagonist) plays Creon, Teiresias, and the Corinthian. Although this is the traditional view, I have always used (when following the three-actor rule) my best actor to play the most demanding *combination* of roles. The division of roles among actors means that Creon cannot be on stage with Teiresias in Sophocles' *Oedipus,* since the same actor cannot play both roles at the same time. Perceptive audiences would recognize the same voice behind the masks of Creon, Teiresias, and the Corinthian; and Sophocles probably arranged *Oedipus* so that the characters who most obviously threaten Oedipus' posi-tion are all played by the same actor.

Not only were the dramatic contests themselves called contests, *agónes,* but many elements within the contests were described as *agónes.* The episodes (scenes) in which two characters dispute an issue are *agónes,* and each of the three actors is an *agonistés,* "a competitor": the protagonist, deuteragonist, and tritagonist (the first, second, and third actors respectively). And there was a competitive prize for the best actor. The word *agón* was also used to describe an athletic contest and a lawsuit. If you were a poor, old, or unemployed male citizen, you knew a lot about the law not only from *agónes* in the theater, but from *agónes* in the law courts. Your best hope of income was to sign up for jury duty, which gave you a small daily fee. Luckily the juries were large. When Socrates was put on trial in 399 BC there were 501 jurymen. More generally, an *agón* was any kind of struggle. Every Greek today knows the words from Aeschylus' *Persians* about the battle of Salamis in which the Persian navy was defeated in 480 BC: "Now the *agón* is for everything!"

Victor Ehrenberg observed that the Greek tragedian was not "a private person writing beautiful poetry in an ivory tower," and that tragedy itself was "an event of public life in which the trends of people's minds were reflected, discussed, and displayed."[87] A tragedian's voice was a powerful influence on politics and could be problematic if, like Sophocles, he were himself a major (and perhaps controversial) political figure. But the raw and democratic audience could be unruly and might laugh, applaud, or otherwise interrupt the performance (so you had to allow for this in your writing). Socrates himself is reported to have applauded the opening lines of Euripides' *Orestes*. Whether they liked it or not, Greek tragedians were faced with an audience ready to interact: thousands of craftsmen, laborers, and peasants attending an "educational" competition for literary honors during a wine festival: an audience that was about to see, in succession, nine tragedies and three satyr plays, not to mention the comedies. A tragedian had to keep all segments of that audience under his spell and sometimes wrote as if inviting a reaction from the audience—unlike directors of modern "serious" dramas, who usually expect their much smaller and more disciplined, bourgeois audiences to remain silent and seated.

I believe we should take it for granted that there were women, resident aliens, and even some slaves present. Of all male gods, Dionysus was least likely to exclude women from his festivals. And if the men left the women to their own devices on the feasts of Dionysus, myth offered some grim warnings about what they might do. Euripides, often taken to task by Aristophanes for teaching women bad habits and giving them dubious role models, was much more likely to be influencing women (for worse or better) in

---

[87] Ehrenberg, *Sophocles and Pericles,* 7.

the theater itself than indirectly, through their husbands' summaries—much less through their reading of the plays in manuscript, since literacy was by no means universal even in the male population. Boys were at least given a basic education; girls, generally, were not. The much more prominent roles assigned to women at all social levels in tragedy than they had in normal Athenian life are probably the best indicators that women are part of the audience the dramatist had to take into account, especially during wartime when military duties kept many men at posts far from home, and when, as Aristophanes indicates in his *Lysistrata,* the casualties of war thinned out the male population.

Many a turning point (*peripéteia*) in tragedy depends not on what a god or a male hero says or does, but on the action of a male or female slave or peasant, or of a strong and resolute free woman. In over thirty percent of surviving Greek tragedies, the principal characters, though played by men, are female. Women had a political role on stage that they were not granted in real life, but which allowed everyone, men and women, to envisage a scenario in which women were empowered. By the time Aristophanes wrote his *Ecclesiazousae* (brilliantly translated as *The Congresswomen* by Douglass Parker) in the early fourth century, he could depict a stage world in which men, at least temporarily, vote for, and acquiesce in, the total transfer of political power to the women. In it the men are faced with new laws that make all property common and require a man to make love to any woman who wants him on the basis of the woman's seniority—a total inversion of the reward system envisaged for Plato's warrior heroes in the *Republic.*

Critics have generally failed to note that the mythical world of Greek drama, both tragedy and comedy, was almost as far ahead, socially and politically, of the philosophers and historians of its day as it was of contemporary realities. Aristotle, in his *Poetics,* which is more often a prescription for what he wanted tragedy to be than a description of what it actually was, felt that women should not be given prominence in tragedy. Had tragedians been writing to his formula, we would have no *Agamemnon, Antigone, Medea, Electra, Helen, Hecuba, Andromache,* or *Trojan Women,* to name only the best known. Fortunately tragedians were not writing to his formula. Sophocles and Euripides were long dead before the *Poetics* was written.

One of the most powerful entrances in tragedy is a case in point. In Sophocles' *Oedipus,* Oedipus and Creon have been disputing high matters of state, of plotting and subversion, and Oedipus has just declared that he intends to have Creon put to death. Then Jocasta arrives and orders Oedipus to go into the house and Creon to go home, like a mother breaking up a fight among children. Both defer to her authority, even though neither leaves the stage. And in due course the quarrel is settled, however grudgingly and temporarily. There are, then, alternatives to execution and war to end disputes, given the right authority figure. This is an opportunity for the women in the audience to cheer, at least for a moment.

Indeed, I have seen audiences struggle to suppress, as they feel they must, a laugh at this point. This is a tragedy, and modern audiences think they're not supposed to laugh, even when something funny happens or is said. For we know Oedipus will eventually conclude that the woman who plays mother here actually is his mother. But audiences usually pay a price for their laughter in Greek tragedy by being made to look foolish in retrospect. Jocasta's successful intervention is disastrous for everyone except Creon, including herself.

Further, this is the second time in the play that someone has ordered the tyrant of Thebes to leave the stage. The first to do so is Teiresias. And after Creon leaves in this scene, even the usually cautious chorus will suggest that Jocasta should have Oedipus taken into the house. Nowhere else in Greek tragedy is a tyrant so ordered around. No one can do this to the kings of Senecan tragedy. Greeks rarely drew the kind of definitive line we tend to draw between the serious and the humorous. They couldn't because their audiences didn't. They would probably be quite baffled by our relentlessly solemn productions of their tragedies.

Although they could express their approval or disapproval of a performance vocally, Athenian audiences were not the judges who decided the contests among tragedians. Voting was restricted to a panel of ten judges, only five of whose votes were actually counted. The deciding votes were drawn by a lottery from among the ten cast. It was, therefore, theoretically possible—though not likely—that a playwright could win seventy percent of the votes and still not win the prize.[88]

---

[88] This procedure made it harder to bribe the judges, since there was no means of knowing how an individual judge voted. You could bribe seven people and still lose; and you would never know if you got the votes you paid for. It also made defeat easier for the two losers to bear. Presumably a second drawing was usually needed to determine second and third place. A. E. Haigh, *The Attic Theatre,* 3rd ed., revised and in part rewritten by A. W. Pickard-Cambridge (Oxford, 1907), 31–37. See also E. Csapo and W. J. Slater, *The Context of Ancient Drama* (Ann Arbor, 1995) and C. Pelling, ed., *Greek Tragedy and the Historian* (Oxford, 1997).

18. Citizens and Non-citizens

The tragedians' audience included the same Athenian citizens who, gathered as an Assembly, were the city's legislative body, and gathered in the various courts, were the judiciary. But the numerous non-citizens could attend tragedies too. Citizenship in democratic Athens was limited, by a law Pericles passed in 451 BC, to those who could show that they were born free and of parents who were both native-born Athenians. That's one of the reasons why Sophocles' Oedipus is particularly worried that he may prove to be the son of a slave. The dramatists seem constantly to be pressing their audiences to see the folly of this law. It is the core of Lysistrata's program of reform in Aristophanes' *Lysistrata,* as it is of the general argument of Euripides' *Ion.* In *Ion,* Euripides represents the founding hero of the Ionian peoples (of whom the Athenians were one) as himself a supposititious child passed off on his non-Athenian father, Xuthus, but nonetheless marked to be ruler of Athens. If you weren't a citizen, but a resident alien (*métoikos*), you could not speak in the Assembly. You had to have a "champion" (*prostátes*) like the popular leader Cleon, who built his career on the voices and power of the less privileged segments of Athenian society, as noted above.

There was no such thing then as Greek "nationality." Citizenship was based on one's ancestral city of birth and one's legitimacy, not on one's Greek ethnicity. Indeed, Pericles became a victim of his own law: his only son who survived the plague was considered a non-citizen, since the junior Pericles was the son of a courtesan, Aspasia. Similarly, in Sophocles' *Oedipus,* Oedipus is not a citizen of Thebes, even though he is the city's tyrant. He is a citizen of Corinth. That is why the Corinthian is so amazed at Oedipus' fear of returning to the town where he is not an outsider. At Thebes he is—as his first interlocutor, the Priest of Zeus, reminds him in his very first words—a resident alien, a non-citizen ruling Theban citizens: "It's my land that you rule." Though the chorus admits that it has treated Oedipus as if he were their ritual king, *basileús,* he cannot claim that title because only a citizen could be elected "king."

The sense of disempowerment that comes with illegitimacy in ancient Greece is hard for modern audiences to grasp. But it lurks somewhere close to the core of Oedipus' fears as it does to the stage reality Hippolytus faces in Euripides' *Hippolytus.* Hippolytus is convinced that his father won't believe his word against Phaedra's because he is a bastard, *nóthos,* a word also used in Greek to describe counterfeit coins. And Hippolytus' dying words to his father, Theseus, who finally realizes, through the intervention of Artemis, that he has unjustly cursed his son are: "Pray that you may have sons like me who are genuine," that is to say, "not counterfeit."

Even more compellingly, and historically rather than theatrically, less than thirty years after Sophocles wrote *Oedipus,* a challenge was mounted to the succession of Agesilaus as king of Sparta, because he was lame of foot. Plutarch, himself an official of the Delphic shrine, says the Spartans consulted the oracle, which replied with a warning:

> Consider, Sparta, though you are greatly proud. Take care that there may not sprout from you, sound of foot [*artipodos*] as you are, a monarchy that is lame. For then diseases [*nousoí*] unexpected will take hold of you and a rolling wave of war that destroys men. (*Agesilaus* 3.4–5)

The Spartans, confronted with their own Sphinx-like riddle of feet, were left free to choose between two competing candidates. Agesilaus was lame. His rival was rumored to be illegitimate. The Spartans (though they were a nation of soldiers) reasoned that Agesilaus' problems with his feet were a lesser obstacle than his rival's supposed illegitimacy (which they declared a greater "lameness") and appointed Agesilaus. Plutarch, I suspect, thinks they chose unwisely. Agesilaus' career marked the end of Spartan power, as his Roman parallel in life is that of Pompey, whose demise marked the end of the Roman republic.

But if we carry the issue of legitimacy of birth over into the Roman world, we find an altogether different picture. Oedipus' citizenship is not really an issue in Seneca's tragedy. In the Roman empire even former slaves could attain citizenship and rise to high positions in governmental administration; and many notable Romans, including Seneca's own family, were not even of Italian, much less of Roman, origin.

19. Plagues and Oracles

Pericles, by the mid-fifth century, had become the architect of an Athenian empire which reached out toward the nearby city-states, across the Aegean, into the Black Sea, and even cast longing eyes toward Sicily; he lived up to the meaning of his name: "The man whose fame [*kleos*] is all around [*peri*]," "the man famous everywhere," rather as Oedipus describes

himself in the opening lines of Sophocles' *Oedipus*. Athens' rapid development as an imperial power enraged other cities in Greece. Many felt each
city had the right to be self-governing. A military struggle between Athens
and these rival states ensued. Two cities prominent in the myth of Oedipus,
Thebes and Corinth, allied themselves with Sparta, the major land-power
in Greece, and began the Peloponnesian War in 431 BC, which ran inter-
mittently until 404 BC when Athens was finally defeated. Athens, therefore, was almost constantly at war throughout the last twenty-five years of
Sophocles' long life.

Shortly after the war began there came a plague that was the source of
charges and counter-charges of blood-guilt between the combatants. Our
sources mention an ancient curse of the goddess Athena that the Spartans
demanded the Athenians expiate. The historian of the Peloponnesian War,
Thucydides (1.126), says an Athenian, Cylon, had attempted (and failed), on
the advice of the Delphic oracle, to establish himself as tyrant of the city over
a century previously. Thus Apollo's oracle had prompted a political action
whose aim was to overthrow the Athenian government. The survivors of
Cylon's debacle took sanctuary with the gods: in front of the altar of Athena
Polias on the Athenian acropolis. Lured out by a promise of safety, they were
killed when they emerged. The Spartans of Sophocles' day demanded that
the descendants of those who killed Cylon's allies be thrown out to expiate
the curse.

But, Thucydides adds (1.127), Spartan motivation was recognized as not
only religious but political: one of those affected would have been Athens'
leader, Pericles, who was related, on his mother's side, to those under the
curse. Plutarch (*Solon* 12.1–3 and *Pericles* 33.1–2) tells the same story. The
Spartans did not expect the Athenians to banish Pericles, says Thucydides;
but they did hope the scandal that made him a "religious" cause of war
would lower him in Athenian eyes.[89]

To mention a plague in ancient Greece not only evokes Socrates' associations of plague and tyranny, but invites mention of Apollo. "Ever since the
Iliad the Greeks had associated Apollo particularly with epidemics, of which
he could be sender and averter. In 430 BC the specially severe incidence

---

[89] As Thucydides assumes a patently political purpose in such dredging up ancient curses against
Pericles, so, when Teiresias declares Oedipus is the blood pollution on the city, Oedipus immediately
assumes Teiresias is involved in a political plot along with Creon ("ruler") to overthrow him and gain
his position as tyrant (*Oedipus* 380–89).

of the plague at Athens, due primarily to overcrowding, was obviously regarded by some as a special dispensation from Apollo."[90] Similarly, some Athenians regarded the end of the plague as a blessing from Apollo. Pausanias (1.3.4) says that the Athenians dedicated a statue to Apollo "Averter of Evil," because he had stopped it.[91] But there was not universal agreement. Greek understanding of medicine had progressed sufficiently that the educated understood, as Thucydides does, that plagues have physical and biological causes and are not visitations of divine anger that can be dispelled by verbal acts of contrition.

The Athenian attitude toward the oracle of Apollo at Delphi was complicated. Although—or perhaps *because*—Delphi produced political oracles and was under the influence of Athens' enemies, the Athenians insisted, when they concluded what proved to be a temporary peace with their enemies in 421, that they should have free access to the oracles and other Pan-Hellenic shrines. They did not like to be excluded from Delphic services. They also went to considerable ritual effort to secure Apollo's favor during the Peloponnesian war by purifying the island of Delos, Apollo's great Ionian sanctuary, not only because, unlike Delphi, it was under *their* control and accessible by seaways they controlled but also in gratitude for the ending of the plague.[92]

Literary evidence suggests that resentment ran high against the Delphic oracle as an institution. Parke and Wormell conclude: "One could suppose that Athenian feeling became embittered against Delphi during the first part of the Peloponnesian War." Similarly John Burnet comments on Plato's *Apology* 21B8: "The ordinary Athenian had no great respect for the Pythian Apollo. The oracle had taken the Persian side [in 480 BC, when Xerxes invaded and sacked Athens] and the Spartan side and generally opposed the Athenians, who were allies of the Phocians [Delphi's enemies]. When, finally, it took the side of Philip [king of Macedonia in the fourth century BC who ended Athenian independence], the Athenians gave it up altogether and sent to Dodona instead for oracles."[93] There is ample criticism of Apollo and his

---

[90] H. W. Parke and D. E. W. Wormell, *The Delphic Oracle* (Oxford, 1956), 1:189. For a different view, see H. Bowden, *Classical Athens and the Delphic Oracle, Divination and Democracy* (Cambridge, 2005).

[91] Calamis' works, however, as Parke and Wormell point out (*The Delphic Oracle,* 190), "are all to be dated to the first part of the fifth century." Pausanias, they suggest, is either thinking of another plague, or he has got the sculpture wrong.

[92] Thucydides 3.87 and 104.

[93] *Plato's Euthyphro, Apology of Socrates and Crito,* ed. with notes by John Burnet (Oxford, 1924), 92.

oracle among fifth-century poets, notably Euripides, whose *Ion, Andromache, Electra,* and *Orestes* lash out at Delphi's corruption and the oracle's lack of wisdom. Such criticism is voiced by ordinary people (Euripides' messenger in *Andromache* 1160–65, for example), as well as by the more powerful and educated. Even the divine Castor comments:

> Phoebus, Phoebus. . . . But he's my lord, I'm silent.
> Though wise, he spoke no wise advice to you.
>
> (Euripides, *Electra* 1245–46)

20. From Pericles to Cleon

When the Peloponnesian War began, the Athenians followed Pericles' policy of not confronting the superior Spartan armies, which attacked Attica most years at harvest-time. They evacuated the countryside and withdrew behind the protective Long Walls that extended the city fortifications down to their harbor, Peiraeus. The Age of Pericles, which began with Athenian forces expanding the city's realms was ending with the citizens' virtual enclosure within their own walls. Pericles had, as Plutarch notes (*Pericles* 33.6), locked the city up tight (*synkleisas*). If his name once suggested "glory [*kleos*] all around [*peri*]," it now suggested "confinement [*kleisis*] all around [*peri*]." In these crowded and unsanitary conditions a plague, which as we now know was typhoid fever, broke out in 430 and lasted through 429 (with a recurrence in 427). It caused numerous deaths, including that of Pericles, and thus marks the end of a political era in Athens.

Perhaps because of the epidemic at Athens, *nósos* ("plague," "sickness") becomes, in Sophocles and other Greek writers, a vivid metaphor for any debilitating and fatal malaise of the individual soul and of the body politic, much as the word "cancer" does in contemporary usage. Plato in *Republic* 5 (470c) describes the conflicts among the Greek states as not just civil wars, but a kind of "sickness." Many in Sophocles' audience may have shared Plato's view that the wars among Greeks are "the ultimate sickness of the city" (*Republic* 544c)—a point Plato makes several times elsewhere in the *Republic*, especially in book 8 (563E; 564B). As we see from a statement attributed to Alcmaeon, disease arises from the sole rule, the *monarchia*, of one of the bodies' powers. Health lies in the balance, *isonomía*, of the bodies' powers;

and *isonomía* is also one of the original words used to describe what we call democracy.[94]

Oedipus is himself described as (foreign) tyrant of his city. Despite the occasional argument by modern scholars that "tyrant" and "tyranny" are not necessarily bad words for a fifth-century Athenian, the majority of ancient Greek writers disagree. Athenian democracy had features of tyranny about it. Statements to the effect that Pericles was a tyrant were common enough, as Plutarch shows in his *Pericles,* and as Victor Ehrenberg has discussed to great effect. One man's great popular leader is another man's tyrant.

After Pericles' death, leadership of Athens was open to newcomers. Pericles' protégé, a young nobleman named Alcibiades, was a contender. But at least as early as 428 BC the heir apparent was Cleon—a popular leader with origins as lowly as Pericles' were aristocratic. No politician earned such hatred from the literary establishment as Cleon did in the years of his ascendancy from 428 until his death in 422. Thucydides saw him as the driving force of Athens' disastrous war against Sparta and her allies, a master of rhetoric, and the agent of Athenian imperialism, who again and again prevented the conclusion of an advantageous peace by stirring up war fever in the gullible populace.

Cleon used his power as a spokesman for the people (*prostátes*) to build the basis of a personal authority in the state that no one was able to challenge successfully until his death. His instruments of power were his formidable oratory and his skillful use of oracles. By the last quarter of the fifth century, the populace was, as we can see from Orestes' comment in Euripides *Orestes* 772, "a fearsome force when it has mischievous champions [*prostátas*]." Cleon was as fearsome a *prostátes* as the people had ever had. F. J. Parsons comments:

> Emancipated slaves, like the *metoikoi* [resident aliens, "metics"], seldom arrived at the dignity of Citizens, or were allowed to manage business in their own names; but were obliged to select some one of the Citizens as their "Patron" [*prostáten, epítropon*], under whose name to be enrolled, and to whose care and protection to be committed. *Compare Sophocles' Oedipus Tyrannus, 411* [where Teiresias remarks that he does not need to be enrolled with Creon as his champion]....

---

[94] Alcmaeon fragment 24B4 (Diehls Kranz), cited by G. E. R. Lloyd, *Polarity and Analogy* (Cambridge, 1966), 20.

The popularity of the demagogue Cleon, of course, caused many to solicit his "Patronage."[95]

Parsons' comment is based on a passage in Aristotle's *Rhetoric* (1408b), which runs as follows:

> The form of one's prose style should not be either metrical or unrhythmical. If it is metrical it is unpersuasive because it appears contrived. It is at the same time distracting because it prompts the audience to look out for when similar occurrences will again arise—the way the children do when they anticipate the answer when the heralds ask: "Who does the freedman choose as his champion [*prostátes*]?" "Cleon!" they say.

When Aristotle warns the public speaker not to use formulaic or metrical diction for fear of prompting an anticipatory response from *children,* Cleon had been dead for more that fifty years. Cleon's popularity as champion of resident aliens was still proverbial, as it was for Aristophanes in *Frogs,* written twenty years after Cleon's death. A hostess who considers herself wronged by Heracles asks to have Cleon as *prostátes* (*Frogs* 569): "Go and call Cleon to act as *prostátes* for me."

Would Sophocles' audience find thoughts of *Cleon* prompted by his character *Creon* in *Oedipus* as Parsons' comment, italicized above, might suggest? Readers must judge for themselves. But it's worth bearing two details in mind: first, "Creon" means "ruler" and Creon becomes ruler of Thebes at the end of Sophocles' *Oedipus;* second, Cleon, as Aristophanes points out in his comedy *The Knights,* written a little after *Oedipus,* was considered by many the new de facto ruler of Athens.

The names "Cleon" and "Creon" are not far apart on the Athenian aristocratic tongue. There was a common aristocratic affectation of speech, specially made fun of in Alcibiades, an opponent of Cleon, and famous as friend and lover of Socrates. It was called labdacism by the rhetorician Quintilian: the substitution of "l" for "r"—a speech affectation or impediment most suitable to the tale of Thebes and the royal house of

---

[95] *The Rhetoric of Aristotle* (Oxford, 1836), in his note on Aristotle *Rhetoric* 3.8 (1408b). The square brackets and italics within the citation indicate my inserted explanations of terms.

Labdacus.[96] For Laius, son of Labdacus, was killed while leaving his native people to consult the oracle at Delphi, as Sophocles' Creon reports. Through Labdacism and Labdacus a link is forged between the myth of Oedipus and Sophocles' Athens.[97]

One way Creon resembles Cleon is in his role as intermediary between Oedipus and the sources of oracular wisdom. In Aristophanes' *Knights* 61, a Paphlagonian slave (often identified as Cleon) is said to bewilder Dêmos (i.e., the people) by chanting oracles. Fontenrose observes: "Kleon is in effect a chresmologue who possesses a collection of Bakis' oracles, which help him to keep Demos under his control (*Knights* 109–43, 195–210, 960–1096)."[98] Curiously, Jocasta's analysis (lines 614ff.) of what she considers Oedipus' ruinous weakness is very similar to the assessment offered of the allegorical Dêmos (the People) in Aristophanes' *Knights:*

Jocasta: For Oedipus lets his emotions run too high
                whenever stressed or pained. Unlike the thinking man,
                he doesn't assess the new from past experience.
                Rather, he's owned by any man who speaks to him,
                provided that man speaks of things that frighten him.

She suggests that Oedipus is "owned by [literally: "is of"] the man who speaks to him." He is the dupe of those who work on his fears. And in Aristophanes' *Knights,* the Paphlagonian slave begs Dêmos (i.e., the Athenian people) not to be the dupe of whoever happens to be speaking to him and uses exactly the same expression (*Knights* 860): "My good fellow, do not be owned by [literally: "of"] the speaker." The same point is made later in the play:

        O Dêmos, you have wonderful
        power. All humans live in fear
        of you, just as if you were

---

[96] For a fuller discussion of Labdacism, see my *Sophocles' Oedipus: Evidence and Self-Conviction* (Ithaca, N.Y., and London, 1991). Also see Michael Vickers' major work on this wordplay in *Pericles on Stage;* also his *Oedipus and Alcibiades in Sophocles, Xenia Torunensia* 9 (Toruń, 2005): 11–32, and his forthcoming *Oedipus, Antigone, and Dionysus: Echoes of Contemporary History in Athenian Drama* and *Alcibiades on Stage: Political Comedy in Arisophanes.*

[97] See Vernant, "From Oedipus to Periander," 22–23.

[98] J. Fontenrose, *The Delphic Oracle* (Berkeley and Los Angeles, 1978), 159.

a man acting as tyrant.
But how easily you're led,
how you love to be flattered,
to be hopelessly deceived.
You always listen open-mouthed
to anyone who speaks to you [*pròs tòn…légonta aeí*].
(*Knights* 1111–20)

Aristophanes' Dêmos strongly resembles Sophocles' Oedipus in this respect. Since the *Knights* probably followed *Oedipus* by no more than five years in the same city, in the same or similar political climate, and addressing the same Athenian audience, it's not impossible that Oedipus, like Dêmos, is a symbolic figure, if not an allegory, of popular credulity, rather than, say, of Pericles in the days when his power was waning.

We may object that all surviving Greek tragedies except the earliest, Aeschylus' *Persians,* take their themes from myth, not contemporary events. True, neither Sophocles nor Euripides wrote directly about a contemporary event. Yet Greek tragedy (unlike Senecan tragedy) is rich in allusions to its own day and we can get a richer sense of Sophocles' *Oedipus* if we take these allusions into account. For Sophocles' *Oedipus* is, in political terms, about how a change in power occurs during a plague; and Sophocles is the first writer known who sets the myth of Oedipus against the backdrop of a plague-ravaged city and the only writer known who places Creon's take-over of the government of Thebes immediately after Oedipus' departure from power. Athens too underwent a change of power during a plague: from the leadership of Pericles to that of Cleon.

Greek tragedies are populated by mythic characters brought forward into the intellectual world of fifth-century Athens, not by the kind of characters we find in modern historical novels. They resemble those in Shakespeare's *Julius Caesar,* who are Elizabethan in dress, manner, and thought, and whose political discussions are highly pertinent to Elizabethan England. Dramatists often address audiences on contemporary issues under the guise of mythic (or in Shakespeare's case ancient, historical) narratives. Traditional ideas about religion, the material world, science, politics, history, and the contemporary human condition came under intense scrutiny in the works of the Athenian tragedians. When Sophocles' Oedipus is given an ambiguous answer about how Polybus of Corinth died, he favors the fifth-century *medical* interpretation.

The dialogue of *Oedipus* is replete with the intellectual discourse of Sophocles' day, epitomized by Socrates, a master of dialectic, of what the Greeks called *élenchos,* "refutation, cross-questioning, cross-examination." He usually began by claiming he knew nothing, and by asking his interlocutors to offer some definition of their own expertise or knowledge, which he would then assail. He undertook this approach because, Plato tells us in his *Apology of Socrates* 21A, his friend Chaerephon consulted Delphi to determine if anyone was wiser than Socrates and was told no one was. Socrates conducted his cross-examinations to determine in what way the oracle was right.

Socrates was accused by his foes of being able to show how an idea they were sure was right was, in fact, less correct than an argument they were sure was wrong. His ability to "win" arguments did not convince all who found themselves logically routed. Rather they came to regard him with suspicion mixed and awe. He was *deinòs légein:* "fearsome (or formidable) in speech," a master of argumentation. He was prosecuted on a charge of making the lesser argument the stronger—and for atheism and corrupting the young—put on trial in 399 BC, found guilty, and executed. And his main prosecutor, Meletus, had some pretensions as a dramatist, having written a tetralogy about Oedipus.

As Sophocles wrote his *Oedipus,* Socrates was at the height of his career. And the formula "fearsome in speech (or thought)" (*deinòs légein*) occurs frequently in Sophocles' play. Oedipus greatly fears those, such as Teiresias or Creon, whom both he and the chorus characterize as fearsome speakers or thinkers and who get the better of Oedipus in argument. And he, like most readers, finally accepts what they say as true.

The extent to which Sophocles' *Oedipus* refracts events of his own day is a complex issue. I have offered only a hint or two here. Those interested in a fuller discussion should turn to Victor Ehrenberg's classic *Sophocles and Pericles* and Michael Vickers' brilliant *Pericles on Stage.* I mention these few points to remind those preoccupied with eternal mythic "truths" that Greek tragedy routinely uses myth as a vehicle for contemporary comment. If we lose a sense of *Oedipus'* timeliness in our obsession with its timelessness, we reduce the full, original force of Sophocles' play. Sophocles' audience, mostly ordinary citizens, understood the politicized myths of tragedy most readily in terms of their own immediate experience of life and of government.

21. Cratylan Man

Greek and Roman attempts to predict the future are a curious mixture of "inspired" prophecy and the meticulous empirical observation of phenomena: the flight of birds, the condition of organs in a sacrificial animal and, though less publicly proclaimed, an understanding of the people who are consulting the expert. All these observations were understood to have the nature and imperfections of forecasts. That is why oracles were almost invariably ambiguous enough to allow more than one interpretation and fulfillment. They are certainly not *decrees,* though, at times Sophocles' Oedipus seems to treat them as if they were.

Oedipus' first mention of Polybus is the very Freudian statement, "Polybus *was* my father"—since he makes this statement while he thinks Polybus is still alive, thus showing he has already at least partially disposed of his father. He does something of the same when he follows this up by saying that he, Oedipus, was thought "the most important man in town." When informed that Polybus is dead, he is delighted by the news, since this means *he* did not kill his father, as the oracle had forecast. Then it occurs to him that his father might have died of *póthos,* of longing for him: he might have killed him indirectly. There is a solid literary precedent. In *Odyssey* 11, the ghost of Odysseus' mother Anticleia says she died of longing for her son. No Greek but Oedipus would have had the slightest trouble accepting that the father-killing part of the oracle was fulfilled by Polybus' death from longing. And, as we have already seen, returning to power in his homeland would have disposed of the other part of the oracle. But Oedipus dismisses the thought, partly because Jocasta has suppressed the Corinthian's report of gossip that Oedipus will succeed Polybus as ruler of Corinth, but partly because he will not stop until he fulfils the oracle more literally.

Perhaps this is because Oedipus has at some point crossed the thin line between fearing things and wishing for them as he oscillates between fearing what will happen and fearing what might already have happened. As a result he is remarkably unconscious of what is (or was at any given moment) the present. For he goes on, by his own account, to tell how he single-handedly wiped out an entire party of travelers who did not yield right of way at an intersection, including a man old enough to be his father. He even tortures and threatens to kill an old slave whom he thinks, for a fleeting moment, might be his father.

Sophocles' Teiresias has a much broader sense of how prophecy and divination work. His prowess resides in his ability to predict by observing the behavior of everything in the world of phenomena around him, including Oedipus. The chorus hails Teiresias not only as "the only human in whom *alétheia* [non-elusiveness] is born" but also as the man who will cross-examine and refute the killer of Laius, as if *alétheia,* what we conventionally translate as truth, were something to be established by Socratic dialectic, as Plato suggests. Yet Teiresias' first words on stage ironically shrug off the chorus' contention that nothing eludes him:

> Reason's power, alas, how fearsome a thing it is
> when insight yields no pay-off for the reasoning man!
> I know this, but forgot it. Or I'd not have come.
>
> (316–18)

He knows that he is about to enter into a verbal contest with the one person who was once able to solve a problem that eluded him: the riddle of the Sphinx.

If we translate *alétheia* as "truth," however, we see no connection at all among these various observations. Greek writers not only explain *alétheia* as *a-léthe-ia,* "non-elusiveness," as if it were the negation of *léthe,* "forgetfulness," "oblivion," but link it semantically with a number of similar sounding words including *aletheís,* "having wandered." Homer's Odysseus and Eumaeus, along with Plato's Socrates, also define *alétheia* as "divine wandering" on the basis of a different division of *alétheia* into two words *theia,* "divine," and *ale,* "wandering."[99] And Plato merges both explanations of *alétheia* in his myth of Er at the end of the *Republic,* where the wandering Er does not lose memory of the world of souls, as others do, when they cross over the River or Indifference and leave the underworld: knowledge is recollection, it is memory, it is that which is not forgotten from one's pre-corporeal existence. Similarly, the paradox that a blind seer has access to that which does not elude one's notice is aided by the similarity between *alétheia* and *aloûn,* "to be blind."

That is why one of Oedipus' most ghastly rhetorical blunders in the play is to mock Teiresias' blindness. As children's taunts make him give credence to a drunk's insult, which is then amplified by the Delphic oracle, so now the

---

[99] The wordplay is as old as Homer, *Odyssey* 14.120–382. See my "Wordplay and Apparent Fiction in the *Odyssey,*" for a fuller discussion and bibliography.

combination of his fears empowers in him the new anguish Teiresias adds, in retaliation for these insults, to the woes Oedipus fears he must face: blindness. And here too we can expect that he will settle for nothing less than literal blindness, just as he will settle for nothing less than literally killing his father and marrying his mother.

Yet when he emerges on stage, having blinded himself, he declares:

> It was Apollo, Apollo, my friends [*phíloi*],
> who achieved these evil, evil sufferings that are mine.
> Yet no man [*oútis*] struck me with his hands
> but I, my wretched self.
>
> (1329–32)

No Greek reader would have missed, as most modern readers miss, the echo of *Odyssey* 9.408. There Polyphemus cries out to his fellow Cyclopes, after being blinded by Odysseus: "Friends [*phíloi*], Noman [*Oútis*] is killing me with treachery or violence." The simple-minded Cyclops has been deluded by Odysseus into thinking that his name is not Odysseus, but Oútis, "Noman," and thus appears to be saying the opposite of what he means. In Greek the negative *ou* has to be replaced by *mé* before certain verb moods. So "Noman" can be either *oútis* or *métis*. But *mêtis*, differently accented, means "thought, mind." So Polyphemus' baffled fellow Cyclopes assume he has gone mad (*Odyssey* 410–12): "if (your) *mêtis* or *métis* [no man *or* your mind] does you violence when you are alone, there is no way you can escape the sickness that comes from great Zeus."[100] Euripides has his chorus of satyrs mock Polyphemus in much this way in *Cyclops:*

Polyphemus:	Noman [*Outis*] ruined me.
Chorus:	No man's wronged you?
Polyphemus:	Noman [*Outis*] blinded my eye.
Chorus:	Then you're not blind.
Polyphemus:	You...
Chorus:	How could no man make you blind?
Polyphemus:	You're mocking. Where is Noman [*Outis poû'stin*]?
Chorus:	Nowhere [*oudamoû*].
	(672–75)

---

[100] For a fuller discussion, see my *Sophocles' Oedipus,* 225–29.

I italicize the whole phrase in line 675 because it is a curious echo of the Corinthian's opening lines in Sophocles' *Oedipus* 924–26, which I will give here in Bernard Knox's translation, with the Greek phrases transliterated to illustrate the points Knox wishes to establish:

> Strangers, from you might I *learn where (mathOIm' hoPOU)*
> is the palace of the *tyrannos OIDiPOUS,*
> best of all, where he himself is, if you *know where (katOIsth' oPOU).*

"These," as Knox comments, are "violent puns, suggesting a fantastic conjugation of the verb 'to know where' formed from the name of the hero who, as Tiresias told him, does not know where he is."[101]

Among the sophists of the fifth century was a man named Cratylus, who argued that the etymology of names explains the identity of people. This is a very curious kind of wordplay based on what modern scholars have labeled "folk etymology," and which they discuss with great caution and considerable discomfort. It is an old phenomenon, found throughout Greek and Latin literature from the earliest days, used both in earnest and playfully, and it explains the "meaning" of proper names in terms of what appear to be the identifiable syllabic elements within a given name. In the *Odyssey*, Odysseus' name is linked with the notion of pain and suffering, *odýne,* and in Euripides' *Bacchae,* the hero Pentheus' name is explained by the god Dionysus as marking him for grief, *pénthos,* which William Arrowsmith nicely translates with a pun on Pentheús and "repent."

This procedure makes some sense, as we shall see, when applied to mythic figures, whose names are often, in all likelihood, derived from the kind of role they have in a traditional narrative. But they become much more suspect when applied, in the manner of Cratylus, to "real" people. When, in Plato's *Republic,* the argument that might is right is advanced by a man named Thrasymachus, "Rash Fighter," the fitness of the name seems too good to be true; and when Julius Caesar's first issue of coins had on it the image of an elephant, with his name CAESAR inscribed beneath it, proclaiming the Punic (Carthaginian) origin of his name, the practice moved into the area of propaganda—though after his assassination *caesus,* "slaughtered," seemed to his enemies the more appropriate etymology.

---

[101] Knox, *Oedipus at Thebes,* 184. See also Gould, *Oedipus the King: A Translation with Commentary,* 63.

Sophocles' Oedipus is something of a Cratylan man: an old-fashioned person who believes that proper names contain within them elements which describe the fundamental nature of the person to whom they are applied. His own experience has taught him that the Sphinx can be disposed of by solving her riddle, though he appears to grasp that the plague currently devastating Thebes is not susceptible of a verbal solution. But the people around him are equipped with advanced skills in the rhetorical language of the fifth century. They are masters of what the ancient scholar Demetrius described as the "formidable" or "fearsome" style of rhetoric, in which the speaker tries not to overwhelm his interlocutor with facts and statistics, but to prompt him toward the desired conclusion while leaving him the illusion that he is seeing through what his opponent is doing and reaching an independent conclusion. It involves letting the "facts" speak for themselves—a mode of argument which, according to the ancients, made the effect of one's criticism more fearsome (*deinóteros*). Demetrius in *On Style* 288 states it this way:

> The effect is more fearsome [*deinóteros*] because it is achieved by letting the fact make itself manifest [*emphaínontos*] rather than having the speaker make the point for himself.[102]

This is much the same point that the Roman rhetorician Quintilian makes when talking of persuasive speech in the courts:

> The facts themselves should lead the judge to suspect. Our job is to remove everything else so that only this conclusion remains. Use of the emotions helps a lot. It's good to break the flow of your speech with silence, to hesitate. Then you may be sure the judge will search out that certain something which he probably would not believe if he heard it actually stated. You may be sure he will believe what he thinks he himself has discovered. . . . In sum: the judge is most likely to believe what is figured in our speech if he thinks we are unwilling to say it [*sic maxime iudex credit figuris si nos putat nolle dicere*]. (*Instructing the Orator* 9.2.71–72)

---

[102] For a fuller discussion, see my "The Art of Safe Criticism in Greece and Rome," *AJP* 105 (1984): 174–208.

Creon is in Oedipus' opinion *deinòs légein,* a fearsome (or formidable) speaker, as his accusers said Socrates was; and Teiresias is hailed by the chorus as a master of *élenchos,* the art of "cross-examination," as Socrates was. As a result, we should ourselves pay careful attention to what they do and say, or we run the same risks as does Oedipus: that their rhetoric will overpower us.

As noted, Creon means "ruler" in Greek, just as Teiresias means, essentially, "expert on prodigies." Their names derive from their role in the story. They are generic, much as are their counterparts in fairy tales. Most of the other characters in Sophocles' *Oedipus* have similarly generic names: Hiereus, "priest"; Angelos, "messenger"; Korinthios, "a Corinthian"; Therapon, "servant" or "slave" (who is also Boter, "herdsman," and, earlier in life, Oiketes, "houseboy"). But we translators betray you readers by leaving some of these names in Greek and translating others into English, which gives you a false sense that Teiresias is an individual person, but that the priest is generic.

There are really only two intruders in this generic world: Oedipus himself and his wife Jocasta, neither of whom has a name that identifies clearly what he or she is or does. Jocasta's name defies any real analysis. And Oedipus' Greek name, *Oidípous,* is variously explained, in the manner of Cratylus, at different points in the tragedy by breaking it into two elements, *oid* and *pou* and attempting to make sense of the whole word in terms of puns or near puns on its constituent elements. The most common meaning of the root *oid* is "know" (and the verb *oída,* "know," in its various forms, is among the most frequently used verbs in the Greek text). The syllable *pou* is more elusive: it can suggest *pou,* "where" or "somewhere"; *poûs,* "foot"; and, with a little drawl, it can suggest *pâs,* "all," "every." Oedipus, in fact, introduces himself at the beginning of Sophocles' play as the man known to everybody, and he is very proud that he knew the solution to the riddle of the feet posed by the Sphinx.

Two-thirds of the way through the play, however, the unnamed Corinthian arrives and offers a different etymology for Oedipus' name, which Oedipus accepts without question as the true etymology of his name: "swollen" foot, introducing the much less common root *oide,* "swell," as an alternative to *oida,* "know." It is obviously not the first time Oedipus has heard it. Like many a child whose name can be assigned an unflattering meaning (e.g., Ramsbottom), Oedipus has been teased mercilessly about it since childhood. When the Corinthian mentions this etymology, Oedipus asks him why he is bringing up this old *deinòn óneidos,* this "fearsome slander"—or, to echo the virtual anagram in *deinòn óneidos,* this "coarse scourge of slander": the verbal abuse that has plagued him from his earliest years and that he recognizes has shaped his life.

Some English versions, we have noted, mistranslate this phrase as if Oedipus were talking of an actual physical ailment he now acknowledges, not about the teasing he got because of his name. Teasing based on a name does not necessarily imply that the victim shares any characteristics implied by the mocking "etymology." But we should note that the Greek adjective Oedipus uses to describe the slander is precisely the same one he uses to describe the fearsome power of Creon's speech and Teiresias' skill at cross-examination, at dialectic: *deinós*. The answer the Corinthian gives offers a formidable or fearsome explanation for the "Swellfoot" nickname that Oedipus has been teased about. And later, when the Slave, under torture, is about to confirm Oedipus' fears, he declares himself to be on the brink of *deinós*, "fearsome" or "formidable" speech. Oedipus is about to accept the full consequences of his Cratylan etymology. He is at last defined (and ruined) by his feet, much as he had destroyed the Sphinx by answering her riddle of feet, which runs, traditionally: What creature goes first on four feet (*tetrápous*), then on two feet (*dípous*), finally on three feet (*trípous*)?

Curiously enough, the other undefined person in the tragedy, Jocasta, also acquires certain sphinx-like qualities in the account that is given of her death. She hangs herself. And, according to Diodorus Siculus (4.64), the Sphinx hanged herself when Oedipus solved her riddle. As Oedipus' self-definition finally situates his identity, it also situates the identities of others. When Sophocles' tragedy opens, Creon is not the ruler his name implies he is, and Teiresias is not the supreme expert on prodigies that his name implies either. Each has been long displaced by the arrival of the undefined Oedipus. They cannot have the roles or identities their names tell us (or Oedipus) are theirs as long as Oedipus is in control. Indeed, Oedipus' suspicions of Creon and Teiresias may well have their basis in his Cratylan thinking. If *his* name is *his* destiny, so too are theirs. And, before the play ends, Creon becomes what his name suggests, and Teiresias is restored to his religious supremacy. The individualistic intruders are eliminated and the generic model is established firmly and totally with each in his proper, Cratylan place.

Sophocles' *Oedipus*, then, conforms outwardly to many aspects of the shape of the Oedipus myth as we know it from other Greek sources. But it necessarily differs from Seneca's *Oedipus* because the Latin language is different from Greek and does not accommodate the particular etymologies deployed in Sophocles any better than English does. There is simply no way to produce anything even remotely plausible in Latin or in English from the name "Oedipus" without descending into such grotesqueries as "eddies of pus"—which, I admit, I toyed with. I conceded, finally, that without renaming all the characters to accommodate comparable English wordplay, there was little I could do to convey these essential aspects of Sophocles' tragedy. I contented myself with adding an occasional epithet to remind the reader that the names Oedipus, Creon, and Teiresias have important "meanings."

22. Some Differences between the Two Oedipuses

While Greek myth was more familiar to Romans than it is to us, the wordplays integral to the fabric of Sophocles' drama work no better in Latin than in English. Seneca faced the same problems we face, except in one respect: he was not trying to *translate* Sophocles, but to retell the story of Oedipus in his own drama. Seneca is no stranger to etymologizing wordplay. In *Medea,* for example, his Latin deploys a wealth of wordplay to compensate for the lost Greek wordplay on the heroine's name, from *me* (me) and *dea* (goddess) to the anagram *eadem* (the same).[103] Many differences between Latin tragedies and Greek tragedies result from something as elemental (and as complex) as the way syllables can be inflected and arranged in the two languages. It's much harder to redeploy the sounds in Oedipus' name than in Medea's, since "Oedipus" carries no etymologizing potential in Latin. Seneca chooses different aspects of the myth to emphasize, and thus refocuses the drama and reshapes the issues and characters involved.

Seneca's main characters are more overtly introspective and self-analyzing than Sophocles' Oedipus. Their most critical battles on stage, like the critical battles of many a Shakespearian character, are often those they are represented as fighting *within* themselves. Senecan drama constantly takes us beyond a character's publicly spoken words into his or her thoughts, which are dramatically verbalized for us in "asides" and soliloquies. These features of Senecan (and Shakespearian) tragedy keep us aware of the tension between what someone does and says to others, and what that same person sees as the reason for what is said and done. We see characters' hopes, illusions, and delusions played out in the personal worlds that they create and within which they so imprison themselves that they find it difficult to grasp that others are not

[103] See F. Ahl, "Seneca and Chaucer," in *Seneca in Performance,* ed. G. W. M. Harrison (London, 2000), 151–71, for a fuller discussion.

somehow extensions of themselves. The psychology of the characters is thus quite frequently made explicit, as in a novel, but as it rarely is in "real life."

In Sophocles' *Oedipus,* in contrast, we—the audience, the readers—are more often left to decode a character's inner thoughts, as we are in "real life." Sophocles restricts our knowledge of Oedipus, Jocasta, and Creon to what they are prepared to say publicly to others on stage. He keeps us on the *outside,* much as we would be at a trial. The inconsistencies and contradictions in a character's utterances are what provide the clues as to the inner thought processes. Unfortunately such inconsistencies are often mistaken by critics for compositional errors on the poet's part and are routinely "corrected" or otherwise disposed of in translations.

Unlike the playwrights of Athens in the fifth century BC, Seneca addresses his work not to a wide, general audience, but rather to the literate elite. While his tragedy resembles Greek tragedy, because it directs itself to the powerful in mythic, poetic discourse, it differs from it for precisely the same reason. It is the tyrant who must be addressed and persuaded to act sensibly, not the people. For the Senecan tyrant, however insecure he may be psychologically, never doubts, or hesitates to use, his absolute political power. Sophocles' tyrants, even Creon in *Antigone,* are rarely so absolute. They are aware that the people have the power to remove them. Tyranny was an intermittent menace in Sophocles' world. In Seneca's it was an entrenched and arguably immovable reality. Oedipus, in Sophocles' *Oedipus,* is easily talked out of punishing Creon. In Seneca, Oedipus has Creon taken to the dungeons.

In writing tragedy, however, Seneca is not following the predominant poetic fashion of his day, as was Sophocles. If surviving literature gives us even an approximation of what Roman imperial poetry was like, Roman poetry of the Early Empire (27 BC–AD 96) was *not* dominantly theatrical. Its major production was the hexameter verse of epic and satire, written with an eye to (1) listeners at a given performance or recitation; (2) Latin-speaking *readers* throughout a vast and culturally diverse empire; and (3) readers of a possibly far distant posterity. Tragedy had, by Seneca's time, ceased to be a major vehicle of poetic or political statement, and Seneca usually avoids specific references to his own day. Among the ten plays attributed to him, only the spurious *Octavia* deals with a contemporary subject.

Seneca's Thebes is not a living, nearby city with which the poet's land is at war, as it is in Sophocles. Thebes, for him as for us, belongs to a distant and foreign culture, albeit one familiarized over the centuries through literary and political contact. The real Thebes had been destroyed by Alexander the

Great. Troy, in contrast, had been given new life in the Caesars' propaganda. Seneca's Theban characters become somehow larger and more universalized than their predecessors in Greek tragedy because they are severed from a readily identifiable contemporary world. But, despite their Greek names, they speak Latin, are Roman, and think like Romans.

Lack of contemporary historical allusion makes dating the plays virtually impossible. The prose works of the Younger Seneca, in contrast, are of much more certain date, ranging from his *Consolation to Marcia* (included among the *Dialogues*) in AD 41, to the publication of his *Natural Questions* and *Letters to Lucilius* between AD 63 and 65. Although the traditional, mythical topics Seneca selects for his plays have an obvious appropriateness to the world of the early emperors at Rome, we can hardly move beyond such a broad generalization. True, with the exception of *Phaedra,* the plays mirror a top-heavy Roman world of absolute power as surely as Athenian tragedy mirrors the often chaotic Greek democracy and intellectual pluralism of Athens. Since Seneca lived his whole life under the imperial autocracy, we have not said much when we have said that. The best we can do is establish some probable sequence of their composition based on internal stylistic considerations, as John Fitch has done.[104]

Fitch accepts the general dating of *Hercules in His Madness* to before AD 54. This was the year of Claudius' death and Nero's accession to the throne. And *Apocolocyntosis* (The Pumpkinification), believed by some scholars to be one of Seneca's own works, parodies a lament from *Hercules in His Madness.* Fitch's study suggests that *Trojan Women* and *Medea* belong to approximately this same period and that *Phaedra, Oedipus,* and *Agamemnon* are earlier. How much earlier, however, we cannot say. The *Phoenician Women* (a fragmentary play) and *Thyestes* were, according to Fitch's analysis, written later, during the last decade of Seneca's life. If Fitch is right—and there is no certain means of knowing it—Seneca's plays were written at various points throughout his life, but mostly *before* Nero's reign. If this is so, they cannot have any connection with any known contemporary plague.

Therefore, although Seneca is a half millennium closer to our time than Sophocles, we know far less about the circumstances under which he presented his tragedies than we know about Sophocles' theatrical world. Seneca was writing when Rome was an imperial autocracy. Republican

---

[104] J. Fitch, "Sense-Pauses and Relative Dating in Seneca, Sophocles, and Shakespeare," *American Journal of Philology* 102 (1981): 289–307. See also A. J. Boyle, *Roman Tragedy,* 189–218.

government had been destroyed in a series of civil wars in an earlier generation, though the senate and other elements of the republic had not been entirely disempowered, and the fiction was maintained that the republic still existed. The emperor designated the chief annual officials himself and was usually the chief priest (*pontifex maximus*). Much major political and administrative business was handled by the emperor's personal staff (many of whom were slaves, former slaves, and non-Romans) who had never held any traditional public magistracy.

There was no constitutional means of getting rid of an emperor since, officially, there was no emperor. The emperor was much more than a tyrant in the Greek sense. He commanded huge armies whose hundreds of thousands of soldiers were loyal to him or to his legates rather than to the state. Assassination and armed insurrection by disaffected troops were the only means of securing a change of regime. But there was no full-scale armed insurrection in Rome between 30 BC and AD 67.

Citizenship, however, was more easily attained in the Roman empire than in Sophocles' Athens, and it conferred, arguably, more important privileges outside Rome than within Rome for the ordinary person. Yet since the Roman populace, citizen and non-citizen alike, was largely disenfranchised politically, the contrast between the political status of men and women at the lower social levels was probably less stark. It has been argued that the city's poor, in fact, were worse off than many of the slaves. They were often left unpaid and unemployed, diverted by public entertainment, and surviving on a free allowance of flour. The most important priesthoods, however, were held by men and not by women, as in the Athens of Sophocles. The chief religious role reserved for women was as Vestal virgins. But if they were unchaste, they could be (and were) buried alive.

23. Seneca and the Roman Theater

There were no permanent theaters in Rome until Pompey built one in 55 BC. And he built it to give himself, not dramatists, a stage. Actors were often slaves or former slaves (as were some of the playwrights) and therefore not members of a respectable, much less fashionable, profession. Further, dramatists had to compete for the public's attention with live spectacles of increasing scale and extravagance that were underwritten by the wealthy and sanctioned by ritual practice: gladiatorial shows and wild beast hunts. The Latin word *munus,* suggesting a public offering or service, came to be shorthand for a gladiatorial "offering." Such ritual and circus-like entertainments were features of Roman life from the middle of the third century BC.

The ruling classes stressed the spectacular and underplayed the verbal and intellectual dimensions so fundamental to Greek drama. Holding one's own against a gladiatorial "offering" would have been even less easy. The poet Horace, writing toward the end of the first century BC, tells Octavian, the imperial Augustus, that Democritus, "the laughing philosopher" as he was called, would guffaw at the notion that a dramatist could win the attention of his restive audience: "He would think the writers were creating their play for an ass—and a deaf one. What voices have had power enough to overwhelm the noise which echoes round our theaters?" (Horace, *Epistles* 2.1.199–201). Pleasure, Horace adds, has "shifted from the ear to eyes that are not good at seeing" (*Epistles* 2.1.187–88), and this speaks to even the Equestrian order, the Roman Upper Middle Class. And, he adds immediately following, not only games but triumphal processions celebrating military victories have intruded upon the dramatist's stage.

The theater is owned by the emperor and stages his shows. Hence Horace's expressed desire to entrust himself to a *reader* rather than to a spectator (*Epistles* 2.1.214–18). The language and metaphor he uses suit the arena and the hippodrome better than the muses and god of poetry. They suggest that Octavian wants books that will fight for him like gladiators, that will serve his glory. The theater already exists for the emperor's glory; the threat lurks that all literature will come to serve the same purpose.

Octavian was, in fact, more eager to censor published and *durable* poetry than the more fleeting criticism which might occur in a public performance. Ovid, who died in exile when the Younger Seneca was in his teens, chastises Octavian for being so concerned about morality in poetry, but so unconcerned about the blatant immorality of what is represented in the theater and at the emperor's own games before his very eyes (*Tristia* 2.497–546). In *Tristia* 5.7.25–30, Ovid comments on the irony of his own situation in this regard. Some of his poetry has been adapted for and performed in the theater, although he himself claims that "I have—and you know this yourself—written nothing for the theater"; he is kept away from Rome in exile. He has, he says, some consolation in the thought that his poems, adapted for the theater, keep his memory and name alive in Rome. If we take Ovid at his word here, the two surviving lines cited from what is supposed to be his play, *Medea,* would seem either not be genuinely his, or to come from an

116

adaptation of his treatments of Medea elsewhere in his poetry. He may have written it for reading or performance elsewhere than in the public theater.

The theater, then, was seen by both poet and political leaders not only as a noisy place, unconducive to poetry, but as the vehicle of corruption and political propaganda. Succeeding Roman emperors were also well aware of the theater's power, particularly Nero and Domitian. Domitian banned actors from using the public stage. Nero adopted a much different approach. Part of his own immense popularity—and much of the contempt that men of letters felt for him—stemmed from his appearances as a performer in the theater and the hippodrome. And he encouraged others to emulate him.

Despite their reluctance to write for the popular stage, Roman writers were aware that theatrical performance has a power over popular imagination that "pure" poetry lacks and regularly present human activity in terms of the theater or amphitheater. In his *Aeneid,* Virgil describes the landscape of North Africa as a *scaena,* a stage set, and compares the nightmares of Queen Dido to the horror experienced on stage by Pentheus or Orestes. Virgil's Aeneas describes a visit to the New Troy built by Andromache in Epirus as a tragic tableau, a mock Troy frozen in time, as if in a painting or stage set with Andromache lamenting as ever over an empty grave honoring her dead husband Hector. In Lucan's epic *Pharsalia,* Pompey, builder of Rome's first permanent theater, recalls his past triumphs in theatrical terms as he dreams. Later, as he dies, he behaves like an actor who must win approval for his final scene.

Seneca presents life in terms of the arena in his philosophical works. In his essay *On Providence* he dismisses ordinary gladiatorial shows as "the childish delights of human vanity" and asks us instead to contemplate the greatest contest of them all: "a matched pair worthy of god's eyes—a brave man matched against evil fortune, with the brave man as challenger." In the Senecan tragedies, particularly the *Trojan Women,* many motifs suggest a theater far different from that of Sophocles. The sacrifice of Polyxena on Achilles' tomb, for example, is described as if it were part of a *munus,* an offering, in the amphitheater:

> on the other side,
> it [the tomb] is encompassed by a plain, rising
> gently at the edges to create
> a valley in between—the shape suggests
> a theater, in fact.
>
> (*Trojan Women* 1123–26)

Astyanax's death has the same "theatrical" quality. The dramatist asks us to envisage the scene from Greek myth in terms of the horror of ritual death in the Roman theater. And he asks us to censure those who hated what they saw but watched anyway. Roman readers could hardly fail to see themselves reflected in the Senecan mirror.

To interest a popular Roman audience in a stage "death" when the games afforded ample opportunity to see real death must have been difficult, and perhaps the horrendous on-stage suicide of Jocasta in Seneca's *Oedipus* is an attempt to do so. But the dramatist could not compete, and probably would not have wanted to compete with the grim spectacles Martial, a poet of the next generation after the Younger Seneca, describes in his *Book of Spectacles*. The Roman amphitheater imparted to even the grossest and most grisly myths a certain air of reality.

It was difficult and dangerous to address a popular audience under the Roman emperors as well as, apparently, futile. If a popular audience detected a covert insult or jest at the emperor's expense, it might be unsophisticated enough to roar its recognition, approving or disapproving—to the great peril of the writer. Smaller, more refined audiences, meeting in times of tyranny and in gatherings where names are known, react more cautiously. Experience teaches them that to acknowledge an insult or jest, even to be present when it is made, imperils the listener as well as the author.

The currently increased theatrical interest in Senecan tragedy contrasts with scholastic insistence that Senecan tragedy was never actually staged at Rome. We will never know if and how it was staged. It is probably correct that the Senecan *Oedipus* was not produced before the massed citizen body of Rome as Sophocles' *Oedipus* was produced before the citizen body of Athens. But this does not mean it was not designed for performance—and actually performed—in other venues. Much modern drama is not aimed at, or performed before, a massed national audience either. Despite the availability of mass audiences through television and cinema, the writer often chooses to address a literary and artistic elite in a small theater.

24. Staging Seneca

Senecan tragedy demands performance, not just recitation, by two or three readers. The rapid interchanges between, say, Medea (or Phaedra) and her nurse need actors, not just voices. The commonly held view that the plays were declaimed by a single voice assumes that the Latin *recitare* and *recitatio* carry the same sense as the English "recite" and "recitation." There is no reason, however, to suppose that these words preclude the notion of performance by multiple actors. In modern Italian theatrical parlance, *recitare un dramma* means "to perform a play," not "to recite a play."

I can do no better here than echo William Calder's observation that "Seneca wrote his tragedies to be performed," and for the same reason: "I have read no cogent argument to the contrary."[105] What is sometimes called the "Recitation Theory" of Senecan tragedy owes much not only to the restrictive Anglo-German-French sense of *recitatio* as "recitation" but also to the low opinion scholars hold of Senecan tragedy as theater. Many Latinists, I am sure, would agree with Elaine Fantham's observation that Seneca's tragedies "are not well-crafted stage-plays."[106] I disagree. Having staged several Senecan plays, I have seen how effective they are as theater. Scholars exaggerate the difficulties in staging them and undervalue their theatrical innovations.[107]

None of the complete plays attributed to Seneca presents insuperable problems to modern directors, even *Oedipus*, with its scene of animal sacrifice. Film directors would have no difficulties whatsoever. I have offered, as stage directions, some suggestions as to how this scene can be managed effectively and legally. Once we accept Senecan tragedy as designed for performance, we may appreciate some of the remarkable effects actual and potential in, say, the staging of *Oedipus, Thyestes, Phaedra, Medea*, and *Trojan Women*.

Yet if the plays were designed for performance but not performed in public theaters, were they only plays in search of a stage, or were they presented in a less public manner? The germ of an answer is found in Suetonius' *Domitian* 7. Domitian, we are told, "forbade actors from using the (outdoor, public) stage, but conceded to them the right to practice their art indoors." Domitian's action, of course, was taken some thirty years after the Younger Seneca's death. But the practice of "in house" performances may well have been going on for some time before Domitian's decree: he was decreeing something even he couldn't prevent. And this, I believe, is how Senecan tragedy was performed—in the more than ample homes of well-to-do Romans

[105] W. M. Calder, "Secreti Loquimur: An Interpretation of Seneca's *Thyestes*," in *Seneca Tragicus*, ed. A. J. Boyle, 184–98, and A. J. Boyle, *Roman Tragedy*, 189ff.

[106] *Seneca's Troades: A Literary Introduction with Text, Translation, and Commentary* (Princeton, 1982), 49.

[107] For a variety of different views see G. W. M. Harrison, ed., *Seneca in Performance*.

with their more than ample fortunes. I emphasize that my resolution of the problem is no more than a matter of personal opinion—as are other theories about the performance or non-performance of the plays. I also warn the reader that stage directions given in the translations are only suggestions.

Ultimately the question as to how Senecan tragedy was presented matters more to a historian of the theater than to a director. The real question for the director is whether these plays are worthy of being staged, given a workable script.

Tragedy is about power and those who exercise it. It addresses the issues of power through the language, persons, and landscapes of myth, all of which are more exotic to Roman than to Greek audiences, since many educated Romans had never been to Greece, much less to the famous crossroads where Laius supposedly died. Athenian soldiers, on the other hand, would have passed them on several occasions during the Persian and Peloponnesian Wars. So Seneca's characters insert descriptions of landscapes, which might be unfamiliar, and even describe the Sphinx (alluded to only obliquely in Sophocles).

Senecan tragedy, like the *Aeneid*, is notable for its very Roman preoccupation with ritual and sacrifice—a feature prominent in *Oedipus, Medea, Thyestes*, and *Trojan Women*. Whereas Sophocles lived in a society where the ritual killing of humans was more a feature of the world of Homer and myth than of contemporary reality, and the large-scale ritual killing of animals more or less limited to special feast days, in imperial Rome ritual death was a more common spectacle, chiefly at the gladiatorial games. Although Cicero decries human sacrifice as "a monstrous and barbarous custom" (*Pro Font.* 31), and Julius Caesar says much the same (*BG* 6.16), Octavian is said to have sacrificed humans on the anniversary of Julius Caesar's death (Suetonius, *Divus Augustus* 15; Dio 48.14.4). So when in *Aeneid* 10.520 and 558 Aeneas is represented as taking prisoners for human sacrifice he may have had a contemporary, not simply a Homeric, precedent. The closeness of the Latin words for "enemy" and "sacrificial victim," *hostis* and *hostia* respectively, built the idea into the language.

It is sometimes claimed that Seneca presents his scene of animal sacrifice and inspection of entrails in *Oedipus* because of a personal predilection for gory descriptions. It would be fairer to see it as part of Seneca's attempt to *Romanize* the myth of Oedipus.

Seneca has to adjust the Sophoclean *Oedipus* in many details to make his tragedy work for Romans. Not least, he has to find some way of presenting prophecy to his Roman audience, since, from Cicero's time onward, the Delphic oracle was essentially defunct. Cicero, Lucan, and Plutarch, among others, all mention, lament, even satirize the disappearance of Delphic prophecy from the world.[108] And there is a story told of Nero's attempt to consult the oracle: that the Pythian priestess refused to respond on the grounds that he had killed his mother.

While Seneca does have Creon visit Delphi and report an oracle verbatim, he also foregrounds other prophetic activities that Sophocles mentions but relegates to the background.

Various forms of divination were institutionalized by the Roman state in ways they never were in Athens. There was, for instance, a College of Augurs at Rome whose special expertise was in the prophetic lore derived from birds. Cicero was himself a member of this board. Two other forms of searching into the future were thriving, though neither was officially sponsored by the state. One was necromancy: the calling up of the spirits of the dead to prophesy; this was taken seriously enough to be practiced even by prominent political figures such as Pompey's son Sextus (see Pliny, *Natural History* 7.178–79)—though such actions were not always favorably regarded. Necromancy and other conjurings of the dead are at least as old as *Odyssey* 11 in the Greco-Roman world. They also find their way into the New Testament and are alluded to in various forms by most Latin epic poets. Most famously, Aeneas visits the dead in *Aeneid* 6; Scipio Africanus consults the dead in Silius Italicus' *Punica* 13; the witch Erictho reanimates a corpse in Lucan's *Pharsalia* 6; and in Apuleius' *Golden Ass*, a murdered man is brought back to life by an Egyptian priest to denounce his murderer. So the conjuring of Laius' ghost in Seneca's *Oedipus* is very much within a continuing Roman tradition. Closest of all to Seneca's is that done by Teiresias in Statius' *Thebaid* 2 on behalf of Oedipus' son Eteocles.

Another form of divination was *haruspicina*, one of the most common and widely accepted modes of enquiring into the future. Though not officially approved, the old Etruscan practice of *haruspicina* involved examining the vital

---

[108] See Lucan, *Pharsalia* 5.111–14: "Our own times feel the loss of no gift of the gods more than this: the fact that the Delphic oracle has fallen silent, after kings came to fear the future and forbade the gods to speak." See Juvenal, *Satires* 6.553–56. The oracle was probably not completely closed throughout the period, since Plutarch, himself an official at Delphi, tells us that the number of priestesses had been reduced from three to one because of failing interest (*On the Obsolescence of Oracles*, 411.Eff.). See my *Lucan: An Introduction* (Ithaca, N.Y., and London, 1976), 121–30; S. I. Johnston and P. T. Struck, *Mantikê* (Leiden, 2005), 283–306 and passim.

organs, particularly the liver, of a sacrificed animal, a procedure that interested the emperor Claudius. And, if we accept the Younger Seneca as author of *Oedipus*, it may be tempting to suggest that the scene of *haruspicina* gained special dramatic force because of the emperor's supposed interest in it.

Modern readers are prepared to countenance prophecy and often treat the prophets and prophecy of tragedy with more respect than did the Greeks themselves. Prophets and prophecy are so much a part of Christian tradition that we sometimes assume, quite wrongly, that all ancient Greeks believed in them, despite the often scathing comments about them in Greek tragedy and comedy, even by Oedipus in Sophocles' *Oedipus*. We are also prepared to countenance ghosts and necromancy. But animal sacrifice and *haruspicina* are too much for us. Although we slaughter many more food animals than the Romans did, the idea of animal sacrifice offends our sense of piety, thereby causing us to condemn rather than figure out the rationale for Seneca's use of it.

Seneca's Teiresias seems to anticipate some surprise even among his Roman audience. He more or less apologizes for not, rather, going into a Delphic trance on the grounds that he's too old for it! Seneca is doing something rhetorically interesting here. The timeless Teiresias has adapted his methods to the writer's contemporary Roman world here as he adapts himself to fifth-century Athens in Greek tragedy. In Sophocles' *Oedipus* Teiresias is the master of Socratic *élenchos*. In Euripides' *Bacchae* he is a sophist who rationalizes the tradition that Dionysus was born from the thigh of Zeus as an error in the oral transmission of myth. Now, in Seneca's *Oedipus*, he is ready for the Etrusco-Roman world of *haruspicina* and is accompanied by a clinically expert daughter who can see and describe the symptoms his blindness keeps from him.

Seneca's Teiresias and Manto detect in the entrails of the sacrificial animals what is obviously a reference to *future* events—the wars between the sons, even perhaps the grandsons of Oedipus. Indeed, the "truth" of the predictions manifest in the entrails inspected in Seneca's *Oedipus* is enhanced, paradoxically, by the fact that neither Teiresias nor Manto can understand them, whereas the mythically aware audience grasps their import immediately.

What Manto and Teiresias observe has little to say about any criminality in Oedipus' past actions, since *haruspicina* does not generally reveal the unknown past. And this may well be Seneca's most important point: that the obsession with self and personal past history can blind people, as it blinds Oedipus, to a larger future problem. And it is the most Roman element in prophecy that encompasses this larger future and to which Oedipus himself remains resolutely and selfishly blind.

25. Seneca's Dark Universe

The Younger Seneca makes it clear in his prose works that he was a follower of the Stoic school of philosophy. We have already pointed out some of the most obvious features of Stoicism. Its followers insisted that the universe is a continuum: all phenomena are bound together in a material and causal network whose behavior is determined by a pre-set formula, "fate," presided over by a benevolent force they called Providence. There is no such thing as "chance" or randomness.

In the Senecan tragedies, however, there is little trace of any benevolent Providence. On the contrary, the plays often show us a dark universe where evil, devised by the human mind and emotions, and activated by despotic power, overwhelms nobler impulses or ideals, and marginalizes the gods. There is no force external to mortal life capable of acting in a corrective, moral capacity. If this is still Stoicism, it is a far remove from the more optimistic determinism in Seneca's letters.

Even if we choose to believe that Seneca was, at heart, a convinced Stoic, we do not have to see him as a soul confident and at spiritual peace with itself. The religious and philosophical agonies of Milton or, no less poignantly, Donne, should warn us of the terrible "laceration of mind," as Samuel Johnson calls it, with which deep-seated religious feelings and conversions are associated. The same John Donne can, in different moods and times, produce the erotic flippancy of *The Flea* and the melancholy religious brilliance of *A Hymne to God the Father*. As Max Brecher has pointed out to me most eloquently, this is "you alone in the arena with all the beasts of your contradictions coming at you all at once. They are, of course, not only your contradictions, but also those of the society (or societies) you have grown up in and live in."

It is mostly in Seneca's prose works that we are assured of the invincibility of good; in the tragedies we see more often the triumph of evil. Seneca, then, gives us two separate visions of himself: the rational, philosophical obverse of his paradoxical coin, and the poetical reverse, assuming, that is, that they are different faces of the same coin, that the author of the tragedies is the same person as the philosopher.

It is possible, nonetheless, to contemplate each face separately. We will, I would argue, gain a better picture of Seneca's poetry if we consider his tragedies *apart from* his prose works if only to counteract a widely held but usually false assumption that poetry begins its existence as prose, and is, essentially, a kind of ornate prose.

In the philosophical world of Roman Stoic determinism, the future ought to be predictable if one can gain insight into the nexus of causality in which all things are bound together. For the Stoic school of philosophy held that the universe is one entity, infinitely subdivisible and totally interconnected: a kind of dynamic continuum. There are no "forms," as in Aristotle, which isolate one object or being from another. Thus the entire universe can react, as does a pond to a stone thrown into it.

Heaven reacts to earth and earth to heaven. The action of an individual man can affect the stars. Such thinking is fundamental to the megalomania of Atreus in Seneca's *Thyestes*. Atreus sees the universe reacting to his crimes, and the chorus in the same play even envisages a collapse of the constellations in response to human criminality. Such megalomania is also fundamental to Oedipus' thinking in Seneca. For he believes that destiny is reserving him for something important and big.

Not all the Senecan plays are as dominated by characters and choruses with such darkly inverted Stoic attitudes (or fantasies) as are *Oedipus* and *Thyestes*. Elsewhere we find views suggestive of the Epicurean school, where humans are combinations of atoms whose bonds are shattered irrevocably at death. In *Trojan Women*, for example, the chorus has a decidedly Epicurean outlook. Death is utter non-existence. It is sweet, they say in a passage echoing Lucretius 2.1–6, to see others suffering not because you delight in their misfortunes, but because it is nice to know you have not been singled out for suffering. And while Calchas argues that it is the will of the gods that Andromache's child Astyanax be killed, Ulysses takes the more pragmatic view that it is wise to eliminate the possibility that Astyanax will grow up to be another Hector whom his own son Telemachus will have to fight. Much the same is true of characters in *Phaedra*, *Agamemnon*, and *Medea*.

Seneca was fully aware that different people thought about themselves and their relationship to the world in different ways. And he was writing dramas, not doctrinal treatises. The fact that Seneca's Oedipus thinks of himself as an instrument of some kind of destiny does not mean that he is such an instrument in any objective way. But because he thinks of himself in deterministic terms, he is capable of accepting the outcome of events as a Stoic would. He has, he believes, discovered his "purpose" in life, his role in the causal nexus of *fatum*, "fate," and he is proud of it.

Sophocles' Oedipus, in contrast, talks of himself as the child of *tyche*, chance, rather than the child of fate. But, like Aeschylus' Eteocles in *Seven against Thebes*, he allows his life to be controlled, to an exceptional extent, by his irrational fears, by random circumstances, and by the manipulation of others. Even in a non-deterministic world, non-predetermined outcomes are predictable on the basis of observed behavior.

There is no more stunning difference between Seneca's *Oedipus* and Sophocles' than in the concluding scenes of the plays. Sophocles' Oedipus, now blind and deprived of the company of his daughters, is ordered back into the palace by Creon, who has taken control of Thebes. The plague afflicting the city is long forgotten. The focus, narrowed to Oedipus and Creon, is given some expansion by the chorus' concluding meditation, if it is genuine, on the mutability of mortal affairs. The words echo the Athenian sage Solon's advice to king Croesus: "Count no man happy until he is dead." But Oedipus is not dead. The story, his sufferings, and those of Thebes are not over.

In Seneca, Oedipus himself delivers the concluding words. He addresses the audience with the sure confidence of a man who feels he has "saved the world," who has purged his own guilt and lifted the blight of sickness and death from his city. Seneca's Oedipus seems intent on making much of the distinction between the conscious and unconscious commission of crimes. He stresses the fact that he is, in a sense, a criminal without being guilty, since he is not aware of the nature of his crimes. Like his counterpart in Sophocles, he has never considered his killing of an old man at a crossroads a crime, regardless of who the man was. He sees his action as criminal only when he concludes that the man was his father.

Nonetheless, Seneca's Oedipus is far less prone to make irrational judgments and draw whimsical conclusions than Sophocles'. And while he never loses his megalomaniacal sense of his own *grandeur* in suffering, neither does he lose sight of all his responsibilities to the state—so quickly forgotten by his Greek predecessor. His death becomes something of a Roman *devotio*—a general's ritual dedication of himself to sacrificial death on the battlefield— long held to be a noble and praiseworthy action at Rome.

As Seneca's Oedipus differs from Sophocles' Oedipus, so too do his chief interlocutors. Creon's pose as the loyal friend is more transparent than in Sophocles, and his Teiresias is at a great remove from Sophocles' master rhetorician. Seneca's man from Corinth, though nudging Oedipus to the conclusion that he is a Theban foundling, is far less rhetorically devious. Yet though the Roman Oedipus performs a kind of *devotio* for his city, he leaves Creon in prison and makes no further provision for the city's future than the removal of himself. His triumph is one of a grandiosely selfish heroism no less ruinous to Thebes than the rather sadder delusions of Sophocles' hero.

Manto's examination of the entrails warns the audience that civil war lies ahead. And if this is in any way the poet's warning of impending danger to the Roman state, much as Sophocles' *Oedipus* hints at the danger of a tyrannical coup in Athens, Seneca's play makes most sense if seen as written at a time when such a dynastic civil war seemed possible, even if it turned out to be a false alarm. And, curiously enough, after each of the historical plagues within the lifetimes of the two Senecas, there was no clearly indicated successor to the ruling emperor. So civil war was indeed a threat.

26. The Roman Plague

I now return, as promised, to the problem of the plague in Seneca's *Oedipus*, if only to satisfy those readers who, like myself, incline to link the dramatic plagues in both *Oedipus* tragedies to historical occurrences of plague and who find the notion that Seneca is simply imitating Sophocles unsatisfactory. For there are other factors which might have been prompting him to include a plague.

Not least among these factors is the tradition, mentioned by the Roman historian Livy (7.2), that the first official dramatic performances at Rome were staged in 364 BC in response to a plague: a rite, imported to Rome from Etruscan culture, to appease angry gods.[109] Seneca could be reflecting a Roman tradition in which the performance of a play is itself an act of appeasement in a time of plague. And some such tradition may also have prevailed at the small city of Epidaurus in Greece, at the shrine of Asclepius, god of healing, the most impressive part of whose archaeological remains is a disproportionately huge theater, still used for performances today.

Certainly Seneca's Oedipus is represented at the end of the play as believing that the city is cleansed by his self-expulsion in an act of self-sacrifice to secure the safety of the state as a whole. There is no clearer example of what

---

[109] See A. J. Boyle's discussion in *Roman Tragedy*, 27 ff.

is meant by the term *pharmakós*, "scapegoat," in all ancient tragedy: a person who shoulders, or thinks he shoulders, the offenses, known and unknown, of the entire community and who, by his death, erases the record of all wrongdoing, a kind of communal cleansing, or, in Greek terms, *kátharsis*.

The notion of *devotio*, the offering up of his own life as a sacrifice by a leader in time of crisis, was deeply ingrained in Roman culture. Early tradition (Polybius 6.55.1–4) has Horatius Cocles performing a *devotio* during the struggle against Lars Porsena in 508 BC and consecrating the Sublician Bridge over the Tiber by drowning himself (as opposed to surviving his famous leap as he does in Livy and Macaulay). Two men named Publius Decius Mus, the father in 340 BC and son in 295 BC, gave their lives for Rome in a ritual *devotio*. Lucan, in his *Pharsalia*, depicts Marcus Porcius Cato as wishing to "redeem the peoples with his blood" during the Roman civil wars between Caesar and the forces of the republic (49–45 BC), and Statius in *Thebaid* 10 shows Creon's son Menoeceus leaping to his death from the walls of Thebes to consecrate them as Thebes struggles to repel the attack of the Seven.

If Livy is correct about the ritual performed in 364 BC (and many think he is not), he is describing an isolated event rather than the beginnings of tragedy at Rome. For the performance he mentions is a kind of pantomime rather than a tragedy in the Greek sense. Tragedy itself does not begin to take root in Rome until about a century later and never, as we have noted, enjoyed the official state support it had in Athens.

The Etruscan nature of the ritual Livy describes is itself of at least passing interest, since one of the Latin terms for an actor is *histrio*, which was thought by the Romans to be an Etruscan word. *Histrio* also bears a striking resemblance to two Greek words of uncertain origin: *historeîn*, "to tell a story," and *historía*, "(hi)story," first used in a technically precise sense by Herodotus, whose home was in Caria in Asia Minor, not far from Lydia, the supposed place of origin for the Etruscans. If this is so, then there is a sense in which Herodotus' *Histories* can be viewed as "re-enactments" of the past. And some theatrical re-enactment of a human sacrifice could quite possibly serve as a substitute for a real human sacrifice as was the case in certain Roman rituals where figures representing humans were destroyed in place of living people.[110]

There can be little doubt, then, that Seneca's Oedipus is thinking of himself in terms of ritual *devotio* in the Roman style, to bring an end to a plague. But which plague?

---

[110] See my discussion in *Metaformations*, 164–65 and 300–302.

We may recall that two plagues seem compatible with the Elder Seneca's authorship (23 BC and AD 6) and one with the Younger's (AD 65).

If the play is by the Younger Seneca, the plague of AD 65 is the most likely. The world is beginning to collapse around both the author and his emperor, Nero. Rome had burned in AD 64; there was a plague after the fire in 65, and a conspiracy to overthrow Nero was detected. Nero had no heirs, but he did have many rivals for power who were poised for the attack. And, for the first time in a century, a civil war was menacing the Roman world.

Within two years Nero had to flee Rome and kill himself or face capture. In 69 no fewer than four emperors ruled, and Rome was ransacked by an army for the first time since 390 BC. The last of the four emperors, Vespasian, succeeded in order by his two sons, Titus and Domitian, established peace and a new dynasty, the Flavians, which lasted until AD 96. And, by the early 80s AD, Statius, declaring himself unready to describe the horrors of that war, which had brought the wealth and nations of the whole world under the rule of one man, contented himself with publishing an epic about the Seven against Thebes.

The years following the death of Seneca the Younger, then, rivaled the horrors of any mythic war. But there were signs of impending trouble well before Seneca died; and Seneca was well placed to see them, since he had tutored Nero when Nero was a teenager and had conducted much of the emperor's business in the early years of his reign. But it will be hard for many to reconcile Seneca's Oedipus with the modern popular view of Nero. So, even though, according to otherwise respectable sources, Nero not only had sexual relations with his mother, but also had her killed, most will be likely to find this match unacceptable. And even if it is found acceptable, the case for Senecan authorship is slim. The window of opportunity for the Younger Seneca to write such a tragedy between the time of the plague and the time of his own death is a little too narrow: less than a year.

Richard Tarrant wisely observes that "covert allusions to contemporary Roman figures or incidents, if they exist in Seneca's plays, are not likely to be traceable at this distance, especially since any such references must have been designed to be ambiguous and therefore deniable."[111] But deniable ambiguities are the writer's stock-in-trade in all environments in which direct expression is prohibited in a particular area of discourse, whether that area be politics, religion, or sex. Yet to have any hope of locating such

---

[111] Tarrant, "Greek and Roman in Seneca's Tragedies," 228.

elusive clues, one needs to be looking in the right place at the right time. Most such investigations in Seneca's case have been based on the tenuous assumption that the writer is the Younger, not the Elder Seneca.

A plausible historical connection can be made between the Senecan *Oedipus* and the events accompanying the plague of 22 BC, if we allow the possibility that the author is the Elder Seneca.[112] The Roman emperor in 22 BC had begun life as Caius Octavius but had acquired a new identity as Octavian, when adopted posthumously by Julius Caesar (44 BC). After a series of civil wars, he usurped control of the state and then assumed a further new identity when he took the name Augustus (27 BC). He fell ill and came close to death in 23 BC, considered resigning his powers, and even, symbolically, gave his signet ring to his longtime friend and aide, Marcus Agrippa. For Augustus had no sons of his own. And Seneca makes no mention of Oedipus' sons either. The treatment that worked for Augustus failed on his heir apparent, Marcellus; and the following year the whole of Rome was ravaged by plague.[113]

In 22 BC Augustus also discovered he was the target of a serious conspiracy, led by Fannius Caepio and Varro Murena (possibly the same Varro who was his colleague as consul). These men he arrested and executed. Had Augustus not survived these various threats to his life, civil war could, arguably, have broken out again, as it might have if he had resigned his powers.

Nine years before the plague of 22 BC, Augustus (then Octavian) had won the Battle of Actium and gained control of his mother-country by defeating not just his rival Mark Antony but also Cleopatra, queen of Egypt. Cleopatra had played an important role in Rome's history. She had been Julius Caesar's lover and was mother of Caesar's only biological son, Caesarion, as well as, later, the wife of Mark Antony. In this sense she was herself a very Egyptian Sphinx of sorts. But Cleopatra, Antony, and Caesarion were all destroyed by the future Augustus. Augustus was, as Oedipus comes to believe he is, an adopted son. In taking control of Rome, he had, like Hippias in his dream, "married his mother." No less strikingly, although he rose to power through

---

[112] It is troubling that the epidemic of 22 BC occurred in the aftermath of a great flood rather than after the kind of heat wave and famine to which Seneca's Oedipus alludes—though floods in 23 do not rule out a heat wave the following year. In this respect, the epidemic of AD 6, associated with a famine, might, at first, seem a better match. For Augustus still did not have a successor clearly designated. The specter of a dynastic struggle in the event of his unexpected death was still present.

[113] The death of Marcellus is given special prominence by the ghost of Anchises in his account of the Roman future in Virgil, *Aeneid* 6.683ff. See my *Virgil: Aeneid*, notes on *Aeneid* 6.863 and 873.

his "father" Caesar's name, he was careful to minimize Julius Caesar himself in works that he commissioned. In Virgil's *Aeneid*, in which use of contemporary Roman names seems to have been carefully restricted, "Caesar" always means Augustus, not Julius Caesar (who is referred to only once, and obliquely, as "father-in-law" in *Aeneid* 6). Augustus seems to have pressured his poets, particularly Virgil, not to name certain people in their works.[114] One looks in vain for Virgil's most important contemporaries and their fathers' generation in the *Aeneid*. But some mythical names are oddly absent too.

One of the most curious facts about Roman poetry is that Augustan poets avoid references to either Oedipus or the Sphinx (who is not among the monsters under the leaves of Virgil's underworld elm). Virgil never names her, even though he does, of course, refer to Cleopatra and Egypt. Neither, more curiously, does Ovid in the *Metamorphoses*. Ovid bypasses the story of Oedipus in favor of a series of tales about Teiresias in book 3 and has Cephalus make a brief mention of her where he refers to Oedipus not by name but as "son of Laius" and calls the Sphinx simply a bard, *vates* (*Metamorphoses* 7.759–61). And even then, Cephalus claims that the Sphinx was instantly replaced by another monster of unspecified nature who was pursued by his dog; and both monster and dog were transformed into statues, conferring victory on neither (786–91).[115] The Sphinx is no less conspicuously absent from Augustan art.[116]

Some caution was probably needed in mentioning the Sphinx because Augustus, Suetonius tells us, when he first assumed power, used the Sphinx as the device on his signet ring, presumably to symbolize his victory over Cleopatra and his annexation of Egypt. He later replaced the Sphinx ring with one bearing an image of Alexander the Great, and finally with one bearing his own image—a practice continued by his successors (Suetonius, *Divus Augustus* 50). Augustus used his signet ring as the symbol of his power. He had duplicates made and passed them to Agrippa and Maecenas when he was out of Italy, thereby empowering them to act on his behalf in his absence (Dio Cassius 51.3.4–6 and Pliny, *Natural History* 37.10).

---

[114] Servius records several instances, in particular the changes made to *Georgics* 4 to remove mentions of Virgil's friend Gallus. See my *Virgil: Aeneid,* note to *Aeneid* 6.306–8.

[115] For further discussion of Cephalus, see my "Homer, Vergil, and Complex Narrative Techniques in Latin Epic," *Illinois Classical Studies* 14 (1989): 1–31.

[116] See Jean-Marc Moret, *Oedipe, la Sphinx et les Thébains: Essai de Mythologie iconographique* (Rome, 1984), 1:113, who notes that the Sphinx is relegated to minor places, the small sides of sarcophagi and provincial bas-reliefs, during the Augustan Age.

Augustus' signet ring was, therefore, as J. M. Carter observes, "in use before 29 BC and was inevitably associated with a rule that many Romans considered illegal or tyrannical."[117] Dio mentions it in his discussion of 31 BC. We don't know when Augustus changed the motifs. But when that ring bore the image of the Sphinx, it made Augustus, potentially, either a contemporary Oedipus or a contemporary Sphinx, or both, depending on the perspective employed. For Augustus not only sealed his letters with the Sphinx-seal but *encoded* them (Dio 51.3.7). Even to tell the story of Oedipus, then, took courage.

That is why it may be important that the only definite span of time mentioned in either *Oedipus* tragedy is the very anomalously precise nine years Seneca's Jocasta says has elapsed between the present plague and Laius' death, which is itself set by some of the characters in close proximity to the destruction of the Sphinx. For this is the same interval that exists between Octavian's victory over Antony and Cleopatra in 31 BC and the plague of 22.

If there is an allusion to the plague of 22 BC, then the closer the composition is set to that year, the more powerful the resonances are, since they conjure Augustus much more fully than they conjure any of his successors who did not use the Sphinx ring and were not famous for victories over Egypt. Thus the author is more likely to be the Elder than the Younger Seneca. Rome had newer and more immediate problems to consider by the time we reach the heyday of Seneca the Younger a half century later.

If this hypothesis has any merit, this tragedy has many things to say to both Augustus and Rome. It presupposes, for example, that the king's motivations are noble, that he intends, above all, to serve the interests of his city. Yet it warns that any advice he is given to step aside is likely to be motivated by the ambitions of those who seek his power and that the result will be a disastrous war of succession, however noble he himself will seem as a result. In other words, the play is not necessarily an oblique attack on the emperor of the sort other poets were making, even though it is candid about his cynical understanding of power.

It is not my intent to suggest that Seneca (Elder or Younger) or for that matter Sophocles is making of the tragedy a precise political allegory, but rather that the playwrights are allowing their contemporary audiences or

---

[117] J. M. Carter, *Suetonius Divus Augustus* (Bristol, 1982), 171. Augustus was out of Italy in 29 BC. For illustrations of Sphinx signet rings, see Moret, *Oedipe,* plates 71–74.

readers to see how universal mythic archetypes are by comparing them to events within their own experience. One does not have to look far nowadays for a Sophoclean Oedipus. But a Senecan Oedipus is harder to find.

The Glossary

To help the reader unfamiliar with mythic detail, I have included a glossary of names which includes cross-references to those that are discussed in this introductory essay.

The translations are based on the Greek text of Sophocles' *Oedipus* established by H. Lloyd Jones and N. G. Wilson in *Sophoclis Fabulae* (Oxford, 1990) and on the Latin text of Seneca's *Oedipus,* edited by Otto Zwierlein in *L. Annaei Senecae Tragoediae* (Oxford, 1986), though with frequent reference to the new Loeb edition by J. G. Fitch, *Seneca Tragedies II* (Cambridge, Mass., 2004).

SOPHOCLES

OEDIPUS TYRANNUS

SOPHOCLES

Oedipus Tyrannus

TRANSLATED BY FREDERICK AHL

The Characters: In the original production, all parts except for the Chorus were played by three actors, assuming different roles.

Actor One (*protagonist*): OEDIPUS, *tyrant of Thebes*
Actor Two (*deuteragonist*): PRIEST OF ZEUS
                              JOCASTA (wife of Oedipus),
                              COURT SERVANT (*who brings news from inside the palace*)
                              A SLAVE
Actor Three (*tritagonist*): CREON ("Ruler"; *brother of Jocasta*)
                              TEIRESIAS ("Expert on Prodigies")
                              A CORINTHIAN

Chorus of Theban Citizens

Non-speaking roles: ANTIGONE and ISMENE (*Oedipus' daughters*)
Attendants to Creon and Oedipus, Teiresias' guide, Crowd of Priests and Holy Men

SOPHOCLES

Oedipus Tyrannus

Scene: in front of the palace of OEDIPUS *in Thebes. A crowd of Priests and Holy Men has gathered, led by the* PRIEST OF ZEUS, *holding in their hands branches wreathed in wool—a sign that they are asking help from the gods. Enter* OEDIPUS.

Oedipus:	Children, most recent sons of ancient Cadmus' line:

Why crowd upon me now and sit before me, wreathed
in garlands, bearing boughs, as if you begged for help?
The city clouds with incense, rings to the skies with hymns
pleading for heaven's aid, moans dirges of lament.   5
I've come in person, thinking justice better served
if I hear you myself, and not through messengers,
through others. I am called Oedipus,
   "Nowhere Unknown,"   8
because I can be called upon by everyone.   8a

Tell me, old man—your status makes it right that you
speak for the rest. What prompts you to assemble here?   10
Are you afraid? Do you desire something? I'd like
to do all that I can. I'd need a heart of stone
not to take pity on an embassy like this.

Priest: You, Oedipus, are ruler of my native soil.
You see us sitting here by gods' altars that you   15
administer. What age are we? Some are just fledglings,
too weak to fly far yet, others weighed down by years.

I'm priest of Zeus—and these the pick of virgin youth
who serve the gods. Common folk flock with wreaths
   and boughs
into our marketplaces, into Athena's two   20
temples or Apollo's shrine near the Ismenus   21
where oracles are discerned from ash of altar fires.   21a

You see with your own eyes: the city's floundering
in gales, no longer has the power to raise its prow,
its figurehead, above the violent surge of blood.
It withers in husks and shells of harvests from our soil,   25
it withers in herds that crop the fields, in wombs
   of wives
whose babies are born dead. Then god, with fire's fever,
drives down upon the city as a loathsome plague
voiding the homes of Cadmus of all life. Dark death
becomes our unseen plutocrat of sobs and screams.   30

I do not worship you as if you were a god,
nor do these youths now gathered at your doors. Rather,
we judge you the outstanding *man* in handling life's
perils, in *dealing with* those powers that are divine.
You came to Cadmus' citadel and you dissolved   35
our bonds of tribute set by a relentless bard's
riddles of song, though you learned not a thing from us,
though no one taught you. But you're said, you
   are assumed,
to have restored our life, with god's help, to its course.
Oedipus, figurehead of power, nowhere unknown,   40
Each one of us turns to you, begs you to find
   some strength
for us. Perhaps you've heard some utterance from
   the gods,
perhaps some man leads you to know where
   strength may lie.
Advice, I've seen, produces its most positive
results when spoken by men with experience.   45

Act! noblest of mortals, steady the city's keel:
Act, and with special care! For, as of now, this land
calls you her savior for your *previous* energy.
That's past. Don't let us have this memory
   of your reign:
how it began—that we stood upright, then, later,   50
collapsed. So set this city straight, where it won't slip.

You brought luck with you and fine auspices,
Be just, be like that now. In this land, you have power.
If you're to rule, it's more befitting that your power
Controls a city with people, not just empty space.   55
A castle or ship is nothing, it is meaningless,
when void of humans, living within, to share it with.

Oedipus: My poor sad sons, I'm well aware, not unaware
of what you yearn for, what you've come here
   for. I know
you all are sick with plague; yet, plague-sick as you are,   60
not one of you is sickened as I am. Your pain,
collective as it is, afflicts you one at a time,
As individuals, and no one else, whereas
My soul laments for city, self, and each of you.
I'm not a sleeper that you wake from his repose.   65
No: understand that I've wept many tears indeed,
and traveled many highways in my wandering thoughts,
Reviewing everything. I kept finding one cure.
I've acted on it, and I've sent Menoeceus' son,
Creon, my brother-in-law, to Phoebus' Delphic shrine   70
to delve into what I might do or say to guard
this city. Now I've reckoned up the days. He's due,
it's time he came back. And I'm pained, worried about
what he's doing now. For he's been gone beyond
the usual time, the time needed for such a task.   75
When he arrives, I'd be an evil man if I did not
forthwith do all such things as are revealed by god.

Priest: Your words are timely! Just moments ago these men
began to give me signals of Creon's approach.

(*Enter* CREON, *crowned with laurel wreaths, and responding with a smile to the crowd that greets him*)

Oedipus:	O Lord Apollo, I pray he comes to rescue us 80
	with luck on his side that shines as brightly as his eye.
Priest:	To take a guess, it's fine. He would not otherwise
	have wreathed his head with berry-covered laurel sprigs.
Oedipus:	We'll know in seconds. He's now close enough to hear.
	My lord, my kinsman, and Menoeceus' son, tell me: 85
	What report do you come bringing us from god?
Creon:	A good one. For I say things hard to bear might chance
	to mean good luck—if, by some chance they turn out straight.
Oedipus:	This is it? What kind of utterance is this?
	This statement neither makes me bold nor frightens me. 90
Creon:	If *you* feel you must hear it with these men around
	I'm ready to state it now. Or we can go inside.
Oedipus:	Speak it to everyone. These people's sufferings
	weigh more upon me than concern for my own life.
Creon:	I would be saying what I heard relayed from god. 95

(CREON *pauses, to make sure that* OEDIPUS *wants him to proceed publicly.* OEDIPUS, *with a gesture, has him continue*)

	Lord Phoebus clearly instructed that we should expel
	a curse that's on our country, nurtured on this soil:
	we must stop nurturing an ill that has no cure.
Oedipus:	By what rite of cleansing? How must we deal with it?
Creon:	By banishing a man or paying off killing with killing. 100
	A hemorrhage bloodies this city with its stormy rage.
Oedipus:	Whose mischance was this? Who is the man he means?
Creon:	We used to have a leader of this land called Laius,
	My lord, before you straightened out our city's course.
Oedipus:	I know him well from hearsay, but I've not seen him. 105
Creon:	He died. And now the god clearly instructs a hand
	to make his killers pay their criminal penalty.
Oedipus:	And where on earth are they? Where will their tracks be found?
	Old crimes belay us in our search for evidence.

Creon:	In this land, he insisted. What is sought gets caught, 110
	But what one keeps neglecting keeps getting away.
Oedipus:	Was Laius in his home or outside in the wilds
	or in another country when he met his death?
Creon:	He left home, he insisted, on divine business.
	He never did come home again or send us word. 115
Oedipus:	No messenger or fellow-traveler noticed him—
	some person that one might consult and learn
	things from?
Creon:	All but one were left for dead. He fled, appalled
	by sights seen, he could cite no clues—except for one.
Oedipus:	Which was? There could be many things to
	learn in this 120
	one, if we grasp the short protruding thread of hope.
Creon:	Robbers, he insisted, had waylaid and killed
	Laius. Not one man's strength, but many hands: a group.
Oedipus:	This robber: how would he have come to dare this act
	unless employed and paid by someone
	here in Thebes? 125
Creon:	That was indeed suspected. But, with Laius dead,
	there was no one to help; and we had troubles too.
Oedipus:	What trouble was afoot to stop you finding out?
	A tyrant and his power had just been overthrown!
Creon:	The riddle-singing Sphinx forced us to
	turn our thoughts 130
	from what had disappeared to what was at our feet.
Oedipus:	So I'll start at the top and make it reappear.
	How properly Phoebus, and how properly you
	have drawn
	all this attention to the dead man's cause again.
	You'll see that, as is only just, I'm your ally, 135
	the agent of revenge for this land and for god.
	I shall myself dispel this poisoned cloud, not for
	some distant friends, but for myself. Whoever the man
	who killed him was, he might, as agent of revenge,
	employ his hand in that same way on me. And so, 140
	in doing right by him, I also help myself.
	Be quick as you can, my sons! Up from the altar steps!

140

These boughs you've left in supplication, take
　　them away!
Have someone convene the Theban laity
　　here—tell them
I'll handle everything. What then appears will show　　145
that luck, with god's help, favors us—or we're
　　already lost.

Priest:　Come, sons, let us arise. This man has now proclaimed,
in public, everything we came here to obtain.
So then, may Phoebus who has sent these prophecies
come as our savior now, and bring an end to plagues.　150

(*Exeunt* Priest *and* Priests and Holy Men. *Enter* Chorus
*of leading Theban citizens who assemble before the shrine of Apollo
Ismenios in front of the palace*)

Chorus:　Comforting Voice of Zeus, what words did you shape
when you came into glorious Thebes
from Pytho, rich in gold?
I prostrate myself before you,
Mind quivering with fear, appalled.

Healer, Lord of Delos, hear my cries of pain!

Awed by you, I dread what new demands
you'll place on me—or is it something　　　　　　155
reaching back through whirling years?

Speak to me, child of golden hope,
Word divine.

I call you first, daughter of Zeus, Athena divine!
Next, Artemis, sister of Phoebus,
this land's defender,
enthroned, honored,　　　　　　　　　　　　　160
encircled by our marketplace.
Finally, Phoebus who strikes from far away:
Appear to me, all three!
Keep death at bay!

If ever in the past
you forced beyond our boundaries
the burning fire of misery,
the earlier mad tide of death
surging on our city,   165
Come to us now too.

Alas, I cannot count the miseries I bear.
My legions of people in their entirety are sick.
There is no cutting blade of thought
that will protect a soul.   170
Nothing born from our sacred soil will grow to fruit.
Women find no reward for childbirth's cries of pain
in giving birth.

Look! For if you did, you'd see
life after life surging
like birds with powerful wings, more irresistibly   175
than raging fire
to the sunset god's edge of death.

In their passing
the city dies in such numbers that I cannot count.
There is no room for pity. Children we have borne
lie dead, engender death, across the plain: 180
unburied and unwept.

City wives and graying mothers
shrill their heartbreak
from here, from there, at the altar's edge,
implore relief from grief and suffering.   185
Hymns of praise pipe brightness
yet the flute descants
keening lament.

Send us the lovely face of courage
to stand firm,
golden daughter of Zeus!

Ares with rage of fire,   190
hailed by men crying,
attacks me with
flaming brands:
War—yet no armor, no shields.

Send him away from my land,
turn him back like a running tide
with a wind from the shore
to the nymphs and the ample bed   195
of the Atlantic.
or to the Black Sea,
rough as its tribesmen,
to a harbor
denying haven.

If night loses its grip on anything,
day moves in to finish it off.

Zeus, father, you control   200
the lightning charged with fire.
Use your thunderbolts,
and wither him beneath them.

Lord of Light, Lycaean killer of wolves,
how I wish you'd defend us,   205
shower your unbending shafts
drawn arrowhead to fingertip,
powered from torqued gold
of taut bowstring.

I long for Artemis' silver beaming
torches of light which she
arcs across Lycian mountains.

I call on gold-capped Bacchus,
whose name is so linked to this land,   210
winedark of face,
greeted with wild cheers,

roaming with fierce Maenads:
Come to us blazing
with pitch-torch
gleaming destruction
against the deathgod
despised among gods.   215

Oedipus: You pray for help. And what you pray you
        could achieve
if you've the will to hear and accept my words, deploy
them on the plague. You'd gain strength,
        lighten suffering.
I'll speak out, an outsider with no point to prove,
outside and uninvolved in what occurred. Alone,   220
I couldn't track things far. I have no evidence.
I therefore call upon you all, you Cadmeans,
As a more recent resident to fellow-residents:
If anyone among you knows the man who killed
Laius, the son of Labdacus, I command   225
that he communicate all that he knows to me.

(OEDIPUS *pauses briefly for a response*)

If he fears for himself, were he to bring the charge
against himself, he will evade full penalty:
nothing unpleasant. He will leave the land unharmed.

(OEDIPUS *pauses again*)

If, further, someone knows the man who
        struck the blow   230
came from another land, let him not be silent now.
I will myself reward him; he'll be duly thanked.

(OEDIPUS *pauses again*)

But if you all stay silent—if someone through fear
For his own person or a friend, chokes back his words
he owes it to himself to hear what I shall do.   235

No one in this land whose thrones	
and governments	236
I rule shall take this man, whoever he may be,	237
into his company or even speak to him.	238
No one shall join him in prayers to gods or sacrifice,	239
or share with him the cleansing font. This I forbid.	240
You all shall ban him from your homes.	
This man's the blight	241
upon our land. For so the Delphic oracle,	242
the word of god, has recently revealed to me.	243
I, being who I am, herewith ally myself	244
with the divinity; also with the deceased.	245
I lay a curse on this elusive man, whether	246
he did the deed alone or with accomplices.	247
May he grind out a wretched life, evil among evils.	248
I lay this curse, should he be in this house and share	249
this hearth of mine with my full knowledge:	
may what I	250
just prayed for others fall upon me with its spell.	251

(*Again, a brief pause*)

I set responsibility on you to do	252
just as I ask: for me, for god, and for this land,	253
this withered ruin, stripped of its fruitfulness and gods.	254
Even were this a matter where the gods made no	255
demands, it would be leaving a moral stain uncleansed,	256
to overlook, not hunt, its cause. A priestly king[1]	257
was killed. Since I'm now in control,	
owning the power	258
that he once owned, the bed he owned, the	
wife who drew	259
semen from us both, some bond would have been born	260

---

[1] Oedipus here uses the word *basileús*, "king," an elected and primarily religious public office at Athens that could be held only by citizens. He, a foreigner, is claiming the right to pronounce a curse on the tenuous grounds that he is the husband to the wife of the former "king." I number the lines individually on this page because many editors re-arrange them.

between us, children in common, but for his mischance,
his offspring's failure; and since chance came
   crashing down
on his head too, I'll take their place, as if he were
my own father. I'll fight on his behalf, I'll go
everywhere as I search out the guilty hand,   265
the murderer who killed the son of Labdacus,
the son of Polydorus, who himself was son
of Cadmus, child of Agenor from long ago.   268

For those who don't do what I bid: I pray the gods   269
no produce may sprout up for them out of this land,   270
and thus that their wives bear no children, but wither
with such doom as strikes us now—but even worse.

(*more moderately*)

	For all you other Cadmeans who are content	
	to do my will, may justice be your ally, may	
	all gods be with you and compassionate always.	275
Chorus:	As you have made me subject to a curse, my lord,	
	I'll state outright: I did not kill, I can't point out	
	the killer. But since Phoebus sent us on the search,	
	he should have said just who it was who did the deed.	
Oedipus:	You're right, that would have been just. But not	
	one man alive	280
	could force the gods to say what they don't wish	
	to say.	
Chorus:	Then might I say what I believe is second best?	
Oedipus:	If there's a third best too, don't fail to mention it!	
Chorus:	Closest in power of sight to Phoebus, lord to lord,	
	is, I understand, Teiresias. From him,	285
	one could, my lord, in this search, get clear-cut results.	
Oedipus:	But even this I did not shelve with things deferred.	
	Creon suggested it. I twice sent embassies	
	To him. He's long past due and so amazes me.	
Chorus:	Then there's the silly talk of times past, long ago.	290
Oedipus:	What was that talk? For I'm surveying every word.	

Chorus:	Word was that he was killed by travelers passing by.
Oedipus:	I've heard that: it was seen by someone no-one now sees.
Chorus:	If he's at all inclined to superstitious fears,
	he won't stay round, on hearing curses
	such as yours. 295

(*Unnoticed by* OEDIPUS, TEIRESIAS *enters, guided by a servant*)

Oedipus:	If deeds do not deter him, words won't frighten him.
Chorus:	The man who'll cross-examine him has just arrived:
	the godlike seer these men lead in, the only man
	born with the knowledge nothing known eludes.

(OEDIPUS *turns to* TEIRESIAS *who is moving slowly downstage, deep in thought*)

Oedipus:	Teiresias, observing all that can be taught, 300
	all that defies words, objects in heaven, things
	walking earth,
	though you can't *see* our city that the plague afflicts,
	your reasoned *insight* shows you it. We are, my lord,
	discovering that you alone can be her spokesman
	and savior. Phoebus—if you've not heard
	through messengers— 305
	sent us response. We'd sent to him for his advice.
	Release from this disease could come only if we
	clearly identified the men who killed Laius
	and either killed or sent them in exile from this land.
	Don't hold back on what birds of omen say to you, 310
	or on such other channels prophecy provides.
	Protect yourself, the city—and protect me too—
	protect all that's defiled by blight from this man's death.
	Our life is in your hands. To use what you possess,
	what powers you have, to help: that
	is man's noblest labor. 315

(TEIRESIAS *speaks at first as if he were addressing* OEDIPUS)

147

Teiresias:	Reason's power, alas, how fearsome a thing it is
	when insight yields no pay-off for the reasoning man!
	I know this, but forgot it. Or I'd not have come.
Oedipus:	What *is* this? How despondently you've come to us!
Teiresias:	Let me go home. If *you* do as *I* say *you'll* cope 320
	most easily with *your* affairs and I with *mine.*
Oedipus:	What *you* suggest is both unlawful and unkind
	to *Thebes.* She nursed you. *You* deprive her of your words.
Teiresias:	I see your voice issues from you with words not apt
	to the occasion. I don't want mine to do the same. 325

(TEIRESIAS *turns as if to leave*)

Oedipus:	Don't leave us, man of insight and reason!

(OEDIPUS *now prostrates himself at* TEIRESIAS' *feet*)

We all

Beg by the gods, we shower kisses at your feet.

Teiresias:	Because *you all* don't use your reason! Never will *I*
	State what is best—

        (*to* OEDIPUS)

                to avoid revealing *your* bad news.

(OEDIPUS *rises from his knees*)

Oedipus:	What's this you say? *You know,* but won't speak?
	You intend 330
	to hand us over to our doom, and ruin *Thebes?*
Teiresias:	I cause *myself* no pain and cause *you* none. So why
	Keep cross-examining? You *couldn't* delve it from *me!*
Oedipus:	You evilest of men, you'd temper a heart of stone!
	You just won't speak? You will appear,
	yet show yourself 335
	inflexible and leave your duties unfulfilled?
Teiresias:	*You* mind *my* temperament yet have no eyes to see
	your *own* that lives within you. And *you* then blame *me!*
Oedipus:	Who would not lose his temper when he heard such things?
	You are dishonoring this city with your words. 340

Teiresias:	All will come out the same if I leave silently.
Oedipus:	If it *will come,* should you not spell it out for me?
Teiresias:	I would not add another word. And, if you wish,
	respond with all the wildest temper of your heart.

(OEDIPUS *turns on* TEIRESIAS *with calculated anger*)

Oedipus:	And my temper's such that I'll withhold nothing	345
	I've grasped. For you should know that	
	I believe that *you*	
	helped father this act, and all but did the act yourself	
	apart from killing him with your own hands. If you'd	
	just happened to have eyes, I'd claim you worked alone.	

(TEIRESIAS *remains silent for a moment, then responds slowly and calmly*)

Teiresias:	Nothing eludes you, eh? I tell you clearly now	350
	to stand by your pronouncement: from this very day	
	speak neither to these people nor to me again	
	because this land's unholy, sickly curse is you!	

(OEDIPUS *turns on* TEIRESIAS *with a mixture of surprise and anger*)

Oedipus:	You see no shame in spreading talk like this around?	
	Where do you believe you'll now go to escape?	355
Teiresias:	I *have* escaped. I nurse knowledge that nothing eludes.	
Oedipus:	Who taught you it? Your trade's not known	
	for unelusiveness.	
Teiresias:	You taught me, nudged me to speak against my will.	
Oedipus:	What was it you deduced? Restate it, so I'll learn more.	
Teiresias	(*suspiciously*):	
	You didn't grasp it the first time?	
	Or you're testing me?	360
Oedipus:	Not well enough to understand. Say it again.	

Teiresias:	These murderers, these men you hunt: *I* claim they're *you.*
Oedipus:	You will not speak such slander twice without regrets.

149

Teiresias:	Should I speak on to fan your temper even more?
Oedipus:	As much as you feel need. But you'll
	be wasting words. 365
Teiresias:	It eludes you, I claim, how vilely you engage with those
	most dear; and you don't see the evil that you're in.
Oedipus:	You believe you'll always get away with talk like this?
Teiresias:	Yes, if there's power in knowledge nothing can elude.
Oedipus:	There is such power, but not in you. In you it's dead, 370
	Blind in your blocked-up ears, blunt brain and
	eye-balls blanked.
Teiresias:	*You* are pathetic, slandering *me* with just those taunts
	with which, so soon, no-one will fail to slander *you*.
Oedipus:	Child of unbroken darkness, never could *you* harm *me*
	or any other human life that sees the light. 375
Teiresias:	Your doom is not ruin by me. Apollo can
	manage. It's his concern to get all this fulfilled.
Oedipus:	Creon or who came up with these discoveries?
Teiresias:	Creon's no problem to you; *your* problem's yourself.

(OEDIPUS *turns to address the* CHORUS)

Oedipus:	Riches, a tyrant's throne—and skill surpassing skills 380
	others possess—all making for a deeply envied life,
	how great the jealousy that keeps you under watch!
	I did not ask the city to empower my hands
	as her first lord. She gave me power. And now Creon,
	a trusted friend from my first days as ruler, yearns 385
	to seize control and throw me out. He secretly,
	creeps up, works in a plot-weaving, king-making fraud,
	a treacherous liar with an eye only for personal
	gain but born blind in the skill he would profess.

(*Turning back toward* TEIRESIAS)

Well, tell me: where have *you* proved
   clear-sighted as seer?   390
How was it, when the riddle-singing bitch was here,
you uttered nothing that could save these townsmen then?
That was a riddle which required prophetic skill,

and not an accidental passer-by to solve.
But you did not come forward with
    your birds, or words   395
from any god, that could make sense of it. Yet I,
Oedipus, with no whit of knowledge, then passed
    by. And I
defeated her with shrewd thinking not learnèd bird-lore.
And *you* now try to throw *me* out. For you believe
you will stand close to Creon's clique
    and Creon's throne.   400

But I believe you'll weep, both you and he who planned
this witch-hunt. Were you not, I do believe, senile,
you'd have learned through suffering what your
    insight meant.

Chorus:	Our guess is that his words were spoken, Oedipus,

in temper. So, we believe, were yours. This is no time   405
for such disputes. Rather one should review how best
we all can analyze these prophecies from god.

Teiresias:	Though you're the tyrant, still at least equality

must be allowed in equal time to make response.[2]
In this respect I too have some empowerment,
For *I* live as Apollo's slave, not *yours*. I won't   410
sign in to have Creon, as spokesman, speak for me.
I speak since you have slandered me for *my* blindness.
You *have* eyes, but don't see the evil you are in,
or where you dwell, or who you share your
    dwelling with.
Do you *know* whose child you are? Does it elude   415
you too that you're a foe to your own kin, dead
    and alive?
That your mother's and father's curse now
    stamps doubly
Down on you with fearsome feet and will some day

---

[2] No one has denied Teiresias the right to speak. In fact the whole first part of the scene is Oedipus' attempt to get him to speak. This is a clever rhetorical ploy on Teiresias' part which enables him to cast Oedipus as the stereotypical "tyrant."

kick you out of this land? You see before you now;
then you'll see darkness. Oh, what place
   won't harbor your screams   420
that day? Won't Cithaeron's echo sing with you,
   when you
have learned the melody of your own wedding hymn
with which you sailed such smooth sailing into a wrong
berth? A host of other evils you don't grasp shall then
assess your status as the same assigned your sons!   425

So counter that by smearing Creon and by stuffing
filth into my mouth! No mortal man exists
who'll tread an eviler path than you, or ever will!

Oedipus: Must I keep hearing these intolerable slurs
        from him?
                Just go to hell! Go back where you came from,   430
        leave this house. And make it quick! Get out! Begone!

Teiresias: *(starting to leave)*
        I never would have come if *you'd* not summoned me.

Oedipus: *(calling after him)*
        I did not know you'd spout such idiocy. If so,
        I'd not have hurried to invite you to my home.

Teiresias: *(stopping, but not turning)*
        We are what we were born. Idiots, you believe.   435
        Your parents, however, thought my insight rational.

        (continuing his exit)

Oedipus: Who were they?
                  Stay!
                       Who in the world did father me?

Teiresias: *(stopping, but not turning)*
        This day will father you. It will destroy you too.

Oedipus: Your words are all excessively riddling and obscure.

Teiresias   *(turning):*
        Weren't *you* born best at finding out what *riddles* mean?   440

Oedipus: Keep scourging me with things like this! You'll
        find me great.

Teiresias:	No! It was luck, pure chance, and now it's wiped you out.
Oedipus:	But if I saved this city I don't care. So be it.
Teiresias:	I'm leaving then. You, child, convey me on my way!

(TEIRESIAS *again begins to leave*)

Oedipus:	Conveyed away? Oh yes! Here, on and under foot, 445 you're trouble. If sped off, you couldn't cause more pain.
Teiresias	(*stopping instantly and turning*): I'm leaving—once I've said what I *came here to say.* Your mask does not awe *me.* There's no detail on which you'll wipe me out.

        I say to you: this man you've sought
lately, threatened and publicly outlawed, this man,   450
this Laian killer, he is here. He's with us now.
Word is that he's an alien resident. But soon
he'll show himself as Theban-born, but won't
    be pleased
by the results. For *now* he sees; *then* he'll be blind—
now rich, a beggar *then,* his sceptre a staff, groping   455
his way into a foreign land. He'll show himself
to his own sons as one who's lived as their brother
and father both, as son and spouse to her who gave
him birth; who's sown his seed where his own
    father sowed,
and killed his father.

(TEIRESIAS *lifts his staff and points to the palace*)

        Go inside and figure this out   460
Yourself! And, if you catch me in a lie, claim *then*
that, in the mantic art, I lack reasoned insight.

(*Exit* OEDIPUS *into palace.* TEIRESIAS *remains on stage until he
leaves, then exits to the side, watched closely by the* CHORUS)

Chorus:　　　Who is the man the holy prophetic voice
　　　　　　　speaking from Delphic peaks
　　　　　　　picked out as the accomplisher,　　　　　　　465
　　　　　　　with bloodstained hands,
　　　　　　　of crimes so unhallowed
　　　　　　　they allow no name?

　　　　　　　Now is his hour to take to flight
　　　　　　　with feet more powerful
　　　　　　　than horses swift as hurricanes.
　　　　　　　The son of Zeus has armed himself　　　　　470
　　　　　　　and darts at him with fiery thunderbolts,

　　　　　　　Forces of vengeance invincible
　　　　　　　pursue.
　　　　　　　None can escape them.

　　　　　　　The voice that made it clear blazed
　　　　　　　　　lightning-bright
　　　　　　　from snow-clad Parnassus:
　　　　　　　we must use every means we have　　　　　　475
　　　　　　　to track a man vanished:
　　　　　　　no footprints, no clues.

　　　　　　　He skulks low in the wild bushland,
　　　　　　　lives high among rock caves:
　　　　　　　a lone bull upon slabstone ground,
　　　　　　　in pain, on feet that give him pain,
　　　　　　　Pulling far from earth's umbilical shrine.　　　480

　　　　　　　Yet its prophecies live for ever,
　　　　　　　circle and hover
　　　　　　　as long as he lives.

　　　　　　　Now the wise legislator of omens
　　　　　　　adds fearsome charges,
　　　　　　　fearsome confusion.
　　　　　　　I cannot believe them or reject them.　　　　485
　　　　　　　I'm at a loss for words, fluttering

amid various hopes, seeing neither what's
   in front of me
nor what lurks behind.

I for one have not learned
what basis for dispute
existed ever in the past

or up to today,

on the Labdacid side,

on Polybus' son's side,   490

to serve me as touchstone of worth,
to justify assault on the public good name
of Oedipus,
to make me avenger
of Labdacus' house   495
in deaths with no clues.

Still, Zeus and Apollo
both understand,
both know what mortals do and did.
But when it comes down to men:
Does a seer fare better than *I* do?   500
There is no unelusive way to judge.
One man could surpass another's wisdom with his own.

Never would I, at least,
declare charges proven
before I saw straight talk.   505

There are clear factors on his side:
the wingèd maiden
who once came to us here.
We saw his wisdom:
He tested as gold, as joy to the city.

So then, for my part, he will never stand accused,   510
in my mind or my heart, of evilness.

(*As the* CHORUS *tries to analyze what has passed,* CREON *reenters*)

Creon: My fellow citizens! I've learned that Oedipus
the tyrant has been charging me with fearsome crimes.
I'm here since my position is unbearable.
If he believes he's suffered any harm through me,   515
in words or deeds, in this current catastrophe,
I've lost desire for life prolonged into old age
with this report attached to me. The punishment
I suffer for his speech is no simple issue
between himself and me. It's very large indeed,   520
if I'm to be called evil in the city here,
and worse, called evil by yourself and by our friends.
Chorus: This slanderous insult was more probably forced out
by wrath than by thought planned with
          rational insight.
Creon: Was it said publicly that, influenced by plans   525
which I thought up, this seer spoke statements
          that were false?
Chorus: It *was* said. What the thought or plan was,
          I don't know.
Creon: Did he keep his eyes straight, and was his
          reasoning straight
while he was busy charging me with this offense?
Chorus: I don't know. What men who rule me do, I never see.   530

(*Enter* OEDIPUS)

But notice he's already come outside himself.

Oedipus: You, sir! Why are you here? Do you put on so great
a mask of boldness as to come right to my house,
you, so obviously the murderer of this man,
exposed as robber of my power as tyrant too?   535
Tell me, by god, what lack of nerve or idiocy
you saw in me that made you formulate these plots?

Did you assume I'd not observe your treacherous
Snake-like approach, or that I'd see it, but lack power
to ward it off? And isn't the stupidity   540
yours, attempting a coup, without riches and friends?
The prize you hunt is snared by cash and mass support.

Creon: You know what you should do? You've said your say.
          Now give
Listening an equal chance. Judge when you have
          learned the facts.

Oedipus: You're fearsomely quick with words.
          I'm slow to learn—   545
from you. I've found you hostile, burdensome to me.

Creon: This I must speak to now as I begin. Listen!

Oedipus: This you must not declare: that you are not evil.

Creon: If you reckon a stubborn and mindless attitude's
          worthwhile, you lack insight, your reasoning
          isn't straight.   550

Oedipus: If you reckon a kinsman can be harmed without
just penalty, you lack insight, your reasoning is insane.

Creon: Yes, I agree with you. There's justice in what you say.
          Start teaching me the symptoms of my malady.

Oedipus: Did you argue or did you not argue to me   555
          the case for sending someone for that pompous seer?

Creon: I did. And I maintain my stand on that advice.

Oedipus: And roughly how much time has passed now
          since Laius...

Creon: Did what particularly? I don't grasp your point.

Oedipus: Was struck down by a blow from a man who's disappeared? 560

Creon: Long layers of bygone time could well be
          measured back.

Oedipus: Was this seer practicing his skill in those days too?

Creon: He was: honored as wise, just as he is today.

Oedipus: Then did he mention me at all during that time?

Creon: No: not when I was standing anywhere nearby.   565

Oedipus: You held no inquiry about the man who died?

Creon: We set one up, of course; we didn't hear a thing.

Oedipus: So why did our wise seer not make his charges then?

Creon: I don't know. And, when insight fails me, I don't speak.

Oedipus:	You do know and could say with insight	
	this much, at least.	570
Creon:	And what would that be? I won't deny it if I know.	
Oedipus:	It surely follows that if he had not met with *you*	
	he never would have claimed that *I* caused Laius' death.	
Creon:	*You're* the one who knows if he claims that.	

Since you've

learned from me, it's fair that I should
          also learn from you.   575

Oedipus:	Learn everything! I'll not be proved a murderer.
Creon:	Well then: you're married to my sister; she's your wife?
Oedipus:	There's no denying your account upon this score!
Creon:	You rule this land jointly with her on equal terms?
Oedipus:	All that I have is hers to take, should she so wish. 580
Creon:	Am I not the third partner, equal with you two?
Oedipus:	That's where you show yourself to be an evil friend.
Creon:	Not if you'd do as I do, and think logically.

Consider this first: do you believe that anyone
will choose supreme power with its
          fears if he can have   585
the same authority conferred with carefree sleep?

(*more to the* CHORUS *than to* OEDIPUS)

I have, you see, no inborn personal desire
to *be* the tyrant if I can *do* what tyrants *do*—
nor has *anyone* who understands sane reasoning.

(*turning back to* OEDIPUS)

Now, thanks to you, I have it all without the fear.   590
If *I* ruled, I'd be doing much I'd rather not.
How could tyranny itself be sweeter to me
than painless control, pure power and influence?
I'm not as yet so self-deceived that I would crave
more than prestigious standing and rich benefits.   595
Now everyone likes me, everyone now embraces me;
now people craving things from you call upon me;
Achievement of what they want lies wholly here with me.

How could I give up all these things to grasp at *that*?
A reasoning mind with insight could not become evil.   600
I have no inborn lust in me for plans like this,
nor would I ever dare help someone else who does.

Examine the proof for this! Go to the Pythian seer:
Find out if my report was accurate in pith
and substance. Then, if you catch me in any plot   605
with our omen-inspector, take me and kill me, not
on a single but a double vote—both yours and mine.
Don't damn me on your own for some plan
    without proof.
It is not just so falsely to regard bad men
as most reliable and the most reliable bad.   610
To cast aside a noble friend is like, I say,
casting aside the parallel self one loves the most.
In time you'll come to know this and you won't
    be fooled.
Only time gives proof that any man is just;
but you could recognize a man as bad in but a day.   615

Chorus:	That's good advice for someone worried that he'll fall,
	my lord. And men who rush their reasoning tend to trip.
Oedipus:	When someone rushes forward with his secret schemes
	I too must, in reply, rush my own counter-schemes.
	But if I take it easy and await his moves, 620
	his plots will win success. Mine will have missed
	their mark.
Creon:	What do you crave to do then? Exile me from the land?
Oedipus:	Oh no! I want you not just gone but dead and gone.
Creon:	You make it clear you won't pull back or trust in me. 625
Oedipus:	I won't, since you exemplify what envy is. 624
Creon:	I see your reason's failing...
Oedipus:	Not my own concerns.
Creon:	It should serve mine as well.
Oedipus:	But you were born evil.
Creon:	If you grasp nothing, though...
Oedipus:	The city must still be ruled.
Creon:	Not under a bad ruler.

Oedipus:	Oh city, my city!
Creon:	I share this city too. It is not yours alone. 630
Chorus:	Stop it, my lords! For, just in time for both of you,
	I see Jocasta now emerging from the house.
	Settle this present quarrel with her help. You must!

(*Enter* JOCASTA *from the palace. She moves immediately toward* CREON *and* OEDIPUS *and places herself between them*)

Jocasta:	You stupid fools! Why use your tongues to
	rouse senseless
	civic unrest? Aren't you ashamed to rouse private 635
	wrongs when all the land is sick with plague like this?
	You, get inside the house! You too, Creon, go home!
	Stop turning pain that's nothing into something big!
Creon:	Blood-sister, your spouse Oedipus has deemed it just
	to act against me fearsomely, deciding between 640
	twin wrongs: exile from homeland, or arrest and death.[3]
Oedipus:	Agreed. Dear wife, I've caught him doing wrongful deeds
	against my person with his skill at wrongdoing.
Creon:	May I be lost to joy and cursed if I've done anything
	you're blaming me for doing to you. May I be killed! 645
Jocasta:	Oh by the gods[4] trust him in this now, Oedipus!
	You should indeed respect this oath sworn
	by the gods.
	And then respect both me and these men
	with you here.
Chorus:	Obey her my lord! Be willing, reason with
	insight, I beg!
Oedipus:	What will you have me concede for you? 650
Chorus:	This man was no mere child before.
	His oath now gives him great standing. Respect it!
Oedipus:	You know, then, what you're asking?
Chorus:	I know.

---

[3] Creon cleverly reintroduces the possibility of exile instead of the death-sentence Oedipus has vowed. Oedipus doesn't notice it.

[4] Jocasta quickly inserts the gods that Creon has actually failed to swear by.

Oedipus:	Then put it in words!	655
Chorus:	That you never condemn a friend who's under oath	
	With unclear logic, or dishonor and banish him.	
Oedipus:	Now understand this well: as you beg this for him	
	you're begging death or exile from this land for me.	
Chorus:	No! By the foremost god of all the gods,	660
	the Sun, may I meet godless,	
	friendless, and hideous	
	Death if I foresee	
	this as my goal.	
	But as I'm suffering, my land is perishing.	665
	It all wears down my soul,	
	if I must add the rift	
	between you two, new wrongs upon old wrongs.	
Oedipus:	Then let him go, though this may well decree	
	my death	
	or my ejection from this land: by force, disgraced.	670
	It is the plaintive words from your mouth, not	
	from his,	
	I pity. He'll be hated wherever he may be.	
Creon:	You're hateful when you flaunt your yielding	
	side, and when	
	raging beyond control you are a pain. But then	
	natures like yours are, justly, hardest on themselves.	675
Oedipus:	Leave me alone, then, and get out!	
Creon:	I'm on my way.	
	unknown to you, but in their eyes, your equal. And just.	

(*Exit* CREON)

Chorus:	My lady, why not have him	
	removed into the house?	
Jocasta:	I will, once I've learned what occurred.	680
Chorus:	An ignorant semblance of an argument	
	intruded. Then injustice took its toll.	
Jocasta:	Are both to blame?	
Chorus:	Yes.	
Jocasta:	And what was the argument?	

161

Chorus:	Enough's enough I think.
	The land has suffered enough. 685
	Best let things stand, it seems,
	where they left off.
Oedipus:	(*to the* CHORUS LEADER)
	See where you've got us now, as a man of good intent,
	by parrying my wrath and blunting its sharp point?
Chorus:	My lord, I've said this not just once before: 690
	know that I'd have shown myself
	as lost to insight,
	with no path to insight,
	if I set myself apart from you.
	You set my own dear land on a straight course 695
	when it was mad with suffering.
	Now send a favorable breeze, if you have power.
Jocasta:	By the gods, tell me too, my lord, precisely why
	You've built up such great wrath. What action,
	done by whom?
Oedipus:	I will. You, lady, I revere much more than them. 700
	It's things that Creon has been—and
	keeps—plotting against me.
Jocasta:	Speak—if you'll state your call to quarrel
	clearly now.
Oedipus:	He claims to have determined I'm Laius' killer.
Jocasta:	He knows this for himself? Or learned it from
	someone else?
Oedipus:	He sent a seer to do his dirty work since he, 705
	for his part, keeps his own mouth free from all offense.
Jocasta:	So now acquit yourself of what you're mentioning!
	Listen to me! Learn why no human element
	of the prophet's skill is relevant to you.
	I'll show you evidence of this immediately. 710

There came to Laius once an oracle's response,
I won't say from Phoebus himself, but from his staff,
that doom would visit him as death at a child's hand—
whatever child were born to me and to himself.
Report says Laius was at some point killed: waylaid   715

by foreign robbers at a place where three roads meet.
His child did not survive birth even by three days.
That man lashed his two feet by the ankles in
   one bond
And cast him on pathless peaks—but using
   others' hands.
Apollo, therefore, neither caused that child to be   720
his father's killer nor caused Laius to endure
the fearsome doom at his son's hands that
   frightened him.
So much for how well prophecies mapped out his life!
You must set *no* course by them, none. Whatever goal
god needs pursued, he'll easily reveal himself.   725

Oedipus:	What wandering of the soul, what insights stirred
	possess me, lady, now I've heard what you just said!
Jocasta:	What anxious thought upsets you? Why are you
	saying this?
Oedipus:	I believe I heard you say that this man Laius
	was cut to pieces at a place where three roads meet. 730
Jocasta:	Such was the rumor then and it's still current now.
Oedipus:	Where is the region where the incident occurred?
Jocasta:	The land's called Phocis. And the road, Forked Road:
	where branches from Delphi and from Daulis converge.
Oedipus:	And what amount of time's elapsed since all of this? 735
Jocasta:	A herald, just before you appeared and gained control
	of this land, proclaimed it publicly in town.
Oedipus:	O Zeus, what is it you've conspired to do with me?
Jocasta:	What's this to you, Oedipus, that it so bothers you?
Oedipus:	No questions yet. Describe this Laius. His physique, 740
	tell me: what was it like? His age? How young was he?
Jocasta:	A dark man, hair streaked recently with strands of grey.
	His build was not a great deal different from your own.
Oedipus:	I'm lost! Alas I think that I've, unknowingly,
	been calling fearsome curses down upon myself! 745
Jocasta:	What do you mean, my lord?
	I watch you and shrink with fright.
Oedipus:	The fearsome thought that our seer sees is troubling me.
	You'll make things clearer if you set forth one detail.

Jocasta:	Well though I shrink from it, I'll tell you what I know.
Oedipus:	Was he traveling lightly escorted, or had he 750
	many retainers, as an important ruler would?
Jocasta:	Five was the total number, and that five includes
	his herald. And there was one coach conveying Laius.
Oedipus:	Now it's coming clear, alas. But who on earth,
	dear wife, told all of you the tale you're telling me? 755
Jocasta:	A houseboy. He was the sole survivor to return.
Oedipus:	Is he by lucky chance inside the house right now?
Jocasta:	No, he is not. The moment he came back from there
	and saw that you were holding power and
	Laius was dead,
	he grasped my hand and begged me
	to send him out into 760
	the wilderness to pastures where we grazed our flocks
	so he could be almost invisible from the city's heights.
	I sent him. He was a worthy man, although a slave,
	and he deserved this favor—and much more than this.
Oedipus:	Is there a way he could come back down
	to us quickly? 765
Jocasta:	There is indeed. But why do you press for
	this right now?
Oedipus:	I fear myself: that I have said much in excess.
	And this makes me desire to take a look at him.
Jocasta:	Well, he'll be here. But I am worthy too, I think,
	to find out what within you so troubles you,
	my lord. 770
Oedipus:	You will not be deprived, since I have come so far
	in my anticipations. Who better to tell them to
	than you? For, thanks to chance, I've traveled
	just such paths.
	The father I had was Polybus, a Corinthian,
	My mother, Merope the Dorian. And I 775
	was thought the most important man in town until
	chance assailed me in a way worth a bewildered
	glance, if not the serious thought that *I* gave it.
	There was a man, at dinner, flying high on drink.

In his cups he called me a bastard child who'd
    been passed off   780
on my unknowing father. I took this badly, yet,
that whole day I restrained myself. But on the next,
I cross-examined mother and father face to face.
They were enraged at both the slander
    and the drunken man
who'd let it fly. I was delighted at how the pair   785
reacted.
                Yet it rankled me, constantly. The tale
took hold, got round. Without a word to
    mother or father,
I traveled to the Pythian oracle.
                          Phoebus,
sent me away, though, didn't honor what I'd come
to ask, revealing to me, in my misery, forecasts   790
of other fearsome and appalling acts: I'd mate
with mother, show mankind a brood it could not bear
to see, and be the killer of the man who'd fathered me.
On hearing this I took myself away in exile
from Corinth, measuring my distance from my land   795
from then on, by the stars above. I went to where
I'd never see the slander of evil prophecies
for me made real. I traveled on and reached these same
regions where, you say, this tyrant of yours died.

I'll leave no detail out of my account, dear wife.   800
As in my travels I neared this place where
    three roads meet,
a herald, and a man inside a horse-drawn coach,
the kind you have described, approached
    the opposite way.
The leader and the old man drove violently at me.
Enraged, I struck the driver forcing me off the road.
Seeing me walk right past the wheels, the old man then
aimed at the middle of my head with two-lashed whip
and hit me. *He* didn't get off so lightly. Instantly,   810
struck by the staff held in this very hand, he toppled

165

back and out, though he was in mid-coach. And then,
I killed them, *every single one.*

Yet if there is
Some kinship linking this stranger with Laius,
Who is more piteous than the man before you now?   815
What man could ever be more cursed by
    gods than he?
No one, no citizen or foreigner, may receive
him in his house or speak to him. For people must,
rather, drive him from their homes. And nobody
but I did this: I placed these curses on myself.   820

Then with my own two hands, the same
    vile hands by which
he died, I then defiled the dead man's bed. Was I
conceived as wrongful? Am I not wholly
    a thing unclean?
If banishment is my doom, and if, banished, I'm not
allowed to see my family, or walk my native soil—   825
if bound to marry mother, couple with her, and kill
my father, Polybus, who sired my life and raised me up?
If someone adjudged these things had
    come upon this man
from some crude, raw demonic force,
    who'd set him straight?
See to it, see to it, holy reverence for the gods,   830
that I may never see this day. Let me be gone,
let me vanish from mortal sight before I see
the blight of such disaster for me, once it's arrived.

Chorus: We would shrink from these things too,
                    my lord. Until
            you get *him* here and learn from *him*,
                    though, cling to hope.   835
Oedipus: Indeed, such is today's sum total of my hope:
            to wait round for a man, a herdsman: just the one.
Jocasta: What do you so desire from him once he's appeared?
Oedipus: I'll teach you what it is. If he were
                    found saying the same

	as you do, I'd already have escaped from suffering.	840
Jocasta:	What did you hear me say that's so significant?	
Oedipus:	He claimed, you were insisting, that *robbers* waylaid	
	And killed Laius. If he still states the number as	
	plural, why, then it is not I who killed Laius!	
	My "one man" could not be the same as his "many."	845
	But if he clearly says "a traveler alone,"	
	The scales tip the responsibility to me.	
Jocasta:	Then understand he made this statement publicly.	
	He simply cannot now retract it and back down.	
	The whole town heard him say it, not just I alone.	850

(JOCASTA *pauses*)

Besides, were he to make some change in what
    he'd said
before, he'll never prove that Laius' death occurred
as was foretold, my lord.
         Apollo Loxias
declared that Laius had to die at my child's hands.
Yet that poor thing never killed Laius, but himself   855
died long before. So I would never give a glance,
myself, not this way and not that, at prophecy.

Oedipus:	You're thinking well.	
	But do send someone, nonetheless,	
	to have this worker sent to us. Don't let it slip.	860
Jocasta:	I'll send for him with all due haste. But let's go in.	
	I would in no way act against your interests.	

(*Exeunt* JOCASTA *and* OEDIPUS *into the palace*)

Chorus:	May my portion in life still be	
	reverent purity in all I say and do	
	in matters where Laws, whose feet	
	stride high above,	865
	lie fixed and firm, as children birthed	
	throughout the brilliance of primeval sky.	

Laws have only one father: Olympus.
They're not born of man's fathering, death doomed.

167

Never will they be lost in sleep's oblivion.   870
Great is god within them;
he does not grow old.

Aggression fathers the tyrant.[5]
Aggression, falsely besotted
with holdings unneeded and inappropriate,   875
ascends the very pinnacle
then crashes abruptly into the abyss
where feet we use flail, useless.

Still, I beg that god never
breaks the hold of good contests that satisfy
    the city's needs;   880
I'll never lose strength under god's sponsorship.

Yet if someone comes by,
arrogant in his words
or use of hands,
immune to fear of Justice,   885
mocking holy images,
let his portion be evil and seize him,
pay off his perverted pride—
if he fails to harvest his profits justly
and hold back from irreverence,   890
stains what should stay intact with mindless contact.

When this occurs, who is the man
who'll brag that he can save his life

---

[5] Dawe, *Oedipus Tyrannus,* on line 872 (873 in my translation), reads "tyrant" as the subject and "aggression" as the object. I see Dawe's point; but the manuscript reading makes sense as it stands. His emendation causes the text to read: "The tyrant fathers aggression," which makes a contrast between Olympus as creator of law and order, and the tyrant as creator of aggression and disorder. In the traditional reading, the thought reaches back to "portion" (Greek *moîra*). The chorus desires to live within the boundaries tradition prescribes, not venture beyond that *moîra* through aggressive self-assertion (Greek *hybris*). Living as the chorus prescribes creates a society governed by law; living the aggressive way yields tyranny. The chorus further hopes (line 887) that the tyrant will be carried off by the rather different "portion" that is meted out to those who go beyond the traditional "portion" of reverence, i.e. death, but worries that the gods might not respond to correct human aggression. If they don't, then religion is a waste of time.

from gods' arrows?
If actions such as his are rewarded,   895
Why must I dance for god?

I'll not make pilgrimage again
to earth's intact umbilical,
or to the temple at Abae,
or to Olympia's shrines,   900
unless things fit together now
so mortals can mark them out.
Zeus, in your might, if you can really hear me,
Lord of All, this must not elude
you or your power that lives eternal, beyond death.   905
This very instant men
are erasing the ancient,
the fading prophecies
dealing with Laius.

Apollo is nowhere evident in rites:
Religion is dead.   910

(*Enter* JOCASTA *from the palace, accompanied by a* MAID, *and carrying in her hands the same kind of branch wreathed in wool carried
by the priests and holy men in the opening scene. She approaches the*
CHORUS)

Jocasta: Lords of the land, I do believe it right to come
as suppliant to the gods, and to their temple naves,
taking in my two hands these garlands, this incense.   913

(*Enter a* CORINTHIAN, *who is about to approach the* CHORUS *and
speak, until he realizes he is interrupting* JOCASTA. *He holds back
and bides his time*)

Oh, how I have begged him. I can do no more.   918
For Oedipus lets his emotions run too high   914
whenever stressed or pained. Unlike the thinking man,   915
he doesn't assess the new from past experience.   916

He's always owned by anyone who spells things out   917
for him—provided that man spells out things he fears.   917a

(JOCASTA *turns to the statue of Apollo*)

To you, Apollo Lycaeus, since you are closest,   919
I've come as suppliant, with these offerings, hoping   920
you'll find there's some way out that leaves
    us undefiled.
We all now shrink in horror as we see this man,
  this helmsman of our ship of state so paralyzed.

Corinthian: Could I learn from you, strangers,
    whether you know where
I'd find the home of Oedipus, "Nowhere unknown"?   925
And better, if you know, where the tyrant is himself.

Chorus: This, stranger, is his home, and he himself's inside.
This lady is his children's mother and his wife.

(*The* CORINTHIAN *bows to* JOCASTA)

Corinthian: Then may she prosper, may she always live amid
a prosperous people. She's the perfect wife for him.   930

Jocasta   Greetings in kind, stranger, since that's what you deserve
for all your courtesy.
           But tell me why you've come:
What need you have, and what you wish to indicate.

Corinthian: It's good, my lady, for your home and for your spouse.

Jocasta: What is this all about? And *who* have you come *from?*   935

Corinthian: I'm out of Corinth. And the word I'll soon speak out
could please—how could it not?—perhaps
    upset you too.

Jocasta: What is it? And what double force does it possess?

Corinthian: He'll be the tyrant. The residents of the
    Isthmian land
will set him on the throne. So it was rumored there.   940

Jocasta: How so? Is not the old man Polybus still in power?

Corinthian: Not any more. For death now has him in the grave.

Jocasta: Are you then saying old man Polybus is dead?

Corinthian:	If I've not got the facts correct, put me to death.
Jocasta:	(*turning to her* MAID)
	Maid! won't you go as quickly as you can and tell 945
	your master?

(*Exit* MAID)
>   So, where are you now, you prophecies
> from gods? This is the man that Oedipus has long
> been running from, the man he feared he'd kill. But now
> he's died by a blow from Chance and not by
>   this man here!

(*Enter* OEDIPUS, *accompanied by Jocasta's* MAID)

Oedipus:	Jocasta, dearest and wisest head a wife could have, 950
	Why have you sent for me to come outside the house?
Jocasta:	Hear this man! And while listening, reflect on where
	the solemn prophetic utterances from the god are now!
Oedipus:	Who on earth is this person? What's his news for me?
Jocasta:	He's out of Corinth. He'll officially announce 955
	your father is no longer Polybus he's died!
Oedipus:	What say you, stranger? Tell me of this report yourself!
Corinthian	If, as is clear, I must announce the last part first:
	know well that he has passed on through
	the door of death.
Oedipus:	Was it conspiracy? or contact with disease? 960
Corinthian:	A small scale-stroke tips ancient bodies into sleep.
Oedipus:	The poor man perished of disease then, so it seems.
Corinthian:	And he had measured out so long a span of time.

(OEDIPUS *now draws* JOCASTA *aside*)

Oedipus:	Well, well, dear wife! Why now would anyone consult
	the hearth of Pythian prophecy or ominous birds 965
	cawing above our heads whose guidance showed that I
	was going to kill my own father. For now he's dead,
	buried beneath the earth. And I, this man, am here
	and did not touch my sword.

                                Unless he withered away
because he missed me. Thus I *could have* caused
    his death.   970

But Polybus lics in Hades, taking the literal sense
of all these oracles with him! They're worthless now!

Jocasta: And wasn't *I* predicting this to you for years?

Oedipus: You were indeed. But I was drawn off track by fear.

Jocasta: So don't let any more of them gnaw at your heart.   975

Oedipus: How am I *not* to shrink back from my mother's bed?

Jocasta: What should a human fear? We're ruled by
         chance and luck.
No one can think into the future accurately.
I'd guess our best rule is to live to our fullest powers.
And as to intercourse with mother, don't fear this!   980
Many a mortal before you has, in his dreams,
also slept with his mother. He who places no
significance on this bears life most easily.

Oedipus: You'd be correct in all of what you say if she
who gave me birth were not alive. But since she lives,   985
I am compelled to shrink from this—
                               though you're correct.

Jocasta: But at least your father's death brightens your eye.

(*At this point the* Corinthian *moves over to rejoin the discussion*)

Oedipus: A lot. I know. But she's alive. And I fear her.

Corinthian: So who and what's this woman you both
         so greatly fear?

Oedipus: Merope, old man. Polybus used to live with her.   990

Corinthian: But what is it about her that you both so fear?

Oedipus: A fearsome oracle dispatched from god, stranger.

Corinthian: Can it be stated, or is it wrong for others to know?

Oedipus: Of course.
                 Apollo Loxias once said I must
have intercourse with my own mother, and then said   995
that I would shed my father's blood with
    my own hands.

	Corinth, therefore, has long been kept away from me.	
	Happily so, although it is pleasure supreme	
	to look into the eyes of those who gave us life.	
Corinthian:	You shrank from this? This kept you apart from	
	your home town?	1000
Oedipus:	I wanted not to be my father's killer, old man.	
Corinthian:	Why then, since I came here in all good will, my lord,	
	have I not liberated you from this terror?	
Oedipus:	Indeed you'd get a just reward if you still could.	
Corinthian:	Indeed, I came primarily for this: the hope	1005
	that I'd fare rather well when you came home again.	
Oedipus:	But I will never go where my begetters live.	
Corinthian:	My son, you clearly don't grasp fully what you do...	
Oedipus:	(*interrupting*)	
	How so, old man? Then, by the gods, start	
	teaching me!	
Corinthian:	...if they're the reason why you run	
	from coming home.	1010
Oedipus:	Phoebus. His words scare me. They may turn	
	out correct.	
Corinthian:	Worried you'll earn the curse of those who gave	
	you life?	
Oedipus:	That's it, wise elder. That is my eternal fear.	
Corinthian:	So you don't know there's really no just cause	
	for fright?	
Oedipus:	How could there not be, if I was born	
	these parents' son?	1015
Corinthian:	Because, in your birth, Polybus was not involved.	
Oedipus:	What are you saying? Polybus did not father me?	
Corinthian:	No more, no less, than this man here. But equally.	
Oedipus:	You're nothing to me. How could my father	
	equal you?	
Corinthian:	Well, neither of us begat you; neither he nor I.	1020
Oedipus:	Why did he name me legally then as his own child?	
Corinthian:	You were a gift, you know. He took you	
	from my hands.	
Oedipus:	He got me from someone else's hands,	
	yet loved me so?	

Corinthian:	His previous childlessness was what persuaded him.
Oedipus:	You gave me to him? Did you buy
	me, or get me by chance? 1025
Corinthian:	I found you in the wooded vales of Cithaeron.

(OEDIPUS *pauses*)

Oedipus:	Might I know why it is you traveled to this place?
Corinthian:	I used to watch my flocks there on the
	mountain grass.
Oedipus:	You were a shepherd then, a migrant working
	for hire?
Corinthian:	I also saved your life then, in those days, my child. 1030
Oedipus:	What was my problem when you took me in
	your hands?
Corinthian:	The ankles of your feet could have proved that to you!
Oedipus:	Dear me, why put new life in this bad ancient tale?
Corinthian:	I was the one who freed you when your feet
	were bound.
Oedipus:	That coarse slander's been my scourge since infancy. 1035
Corinthian:	That's how you got your name, recalling
	your mischance.
Oedipus:	By the gods! Who did this to me?
	Mother or father?
	Speak!
Corinthian:	I don't know.
	He who gave you to me has better insights.
Oedipus:	You *got* me from somebody then? You didn't *find*
	me yourself?
Corinthian:	No. A nomad shepherd presented you to me. 1040
Oedipus:	Who was he? Do you know enough to
	describe the man?
Corinthian:	He'd a post with Laius, I guess. Why yes,
	that was his name.
Oedipus:	You mean to say the past, late tyrant of this land?
Corinthian:	Certainly. This man was then a shepherd
	for... this man.
Oedipus:	And is this man then still alive? Could I see him? 1045

Corinthian:	You local residents would know that best of all.
Oedipus:	Does anyone among you bystanders here know
	the shepherd he's referring to? You've seen him perhaps
	either out in the countryside or here in town?
	Give me a clue. It's time for this to be disclosed. 1050
Chorus:	I think he is no other than the man out
	in the wilds,
	the one you were trying to see a little earlier.
	Jocasta here would not be least qualified to say.

(OEDIPUS *summons* JOCASTA *down from upstage*)

Oedipus:	Good wife, are you thinking about the man
	we wanted here
	a while ago? Is he the person this man means? 1055
Jocasta:	What does it matter who he means? Don't
	dwell on it.
	And what he's said, don't try remembering. It's false.
Oedipus:	How could I possibly get such clues as these
	and not disclose through them the mystery
	of my birth?
Jocasta:	Dear gods! I beg you, if you value your life at all, 1060
	then stop this stupid quest. It's made me sick enough.
Oedipus:	Cheer up! Your pedigree won't be discovered bad
	though I'm disclosed a slave, my grandmother
	proved a slave.
Jocasta:	Obey me, nonetheless, I beg you, don't do this!
Oedipus:	I couldn't obey you, and not learn it all clearly. 1065
Jocasta:	My reasoning is sane; I'm picking your wisest course.
Oedipus:	Your "wisest courses" have, of late, just been a pain.
Jocasta:	You doomed fool! I hope you never learn who
	you are!
Oedipus:	Can someone go and bring the herdsman here to me?
	And leave this woman to wallow among
	her wealthy roots. 1070
Jocasta:	Alas, you piteous wretch! That's all I can
	call you now.
	And I will never call you anything else again.

(*Exit* JOCASTA)

Chorus: Oedipus, why has your wife gone rushing
out distraught
And wild with grief? I fear that some catastrophe
will burst forth from this silence she has
vowed to keep.   1075

Oedipus: Let what must burst forth, burst! I'll be
prepared to view
the seed from which I grew, however small it is.
Perhaps she's reasoning like a woman, thinking big,
and is ashamed about my ignobility.
(*grandiosely*)
But I pronounce myself to be the child
of Chance!   1080
I'll not be disinherited; Chance gifts me well
She is my mother and my brothers are the moon's
Phases that make me dwindle small and
fill to greatness.
Such is my nature. And I could never grow to be
other than this and not find out the secret
of my birth.   1085

Chorus: If I'm clairvoyant—endowed
with wise and structured thought—
I swear by Mount Olympus'
pathlessness that you, Mount Cithaeron, tomorrow,
when the moon's full, shall find that Oedipus   1090
will honor you as fatherland,
nurse, and mother too,
and we, proclaiming your great
help for my tyrant's family,
will dance, honoring your name.   1095

Phoebus, healer, may this meet your approval!

Child, which one,
which one of the long-lived
nymphs, moved on by Pan, your father,

leaping among the peaks, gave   1100
birth to you?
Perhaps some mistress of Loxias?
For he enjoys all the high-lying grasslands.
    Or could it be:
Hermes, lord of Mount Cyllene,

Or the god of Bacchanals   1105
who lives upon mountain tops
who got you,
a chance find,
from some sloe-eyed, amusing nymph he loves
    to kid with?

(*Enter* Slave, *escorted by other men similarly dressed, servants of* Oedipus)

Oedipus:	(*to the* Chorus)
	If I must judge, old sirs, I do believe I see 1110
	the herdsman we've been looking for of late, although
	I've not encountered him before. He's very old—
	same age, and same physique as this man next to me.
	Besides, I know the houseboys bringing him:
	they're mine.
	You, I suppose, would be more qualified than I 1115
	to say, since you have seen this herdsman previously.
Chorus:	I recognize him, be assured: he was indeed
	Laius' man, as trusted a drover as he had.
Oedipus:	I ask you first, stranger from Corinth: Is this man
	the one you mean?
Corinthian:	The very man you're looking at. 1120
Oedipus:	You, old sir! Come! Speak and look me in the eye!
	I have some questions.
	Laius:
	Did you once belong to him?
Slave:	Yes. I was his slave. Reared in his house, not bought.
Oedipus:	What work were you employed at? What was
	your living?

Slave:	Grazing livestock. I've followed them most
	of my life.
Oedipus:	And in what regions most particularly?
Slave:	Sometimes on Cithaeron, sometimes in spots nearby.
Oedipus:	This man: you know his features? Familiar
	from somewhere?
Slave:	(*unsure whether* OEDIPUS *is referring to himself or the*
	CORINTHIAN)
	When he was doing what? And which man
	do you mean?
Oedipus:	The man beside me. Have you encountered
	him before?
Slave:	No. Can't say that I have, straight off
	from memory.
Corinthian:	Master,[6] that's no surprise. I'll get him to recall
	clearly these things of which he's ignorant. I know
	that he knows how it used to be on Cithaeron:
	he went with two herds. *I,* with one, was
	close to him
	for three whole six-month seasons, from the
	spring until
	Arcturus rises in the fall. When winter came
	I used to drive *my* flocks back home for shelter; *he*
	would drive his own away to Laius' sheep-pens.
	(*to the* SLAVE)
	Do I or don't I state some part of what occurred?
Slave:	You state the facts, though they're recalled from
	long ago.
Corinthian:	Now tell me: you know you gave some child to
	me back then
	so I could bring him up myself as my own child...
Slave:	What's this? What are you up to, recounting this old tale?

Line numbers: 1125, 1130, 1135, 1140

---

[6] This is the first time *despótes,* "master" (as opposed to slave), has been used in the play, and marks a change of tone in the Corinthian, who has up to now been cheekily familiar with Oedipus. It's also the first time a slave has been on stage. The Corinthian (a free man) is probably trying to intimidate the slave by warning that if there's a dispute over testimony, the slave will be interrogated under torture. Readers familiar with Plato's *Meno* may see here an ironic echo of the Socratic doctrine of knowledge as recollection.

Corinthian:	This man, good fellow, was that child
	when he was young. 1145
Slave:	Damn you! Why don't you just shut up and stay
	that way?
Oedipus:	Oh, don't you tongue-lash him, old sir. Your
	words entail
	a flogger's lashing more than does the tale he tells.
	(*signaling* ATTENDANTS *to approach*)
Slave:	Noblest of masters, what is it I'm doing wrong?
Oedipus:	Not telling the story of the child in his account. 1150
Slave:	He knows his statement's nonsense. He's up to
	something else.
Oedipus:	You'll speak from courtesy or else you'll speak
	from pain.
	(ATTENDANTS *seize the* SLAVE)
Slave:	Don't, by the gods, oh please don't torture an old man!
Oedipus:	One of you, twist his arms behind him now! Be quick!
Slave:	What do I gain, poor wretch?
	What else do you need to know? 1155
Oedipus:	Did you give him the child whose story he recounts?
Slave:	I gave it to him. Oh, I wish I'd died today.[7]
Oedipus:	You'll get your wish if you don't state the honest facts.
Slave:	I'm much more likely dead if I declare the facts!
Oedipus:	This man, it does appear, is trying to stall for time. 1160
	(ATTENDANTS *begin to twist the* SLAVE's *arms*)
Slave:	I'm not. Not I! I just now said I gave it him.
Oedipus:	Where did you get it from? Was it another's—yours?
Slave:	Mine it was not, for sure. I got it from someone else.
Oedipus:	From which of these citizens? And from what
	kind of house?
Slave:	For god's sake, master, don't develop this tale more. 1165
Oedipus:	You're dead if I've to ask you this just one more time.
Slave:	In that case it was among the births in Laius' house.

---

[7] Commentators and translators often render: "that day (in the past)," thereby having the slave, in effect, concede he has been lying. But "that day" makes nonsense of Oedipus' response in the next line. The Greek expression normally means "this day" in drama, and leaves readers free to decide for themselves whether, when, and if he is lying. Note that Oedipus never asks the slave the question he first summoned him to answer: if the slave saw Laius killed and, if so, who killed him.

Oedipus:	A slave or actually born of Laius' own blood?
Slave:	Alas, I'm on the brink of speech with fearsome power.
Oedipus:	And I of hearing it. And yet it must be heard. 1170
Slave:	The child was generally called his. She who's inside, Your wife, could best say whether this, in fact, was so.
Oedipus:	So it was she who gave it you?
Slave:	That's so, my lord.
Oedipus:	With what purpose in mind?
Slave:	That I dispose of it.
Oedipus:	The woman who bore him dared...?
Slave:	No, shrank from prophecies. 1175
Oedipus:	Which said?
Slave:	The statement was that he'd kill his parents.
Oedipus:	So why did you release him, then, to this old man?

Slave:	I pitied him, my lord. And I believed the man
	 would take him to the home from which he came.
	     But he
	 saved him for bigger things. If you're really the man 1180
	 this person claims you are, then know your
	     doom is grim.

(*The* Corinthian, *stunned, makes as if to say something, then leaves quietly under the harsh stare of the* Slave)

Oedipus:	Alas, alas, that it could all emerge so clear!
	 Sunlight,[8] may *this* be my last glimpse of
	     you, exposed
	 as son who came to light from those that I should not,
	 lay with those I should not, killed those
	     I must not kill. 1185

(*Exit* Oedipus *into palace. Exit* Slave, *escorted by attendants, leaving the* Chorus *alone*)

---

[8] The Greek is full of alliterative wordplay involving *phys,* "come into being," *saphê,* "clear," *aph'ôn,* "from whom," *péphasmai,* "I have appeared," and *phôs,* "light" (which itself differs only in tonal accent from *phós,* "human being").

Chorus: Successions of mortal births:
alas, when I add up your lives,
their sum total is nothing.

My thought: who—what man—wins more
than this share of blessing divine: 1190
that he's believed gloriously real
till the belief in glory fades?

My proof: you are, you, the divine in you,
Oedipus, that touched you, wretched man.
In human life, there's nothing I think blessed.   1195

Your shot was far too accurate, won power
over success itself, blessing totally divine,

O Zeus!
Down you blasted her,
that virgin with taloned hands,
Singer of Doom, and you raised up   1200
a fortress against Death. Hence
you are called my ritual king,
and granted greatest honors
in great Thebes, as lord and ruler.

But now, who could one hear called
    more pathetic?
Who can live with you through your trials, savage   1205
ruin on ruin, your life overturned?

Alas, the famous head of Oedipus!
Alas, the same great harbor into which father and son
delighted to come to rest, to spread and set their
    bridal sheets!

How could your father's seedbed   1210
find the strength to bear your sowing,
sad man, and so silently, so long?

All-seeing time has tracked you down against
    your will,
condemns your unwed wedding, long since
fathering children where it was the child.   1215

Alas, O long lost child of Laius,
I wish, I wish,
I'd never seen you.
I mourn for you as if my mouth
Keened dirges for the dead. To tell it straight,   1220
I drew my breath of life from you,
And I have now put my own sight to sleep.

(*Enter the* Courtier, *hurrying toward the* Chorus *leader*)

Courtier: You, men always most grandly honored
           in this land,
what actions you will hear about! What sights
        you'll see!
And what great sorrow you will bear—if you
        stand close,   1225
And are still moved by what affects the
        house of Labdacus!
I don't suppose either the Phasis or the
        Danube would
suffice to cleanse and purify this house. It hides
so many evils soon to emerge into the light:
evils willed by the self not done unwittingly.   1230
And pain hurts most when clearly inflicted
        by the self.

Chorus: What we already knew leaves no more
           room for pain.
What do you have to say that adds to all of this?

Courtier: The most succinct of statements both to
           make and grasp
is this: Jocasta, our divine head, has just died.   1235

Chorus: Poor, suffering woman. Who or what, then,
           caused her death?

Courtier: She brought death on herself.[9] The worst of
    what was done
  is absent from my words. No eyewitness was there.

  But you will learn as much as my memory recalls
  about what sufferings that poor woman
    then endured: 1240

  how, distraught with anger, she passed through the hall
  and threw herself instantly upon her bridal bed,
  ripping her hair out with the fingers of both hands;

  and how she'd slammed the doors shut when
    she went inside,
  calling on the late Laius, already long since dead. 1245
  (For she remembered the late man's sowing, long ago,
  of seed that he would die by, leaving her to bear
  by that same seed the pains of birth for children cursed).
  And she bemoaned the nuptial bed (where she, accursed,
  bore double offspring, husband from husband,
    child from child).   1250

  How, after this, she perished: that I still don't know.
  For Oedipus burst in. His shouts prevented us
  from watching all her troubles to the bitter end,
  for we were watching *him* as he wandered about.
  He pressed us all, begged us to give him
    a sword and asked   1255
  where he might find that wife (who was no wife at all

---

[9] The Courtier's account of what happened to Jocasta is a very intricate rhetorical structure and in some ways a miniature of the play itself. Although he declares there were no witnesses, he describes the scene as if he had seen most of it; he even describes in indirect speech what he imagines were the thoughts subtending Jocasta's actions, which some translators misleadingly transpose into direct speech, thus conveying the notion that the Courtier is reporting words Jocasta actually said and giving the false impression that she is declaring her belief that she is Oedipus' mother. The conclusion she knows Oedipus will draw is going to make her life intolerable, regardless of whether she thinks it right or wrong. And, during her final scene on stage she makes it clear she thinks the Corinthian is inventing the story of finding (or being given) Oedipus, but realizes that Oedipus believes him.

but a maternal cropfield with a double yield:
himself and his own seed). As he raved on, some god—
not any man among us who were standing near—
Showed him the way.

          He, roaring fearsomely, as if   1260
some force were leading him, then hurled
   himself against
the double entrance, bent and burst the hollow doors
and plunged into the room. And there we saw his wife
inside, hanging entangled in a noose of woven cords.
On seeing her, the poor wretch, bellowing
   fearsomely,   1265
released the strangling rope. And then, poor
   thing, she lay
upon the ground.

         What followed was fearsome to see.
He tore from her and from her robes the
   long-pinned, gold
brooches that kept her garments draped, then
   raised them up,
then struck and orphaned the moving
   orbs of his own eyes…   1270
He voiced such words: he'd done this so his
   eyes could see
no more the evils he experienced or wrought;
so that, from then on, they might see only in darkness
those they should not see, might fail to recognize
those he needed to know.

           Not once, but many times   1275
he chanted his lament and raised his hands to strike
clear through his eyelids. Blood-red globules
   soaked his beard,
pulsing, not oozing rheum of murdered eyes,
   but a dark rain
of gore plumped-out like hail that wholly
   drenched the man.
These evils crashed upon both heads, not his alone: 1280
and so, commingled thus, they coupled man and wife.

Let us not lay aside their prior blessedness:
In fairness, they were blessed. But now, this day
   screams out
lament, destruction, death, and shame—of all evils'
multitude of names not one is missing here.   1285

Chorus: Has this poor man found some respite from evil now?
Courtier: He shouts for someone to unbolt the doors and show
to all Cadmeans here this father-killer, mother—well,
he cries obscenities which I cannot repeat.
He says he'll tear himself out of this earth, and won't   1290
stay on accursed, accursed by his own words,
   within this house.
Yet he lacks strength, he lacks someone to guide
   his steps
away. The plague upon him is too great to bear.
But he will show you now. These bolts upon the gates
have been pushed back, and you'll soon see the
   kind of sight   1295
that could stir pity even in one who hates his guts.

(*Enter* OEDIPUS, *one hand masking his face, the other groping for support.* Exit COURTIER)

Chorus: Seeing this pain is such a fearsome thing
For humans, the most fearsome sight
That I have ever seen. O, what insanity
came over you, poor wretch, what force divine   1300
leaped down from dizzying heights upon your
   lot in life
divinely cursed and wholly crushed it so ?

Accursed man, I lack capacity
to look at you, though there's so much I'd like
to ask, to find out, and I'd like to gaze on you.   1305
You make me shudder, overawed.
Oedipus: I am so crushed by misery,
alas. And where, alas,
on earth can I convey my suffering?

185

	Where may my voice take off for in its flight?	1310
	O force divine, how you have trampled me!	
Chorus:	To a fearsome world cut off from sound and sight.	
Oedipus:	Alas, my veil of darkness I would tear away!	
	To say how it sailed in defies all words.	
	It is stone-anchored, unmoved by favoring winds.	1315
	Ah woe on me, and woe again:	
	I feel the stinging lash of real, raw pain	
	compounded with the memory of evils done.	
Chorus:	It is no wonder that in such suffering you feel	
	The pain doubly and your bad reasoning	
	doubly too.	1320
Oedipus:	Alas, my friend.	
	You are the only one who still stands by me, still	
	tends me, props me, tolerates me now I'm blind.	
	Alas.	
	You don't elude me, for, though I'm in darkness,	1325
	I know by your voice at least quite clearly	
	who you are.	
Chorus:	Oh what fearsome things you've done!	
	How did you dare	
	destroy your eyesight? What divine force	
	drove you on?	
Oedipus:	It was Apollo, Apollo, my friends,	
	who wrought these evil, evil sufferings	
	that are mine.	1330
	Yet no man struck me with his hands	
	but I, my wretched self.	
	What need had I to see?	
	If I could see,	
	I'd get a glimpse of nothing I'd find sweet.	1335
Chorus:	It would be as you say yourself.	
Oedipus:	What was there for me to see,	
	my friends, or like? What still exists	
	that is a joy to speak to or to hear?	
	Take me away from here	1340
	as swiftly as you can,	

Take me away, my friends!
I'm the great cause of death,
I am the most accursed,
most hated of mortal men   1345
even to gods above.

Chorus: Your mind and, no less, your misfortune stir pity.
Oh, how I've wished I'd never known you at all.

Oedipus: I hope whoever it was saved me from death,
and rescued me, freed me from   1350
savage bonds around my feet
in nomads' pastures, will fall down dead.
He did me no favor.
For if I had died then
I would not cause such pain to friends, or to myself.   1355

Chorus: Had I my wish, it too would be the same.

Oedipus: Then I would not have come to be
my father's killer, earned fame
among mortals as bridegroom where I was born.
Now I am lost to god, son of unholiness,   1360
a wretch who shared
the very bed
where I was born.
If evil has its hierarchy,
evil's topmost place   1365
falls, then, to Oedipus.

Chorus: I don't know how to say that you have planned
    things well,
for you'd be better dead than living a blind man's life.

Oedipus: Don't keep playing teacher and counselor to me,
saying what has been done was best done otherwise.   1370
Could I still see, I just don't know what eyes I'd need
to use if I came down and sighted my father's face
in Hades' sightlessness, or my poor mother, too.
What I've done to that pair deserves more
    than a rope.
And could seeing my children still be my desire,   1375
considering how their being came about? Never!
Nor could I look upon this town, nor at its tower,

187

nor at the sacred shrines of its divinities—
not with these eyes, my eyes! Though I was
   brought to life
in Thebes as the unique, most blue-blooded
   of men,   1380
from all of this, I, in my utter ruin, cut myself
away! For I decreed that everyone should shun
the impious man, the man the gods had
   shown unclean—
and yet of Laius' blood. Determining the guilt
was mine, was I to stay and look these men   1385
straight in the eye? Of course not.

                            Were there also a means
of blocking off the stream of sound that flows
   in through
my ears, I'd not have stopped myself from
   sealing off
my wretched self so I could neither see nor hear
anything. Having consciousness reside outside,   1390
beyond evil: that would be sweet.

                        Alas, Cithaeron,
why did you take me in? Why did you not kill me
the moment you got me, so I'd not have exposed
myself to humans, or ever shown where
   I was born?
O Polybus, Corinth, my pre-Laian father's home,   1395
in fact! in me you raised beauty cancered to evil.
I find I am both evil and of evils born!
Do you remember me, you three paths, hidden vale,
thicket and narrow track where three roads meet?
   You drank
my blood, my father's blood, spilled by
   my hands. Recall   1400
what I did there, and next what I achieved when I
came here.

             Marriage, oh marriage, yes, you fathered me,
and, done with fathering, conceived the self-same seed
again and showed the world a bloodline that made sons,

fathers, and brothers, one, made mothers
    the same as brides, 1405
brought each most shameful human
    act to consummation.

Yet, one should not persist in talking about things
if they're not things it's also fine to do. So now
I pray you by the gods, make haste and hurl me out
somewhere, kill me or plunge me in the
    hidden depths 1410
of sea, somewhere you'll never set eyes on me again.

(*The* CHORUS *makes no move. So* OEDIPUS *appeals more poignantly*)

Come! Condescend to touch a man in misery.
Do as I say this once, don't be afraid of me.
There is no one, no mortal, who can possibly
bear the evil deeds I've done but I myself. 1415

(*The* CHORUS *remains unresponsive and motionless. As they stand
still, the palace doors open and* CREON *enters, dressed in the tyrant's
robes and regalia. The* CHORUS, *relieved, acknowledges him and
finally speaks to* OEDIPUS)

Chorus: The man it takes to do and plan what you request
    is here when needed: Creon. Only he is left
    to keep the country now as guardian in your place.
Oedipus: Alas! What words shall I pick out to say to him?
    What will emerge to justify his faith in me? 1420
    I've proved evil in all my past dealings with him.
Creon: It's not to laugh at you that I've come, Oedipus,
    to scourge you with slanderous mockery for your
    evil acts.

(*turning to the* CHORUS)

    But, you men, if you've not yet learned
respect for things that come to birth and die, at least

	protect the Lord Sun's fire, which nurses everything,	1425
	from sights that shame the eye. So don't display for him,	
	all unconcealed, a *thing* accursed like this, which earth	
	and holy rain and light won't tolerate. Get it	
	inside the house. It's best that only people, kin	
	by birth, should see and hear evils their	
	kinfolk bear.	1430
	And they will thus be acting reverently and well.	
Oedipus:	By the gods, since you've defied my expectations,	
	coming, supreme in good, to me, a man supreme	
	in evil, *obey me in this!* For your sake, not for mine!	
Creon:	And to obtain what need do you *beseech* me thus?	1435
Oedipus:	Hurl me from this land as quickly as you can,	
	to where no mortal man will see or speak to me.	
Creon:	I would have done so, rest assured, if I'd not first	
	Needed to learn from god precisely what	
	must be done.	
Oedipus:	Surely his prophecy was made entirely clear:	1440
	Destroy the impious man, the father–killer: me.	
Creon:	Such things indeed were said.[10] But given our	
	present need	
	It's better to learn precisely what action to take.	
Oedipus:	So you'll enquire of god about a wretch like me?	
Creon:	Well, even you would now have faith in	
	what god says.	1445
Oedipus:	Well, now I charge you and I beg you on my knees.	
	The woman in the house: bury her as you will.	
	It's right you set your own kin properly to rest.[11]	
	Then let this, my father's town, never assume	
	it right that I be resident here while still alive.	1450
	Let me live in the mountains where	
	Cithaeron's now	
	called mine, and which my mother and father,	
	when they lived,	

[10.] Creon had said them himself.

[11.] Creon never responds to this request. In Sophocles' earlier *Antigone* Creon denies burial to his nephew Polyneices

together chose as grave to keep me down, so I
may yet die at the hands of those who both tried hard
to kill me. Yet I know this much: it won't be plague   1455
or something else that kills me. I'd not have been saved
when on the point of death, unless for fearsome evil.

Let the doom apportioned me go where it goes.

Don't worry yourself, on my behalf, about my sons,
Creon. They're male. They will not lack
      a stake in life   1460
wherever they may be.[12] But my poor, piteous girls,
they were my eyes' delight! Never was this man's table
spread with food with those two set apart from me!
All that I ever touched, this pair has always shared
with me. So please look after them on my behalf.   1465
Permit them, above all, to touch me with their hands,
the two of them, and weep over my evil doom.
Come, my lord!
Come, nobleman nobly born! If my hands could
      just touch
them, I'd believe I had them as when I could see.   1470

(CREON *motions to attendants who usher in* ANTIGONE *and* ISMENE.)

What am I saying?

Oh Gods! Do I not hear my two darlings somewhere,
both streaming out their tears? You pitied me, Creon!
You have sent me the nicest gifts: my two offspring!
      Am I right?   1475

Creon: You're right. I am the one who has provided them,
I know the delight they bring you now, as in the past.

Oedipus: May you be blessed by chance, and on your
      journey may

---

[12] Eteocles and Polyneices caused a civil war and killed one another.

god guard you better than, it chanced, he guarded me!
(*to his daughters*)

Children, where are you out there?
   Here, come over here,   1480
come to these hands of mine, these sisters of
    your own,
the hands of him who did the act of fathering you
and now must be ambassadors of sight for eyes
once full of light. I stand revealed as he who sowed
you in the very womb where my own seed
    was sown,
I neither saw it as it occurred nor in my fantasies   1485
foresaw it. And I weep for you both, as I lack power
to see you; sickened, for I can grasp what still remains:
life's bitter treatment from your fellow
    men which you
must live through. For what contact will you
    come to have
with those in town, what feasts will you
    attend—from which   1490
you'll not come home in tears, instead of staying out
to watch the spectacles? When you're of
    marriageable
age, who will there be? Who'll shrug off the
    slander, children:
the abuse he'll take? The scandal of my parenting
affects you too. What face of evil is left out?   1495
"Your father killed his father, then he
    plowed his own
mother and spurted you where he was
    once conceived
He got you from the selfsame source he got himself."
This is the kind of scourging that you'll take.
    Who, then
will marry you? No one at all, children. Not one.   1500
You must, that is to say, wither in barrenness
and rot away.

(*turning to* CREON)

Menoeceus' son, since you alone
are left as father to these two—for we, the other
pair who brought them into life, are dead and gone,
don't disregard these two as they, your relatives,   1505
wander as beggars, husbandless. Don't bring
   them down
to match in full the abasement of my evil plight.
Pity them; for you see how young they are, bereft
of everything except what you give, for your part.
You're nobly born. Show your agreement
   with your hand.   1510

(*to* ANTIGONE *and* ISMENE)
My two children, were you, as yet, of reasoning age,
I'd give you much advice. Instead, pray this: that I
may live always where each instant allows; that you
may find yourselves a life more prosperous than this,
the one your father, who begat you, has to lead.   1515

Creon: Enough! You've passed your quota of tears.
     Now go inside the house!
Oedipus: I must obey, though the order isn't sweet.
Creon: All things have a moment of beauty.
Oedipus: You know my terms for going?
Creon: You'll tell. I'll hear, then know.
Oedipus: Send me from here in exile.
Creon: You're asking me to give what god must give.
Oedipus: But I'm the man the gods hate most.
Creon: Then you'll get your wish quickly.
Oedipus: You really make that claim?
Creon: What reason fails to prompt, I usually don't waste
     time saying.   1520
Oedipus: Lead me from here right now.
Creon: Go now. But … leave the girls.
Oedipus: No, no! Don't take them from me!
Creon: Don't yearn to be in power all the time!

What power you had did not accompany
    you through life.

(CREON *takes his daughters from* OEDIPUS, *who stumbles off alone
either into the palace or away from it.* CREON *moves to the side of
the stage and watches*)

Chorus: [Look, inhabitants of our ancestral Thebes:
    Here's Oedipus
who understood such famous riddles, the most
    powerful of men.   1525
Who of our citizens saw what chance gave him
    without envy?
Look at how he's now met a wave of fearsome catastrophe.
And so, since you are mortal, watch for that day that
    ends it all.
Consider it with care. Count no one blessed before
    he crosses
beyond the finishing line of life without enduring pain.][13]

Curtain

[13.] Most editors reject these lines as spurious. I remain undecided, but usually include them in performances. Sophocles expresses a similar sentiment in his *Tyndareus,* fr. 646 (Radt).

SENECA

OEDIPUS

SENECA

Oedipus

TRANSLATED BY FREDERICK AHL

The Characters: If this play followed the Greco-Roman practice of having a single actor play multiple roles, it requires four actors in addition to the CHORUS and CHORUS LEADER.

Actor One:	OEDIPUS, *king of Thebes*
Actor Two:	JOCASTA, *wife of Oedipus*
	CREON, *brother of Jocasta*
Actor Three:	TEIRESIAS, *a seer*
	A CORINTHIAN
	A MESSENGER
Actor Four:	MANTO, *daughter of Teiresias*
	PHORBAS, *a shepherd*
	CHORUS LEADER
	CHORUS of Theban citizens, including at least some dancers; for stage purposes a mixture of male and female.

The chorus should seem, in its first appearance, old and predominantly male. Long, black, hooded robes, perhaps. Beneath these robes, one should be dressed, in androgynous style, as Bacchus; the remainder should wear fawn-skins beneath their robes (the costumes of Maenads: young and middle-aged

197

women who, under Bacchus' influence, are capable of savage destruction and fierce sensuousness).

Non-speaking roles:
Attendants to Oedipus, Creon, and Teiresias

The tragedy, like all Seneca's plays, is divided into five acts.

SENECA

Oedipus

ACT 1

Scene: Thebes, before the royal palace. Time: dawn. Enter OEDIPUS,
accompanied by JOCASTA, *his wife*

Oedipus: So soon! Night has been banished, and huge day
comes hesitantly back. His mane of light
rises, shrouded with mourning veil of clouds.
His eye, evil with flames inflicting pain,
will look upon our homes made sonless now
by sickness's blind greed. Night made the mounds
of dead. But day will thrust them on our sight.   5

Can anyone delight in power? How?
Oh, what a treacherous good thing you are,
so sweet a face, masking such wickedness!
High mountain passes always catch the wind;
the tidal flow of even a quiet sea   10
whiplashes a cliff whose rock face separates
vast oceans. So too pinnacles of power
stand towering in Fortune's path.

                             How well
I'd done: escaping my father Polybus'
control, an exile, sundered from concerns,
I wandered without being scared and fell—

I swear by god and heaven—into the power
I hold.

        Now I have fears one should not voice,   15
fears my father may be torn from life
by my right hand. Apollo's prophecies
warn of this and sentence me to still
a greater crime.

Jocasta:[1]   Is there any act
of godless criminality greater
than butchering one's own father?

Oedipus: How grim
a mockery of the loving son I am,
ashamed to name the fate in store for me!
Phoebus threatens that the son will go   20
into his parents' bedroom carrying
a flaming torch no loving son should bear:
into forbidden intercourse, incest.
This drove me from my father's realm and power,
this fear. I didn't go from hearth and home
outlawed for grim deeds done.

                     I'd little trust,
I, in myself. That's why, Nature, I put   25
your laws away, where they'd be safe for you.
When horror runs deep, you might then be inclined
to fear you'd do things that you would put down
as just not possible. I'm terrified
out of my wits at everything. I feel
that I cannot entrust me to myself.
So soon—now as I speak—fate gets prepared
to plot against us. What can I conclude   30
when this plague acts against the Cadmeans,
kills them indiscriminately, spares
only me? I'm being saved. For what?
For what evil? Around me, the city falls,
continuously fresh tears lament the dead:
a land depeopled. Yet I stand unharmed.

---

[1] I have assigned these lines to Jocasta. In the manuscripts they are given to Oedipus.

I am on trial, accused before Phoebus.   35
(*inwardly*)
How could you hope so great a criminal
would be given a healthy power and realm?
I have made Heaven charged with guilt, loaded
with harm. No gentle breeze with icy breath
soothes hearts gasping with fire, no gentle breath
of spring winds breathes life. No! The immense sun   40
expands the bestial blaze of dog days' heat,
bursts in upon the lion of summer.
Moisture deserts the streams, grass yellows,
Dirce's spring burns dry, and Ismenos
trickles thin, tinctures the now parched dunes'
nude shallows. Phoebus' sister moon slips
darkly through the sky, the universe   45
pales grim and sick beneath the shroud of day.
No star twinkles in night's serenity.
Heavy, unearthly vapors ghost the earth,
Hell's deathly mask visors Heaven's battlements
and palaces. Ceres, our mother earth,
though she is ripe, denies her fruit. Golden   50
she ripples with tall, wheaten ears and yet
the stalks are sered dry, harvest and seed-grain
dead.
     No part of our community
is free, empty of death's depleting force,
immune. Impartially all ages, male,
female drop in death. This deadly plague
joins young and old, fathers and sons. One torch   55
marries the bride and groom and lights their pyre.
No bitter tears, no moaning at graveside.
The constant victories of catastrophe,
their massive scope, have by now dried our eyes.
When death is everywhere we pass beyond
tears for things.
        Look now!
               This man is borne
to his cremation by his sorrowing

father, sick himself. A mother brings   60
one child. Mindless with grief, she's hurrying
back for another for the same pyre's flames.
Even as they mourn, a new grief dawns:
for their own burial rites now coincide
with funerals in progress. So they burn
their own kin's corpses on another's pyre.
They steal fire. Abject misery knows no shame.   65
No separate tombs cover and sanctify
dead bones. Enough they've been exposed to flame.
So small a part is really burned to ash.
There's no earth left for graves, no wood for pyres;
prayers and medicine fail to aid the sick.
Disease destroys all those who come to help.   70

Prostrate before the altars, with my hands
bent back in prayer, I beg of destiny:
"Is it not time? May I not race ahead
and die before my homeland is destroyed?
Don't let me be the last to fall or be
the final funeral in my realm, my power!
Will of god, you're too brutal! And fate,   75
too harsh! Is death, so ready to move in
upon this people, not allowed to touch
just me?"
                   Disavow this realm, this power
your lethal hand contaminates! Leave tears,
leave funerals and this deadly poisoned sky
you bring wherever you go, accursed guest!
You should have been made outlaw long ago,   80
banished, yes, even to your parents' home.

Jocasta: What use is it, my husband, to complain
about evil? Complaining makes things worse.
Being king, I think, means this: coming to grips
with what confronts you. The harder it is
to stand, the more power's burden slips
    and slides,
the more determinedly you must take

	your stand. Be brave! Step confidently now!	
	A man does not retreat from Fortune's blows!	85
Oedipus:	Charge me, or shame me with faint-heartedness?	

No, no! My manliness does not know how
a coward fears! If swords were drawn on me,
if the sharp-pointed violence of war
were rushing in on me, I'd have the guts   90
to steel my hands to meet even the gods'
giant enemies.
                                        I did not run
from the Sphinx, who knotted words in blind,
noosed riddles. No, I faced her bloodstained jaws,
this prophetess too hideous to describe,
the soil beneath her white with scattered bones.
High on her cliff-top perch she flexed her wings,   95
hovered above her prey, coiled her whiplashing tail
to goad her menacing fury to full force,
like a fierce lion. "Sing me your riddling song,"
I said. She, screaming hideously from above,
her evil jaws grinding noisily, her claws
tearing at boulders, could not wait to rip   100
into my vitals. But I did unlash
the knot of her enigma's webbed deceit,
the grimly riddling song of the winged beast.

Jocasta:[2] Why make your prayers for death now? Are you mad?

It's too late. You had your chance to die.
Thebes' scepter was your prize for glorious deeds,
your payment for destruction of the Sphinx.   105

Oedipus: That shrewd monster's ashes fight again

against me, in me. The plague that was destroyed
now wipes Thebes out, and there is only one
surviving hope of safety for the town:
if Phoebus offers any safe path now.

---

[2] I have assigned these lines to Jocasta also. In the manuscripts they are given to Oedipus.

(*Exit* JOCASTA. *Enter* CHORUS, *dressed as, and appearing to be, Theban Elders, and predominantly male in appearance. They may speak either as a group or individually, as suggested by the notations* LEADER, VOICE 1, VOICE 2, VOICE 3, VOICE 4)

Leader:	Your sun is setting, glorious house of Cadmus.	110
	Thebes, your whole city sets. How we lament you,	
	as you gaze over fields widowed of farmers.	
	Bacchus, your famous troops are cropped by death now:	
	those who accompanied you to distant India,	
	dared gallop horses on the plains of sunrise,	115
	planted your standards in front of heaven's portals.	
Voice 1:	They saw the Arabs, blessed with cinnamon forests,	
	then Parthian horsemen, feared for the arrows	
	Fired when they've wheeled round, treacherously	
	retreating.	
	They trod the shores of India's red Ocean	120
	Where Phoebus rises unshuttering the day's light.	
Voice 2:	His fire, much closer here at his first birthplace,	
	darkens nude Indians.	
Voice 3:	(*to* OEDIPUS)	
	We, though the offshoot of triumphant root-stock,	
	wither and die now; raw fate devours us.	125
Leader:	New-formed processions, endlessly marched off	
	deathward: a straggling column trooping glumly,	
	hustled to ghosthood, but halting, grim and	
	dense-packed.	
Voice 2:	All seven gates can't yawn wide enough for	
	crushes of people streaming toward gravesites.	130
	Corpses in piles stand, heavy and compacted:	
	Burial on burial.	
Voice 4:	Pestilence first struck shepherds' slow yearlings:	
	woolbearers cropped herbs fattening but fatal.	
Leader:	Hand high, a priest stands poised for the death-blow	135
	over the victim's neck, but sees the bull slump	
	listless, his only fire his consecrated	
	horns' glint of gilding. When struck by the massive	
	axe-blow his neck cracks, snapping under huge force,	

not blood but vile pus gushes from the dark wound,   140
staining the sharp blade.

Voice 4:   In a race a stallion,
making the home turn, slows and then collapses;
hurling his rider over slumping shoulders.

Leader: Ghostlike in pastures cattle lie untended;   145
And, while the cows die, sorrow wilts the stud bull.
As the herd's size wanes, herdsmen fade and vanish
dying among their ulcered bulls and heifers.
Wolves' jaws no longer scare their prey, the buck deer;
lions' fierce roaring stops; bears' matted fur sheds   150
all its raw violence.

Voice 2:   Snakes that lurk in hiding
lose their own poison, burn with fever, dying,
venom sacs dried out.

Voice 3: No glorious leaves crown woodlands, pouring cool
     shade
on darkened hillsides,   155

Voice 4:   no fresh turf greens fields
Voice 1: no vines bend boughs down plumped out by Bacchus.
Voice 2: All nature tastes our ripe fruits of evil.
Leader: Hell's sister Furies break bolts in darkness'
deepest abysses, riot with Hell's torches,   160
Voice 1: Hell's fiery river leaps over its banksides
mingling death's waters with those of our own Thebes:
Leader: Styx flows to us as we once sailed from Sidon.
Voice 4: Greedily black-clad Death gapes with blind jaws,
Voice 1: batlike, unfurling all wings in full spread.   165
Voice 2: Death's ruthless boatman, old, raw, and mighty,
plying his monstrous skiff through turbid waters,
Tires, his arms hardly tug back on his laboring
boatpole,
Voice 1:   exhausted
Voice 2:   by constant shipment
of teeming new dead.   170
Leader: Some say Hell's guard-dog broke chains of Spartan
steel and, at large now, roves within our lands;
some say that earth roared, others say that phantoms

huger than humans have been sighted,
  wandering
our holy woodlands,   175

Voice 3:   that Cadmus' grove twice
shuddered its snow off, shivering in terror,

Voice 1: that Dirce twice streamed fountains shooting
    bloodspurts,

Voice 2: that Amphion's hunting
hounds have made silenced
night resound with howling.

Leader: Graver than Death herself are the hideous   180
new masks Death wears. Limpness insensate
paralyzes locked limbs. Blotches of redness
ravage sick faces; scattered, tiny pockmarks
measle the whole head, then infection's fire
burns, fevers, ruins the brain, the body's fortress, 185
bloats cheeks suffused with blood in profusion.

Voice 1: Eyes stiffen, staring; and accursèd fever
gnaws at the limbs' joints, ears are set ringing,
black gore drips from blocked, ravaged nostrils,
bursting through stretched veins.   190

Voice 2:   Coughing's relentless
rasping convulses lungs and intestines.

Voice 1: Men cling to ice-cold boulders in embraces,
till the stone warms too.

Voice 4:   Quarantine guards die,
borne off as corpses. Those imprisoned, free now,
steal out to fountains,   195

Voice 3:   gulp down their waters,
quenching their deep thirst.

Leader: Crowds sprawled like victims lie at the altars,
praying for death—the only prayer
  gods always
quickly respond to.
            Hordes throng the temples
not to appease heaven's powers with
  their offerings   200
No, they take joy in glutting gods to fullness.

ACT 2

CREON enters and is noticed by OEDIPUS

Oedipus: Someone is hurrying to the palace. Who?
Is it Creon, distinguished for his deeds
and his nobility of blood? Perhaps
my mind's eye is so weakened and so ill
that it mistakes delusion for truth.

Leader: Creon has come, as we all prayed he'd come.   205

Oedipus: I feel a shudder of anxiety,
my mind afraid of what fate moves toward.
My heart sinks quivering between two matched
emotions. When and where delight lies coupled
with grim reality one is torn both ways,
one's spirit lacks clear vision. The soul
both fiercely longs to know—and is afraid.

Brother of my wife, if you bring back
some help to us in our exhausted state,   210
hurry to give it voice. Explain it now!

Creon: The oracle makes no sense: it is inert,
entangled in its enigmatic words.

Oedipus: Give sick men help that offers no clear sense
and you deny them any help at all.

Creon: It is the practice of the Delphic god
to hide secrets in malleable words
that bend both ways.   215

Oedipus: Then speak them, even if
they make no sense. For Oedipus alone
is blessed with skill to know which way is right.

Creon: A king was killed. God bids this sacrilege
set right by exile. The man murdered, Laius,
must be avenged. Not until then will day
bring daylight rushing back into the heavens
and give us safe air from clear skies to breathe.   220

Oedipus: This king was famous. Who killed him? Spell out
the name Phoebus declared. He'll pay the price.

Creon: I hope I may safely tell things that, when I heard and saw,
        sent shudders through me: my limbs paralyzed, blood
            thickened and icy.
        I entered Phoebus' shrine, a petitioner on humble feet,   225
        formally invoked his power divine, hands purified
            and raised.
        Double-peaked, snow-capped Parnassus roared its
            hostility,
        Phoebus' laurel quivered threateningly above my head,
            shaking
        her tresses of leaves, the sacred Castalian springs ceased
            flowing
        instantly. Then the priestess, prophetic voice of
            Leto's son,
        tossed free her shock of hair and, roused to frenzy, let
            her god take her   230
        before she reached his cavern. A voice huger than any
            human's
        crashed out like lightning's flame with the shattering
            vastness of thunder:

        "Gentle to Cadmean Thebes will the stars return in
            their motion
        if the fugitive guest leaves the springs of Ismenian Dirce.
        He killed the king and brought plague, marked out as an
            infant by Phoebus.   235
        Villainous killer, you will not enjoy your pillage much
            longer!
        You'll fight a war with yourself, leave war to your
            sons as their portion,
        son, who vilely returned to rise back in the womb of
            your mother."

        (OEDIPUS *pauses for a moment, then addresses* CREON)

Oedipus: What I prepare to do at gods' command
        would have been done more decently back then,
        when the dead king was cremated and laid to rest,   240

in case it crossed the mind of anyone
to plot more violence against the sanctity
of royal power. One king must tightly guard
another king's security. Once dead,
no matter how they feared you while alive,
you mean nothing at all to anyone.

Creon: He meant a lot. But, after he had died,
a greater fear made us neglect his rites.

Oedipus: Could any fear for safety keep you from   245
what was your solemn duty to your kin?

Creon: The Sphinx: grim threats from her accursèd spell.

(OEDIPUS *moves forward to address both* CHORUS *and audience*)

Oedipus: Well, now it's time to make proper amends
for this crime done. Divine will so commands.
If there's a god who looks on kings and power
without anger, be with us.

                    Jupiter,
you who keep the speeding stars on course!

Phoebus, the sun, symbol supreme of order   250
in heaven, who can adjust your path to rule
the zodiac! Your swift rotations power
time's slow wheels.

                    Phoebe, moon's light wandering
at night-time, sister racing in relay with
your brother sun.

                    Neptune, ruling the winds,
driving your sea-blue course across the salt   255
ocean's width and depth.

                    Death, housing us
when we can see no more.

                    I pray that he
whose hand killed Laius may never know
a house at peace, forces of hearth and home
that he can trust, a land to shelter him
when he's expelled. May marriage bring him shame

and pain and children who dishonor him, 260
may he, with his own hand, kill his father,
may he do all that I escaped doing.
I can invoke no stronger curse than this.
There'll be no chance for pardon and no place,
I swear this by the power I wield as king
over this land that sheltered me. I swear it
by the land I left, and by the gods
who guard my family, and by Neptune, 265
my homeland's father in a double sense.[3]
Your waves break playfully and close to it
on either side, this land I call my own.

Phoebus, who breathes words through prophetic lips
of Delphi's priestesses, bear witness now
to what my voice says. On it I pin my prayers
that my own father thrive until old age
at ease, and that he'll see his life's last day 270
secure on his high solitary throne:
that Polybus will be the sole husband
his Merope will ever know.

(*He glances at* CREON)

                              I swear,
no special favors and no personal ties
will tear the guilty party from my grasp.

Explain to me where this outrage occurred.
Was it a fair fight or a planned ambush? 275

Creon: While heading for the woodlands at Delphi
by the holy Castalian spring, he went
on foot along a pathway all closed in
by scrub and thicket. The road then branches out
crossing the fields along three different routes.
Of these, one cuts across the soil of Phocis,
Bacchus' lands. Parnassus, at its end,

---

[3] Corinth, situated on the Isthmus, had ports on either side.

cresting a gently rising ridge of hills,
towers its twin peaks up toward the sky,   280
leaving plowed fields behind.
                              Another road
leads to the lands of lying Sisyphus
with seas on either side.
                              The third, a track,
snakes through a deep hollow to Olenus' lands,
follows and finally crosses the ice-cold
Evenus on its shallow, meandering course.   285
It was peacetime; the attack was a surprise,
as, out of nowhere, a band of thugs sprang forth
and put him to the sword. No one saw it.

(CREON *is interrupted by the arrival of* TEIRESIAS, *accompanied by*
MANTO, *his daughter*)

Leader:[4]	Teiresias chooses his moment well.
	He gives what speed he can to trembling limbs,
	enlivened by news of the oracle.
	Manto, who guides him, serves as his escort now,
	his window on the world, since he himself,
	widowed of sight, perceives no trace of light. 290
Oedipus:	Since you are someone even gods revere,
	second in wisdom to Phoebus alone,
	explain the oracles and name the man
	whom they are marking out for punishment.
Teiresias:	It does you, of all people, no credit,
	you, a thinking man, that you're surprised
	how slowly my tongue expresses thoughts as words,
	how it plays for time. When you lack sight 295
	a large segment of truth conceals itself.
	Yet I will follow where my country calls,
	where Phoebus calls. So let the words of fate
	now be deciphered. If my blood ran hot,
	pulsed strong, I'd take god's force into my lungs.

---

[4] The lines given here to the Chorus Leader are usually assigned to Creon.

But it does not. So bring a white bullock,
one never broken to a curving yoke,
before the altar. Guide your father, child.   300
Light is no use to him. Report to me
the clear signs that spell out fate's sacred words.

(*Two attendants bring in a bull's head with gilded horns to represent the living animal.* TEIRESIAS *and* MANTO, *joined by* OEDIPUS,
move toward the altar)

Manto: The perfect victim is already here,
                standing before the holy altar now.
Teiresias: In ritual invocation, call the powers
                of heaven to witness our votive act.
                Place gifts of incense from lands of sunrise
                upon the altar flames as offerings.   305
Manto: I've set the incense on gods' holy fires.

(*The incense flares suddenly and brightly in the darkness, but only
for a moment*)

Teiresias: Does the flame devour our offering now?
Manto: Light flared up instantly, instantly died.
Teiresias: But did the fire shine out distinct and bright,
                raising a sharp apex straight up to heaven,   310
                exploding a crown of brightness in the air,
                or did it flicker sideways and around,
                as if it could not see its way, then fall
                lost in darkness and streams of billowing smoke?
Manto: The flickering flame had no consistent shape,
                but wove within itself many colors,
                like Iris who brings rain and paints an arc   315
                curving across a huge expanse of sky,
                heralding storms. You'd hesitate to say
                which colors were present and which were not.
                Deep blue, chevroned with yellow, flickered first,
                and then the red of blood, and finally
                all vanished into darkness' binding grip.   320

But look! the fire now splits into two flames,
as if to fight. Embers of what was once
a sacred mound sunder in hate. Father,
I look and shiver. Bacchus' wine thickens
within the cup to blood, thick smoke encoils itself   325
around the king's head, settles more densely still
upon his face, its thick cloud first veiling
then blocking out the light. Father, explain
what all this means.

Teiresias: But how can I explain?
My mind is thunderstruck, it leaves me dazed,
aimlessly drifting in tempestuous thought.
What can I say? It bodes evil, terrible   330
but unfathomable. Usually
the powers, when angered, show it by clear signs.
But here they wish, and, then again, don't wish
to state the cause. Their rage is violent.
Why then do they hide it? Something lurks here
that shames the very gods. Hurry, bring up
cattle ready for sacrifice, sprinkle   335
their necks with milled grain and with salt. Tell me:
are their eyes calm? Are they willing, ready
for the ritual and for the knives that wait?

(*A heifer's head is now brought to the altar to stand next to the
bullock already there*)

Manto: The bull, positioned facing toward the east,
where the sun rises first at daylight's birth,
raises his head high, then, frightened by day,
turns it aside in fear and shuns its rays.

(*The animals are sacrificed*)

Teiresias: Do both sink to earth as the first blow is struck?   340
Manto: The heifer falls on the poised blade herself,
is dead at the first blow. The bull, struck twice,
charges this way and that without purpose.

	He's weakening now, but finds it hard to force	
	his life to leave him, for it fights back hard.	
Teiresias:	But does the blood spurt quickly from precise	345
	incisions or seep slowly from deep wounds?	
Manto:	The heifer's blood gushes out where she was cut.	
	The bull's gashes, though massive, are just flecked	
	with light, red trickles. But, as he backs off, blood	
	floods out through his mouth and through his eyes.	350
Teiresias:	(*to* OEDIPUS)	

Such inauspicious sacrifice is cause
for great anxiety.
(*to* MANTO)

                           Nonetheless, proceed.
Describe the features of the viscera.
(MANTO *inspects the heifer's viscera*)

| *Manto:* | Father, I do not understand. Most times | |

the entrails pulse and quiver gently. But not now.
They make my hands shake violently. Dark blood,   355
new blood, keeps spurting from the veins.

                                   The heart
is deep inside and very hard to find.
It's shrunken with disease. The veins: livid.
The entrails: largely gone. The liver: diseased
and foaming with black gall. On it, an omen
always bad for individual power:
On two identical beds or lobes, two heads.   360
protrude, each split. The covering membrane's thin,
denying secrets to its secrecy.
The left, the hostile side, swells up, derives
its power and strength from seven veins. But then,
cutting across each one there is a ridge
that intercepts the blood's returning flow.   365
Nothing is placed where it's supposed to be:
the organs are reversed, their order changed.
The lungs are on the right, engorged with blood,
compressed. They cannot breathe. The heart's not on
the left. There is no caul to give protection,
gentle and complete, with fatty tissue

to the viscera. Nature's birth organs   370
are all inside out: the womb's not structured
as a womb. Let me look closer. For within
There's some hard tumor. What anomaly
is this? The heifer was unmated, yet
there is a fetus, and the pregnancy
is not, as usual, in the uterus.
It's moving and groaning, flexing feeble limbs   375
in quivering spasms.
                                    Now a dark flood of blood
invades the innards, and the wretched beasts,
just butchered, try to rise back to their feet,
raising hollowed bodies, trying to gore
the priests who slaughtered them. Their viscera
keep slipping from my hands.

                                    Yet the deep sound   380
that drives you back is not their bellowing
nor that of frightened cattle somewhere around.
It is the cry of terror from the altar fires.

Oedipus: Explain what these portents of fire forebode,
those we have witnessed in this ritual
of terror. I am not afraid to hear   385
your words. People, I've observed, attain
a calm indifference when great evils strike.

Teiresias: You'll soon look back with envy's evil eye
upon these sufferings you seek to cure.

Oedipus: Let me at least know what the powers of heaven
want me to know. Who has bloodied his hands
with the unholy killing of the king?

Teiresias: Neither the birds who cut through heaven's heights
on their light wings nor viscera ripped out   390
from bodies still alive have power to conjure
that name. We must try another path.
We must call Laius back from Erebus,
back from the shores of night's eternity,
so that he can, on his return, himself
denounce his killer. We must unseal the earth,

implore the help of death's implacable
lord, Dis. We must draw out to us from there   395
the populace entombed beyond the Styx.
Tell me to whom you would entrust this task,
this ritual. You cannot go yourself:
For the king and head of state to visit
and to see the ghosts of darkness would be
sacrilege.[5]

Oedipus: Creon this is a task
that cries for you. My kingdom and my power
now look to you as second in command.   400

Teiresias: While we loosen the locks that dam the deep
waters of Styx, have people sing a hymn
beguiling Bacchus with its words of praise.

(*Exeunt* TEIRESIAS, MANTO, *and* CREON, *leaving* OEDIPUS *and
the* CHORUS *together on the stage. What follows is a dithyramb, a
Greek hymn performed somewhat in the style of a Jacobean masque,
narrated by the* CHORUS LEADER. *To convey its impact, its mixture
of the seductiveness and violence that characterize Bacchus and his
worshippers, at least some dance-action is required. The* CHORUS
*mimes various stages of Bacchus' life. One dancer should mime Bac-
chus himself, shedding his (her) long, black-hooded robes, to reveal
beautiful long hair and a flowing dress. As each episode unfolds, other
members of the* CHORUS *should slip off their long robes—and with
them all appearance of age and conventional masculinity*)

Leader: God whose streaming tresses are bound back by fluttering ivy,
You whose soft hands are armed with a wand made of pine
    from Mount Nysa,
Brilliant glory of heaven, hear the prayers   405
that we, Bacchus, your noble Thebes,
offer you, palms outstretched
in supplication. Turn to us.

---

[5] Certain Roman officials, such as censors, were forbidden to look upon the dead during their
terms of office. Teiresias' remark also reminds us that Virgil's Aeneas could be seen as acting impi-
ously by consulting the dead in *Aeneid* 6.

(The Chorus *moves away from its* Leader, *who takes up a position dominating, but separate from, the others for the remainder of the choral song. All but two of the remaining members of the* Chorus *uncover their heads and assume a more youthful posture. Each takes up a Bacchic pine-spear [thyrsus], reveals youthful hair and a face younger and more feminine than would have been assumed. Of the two remaining dancers still fully gowned and hooded, one representing Bacchus, stands aloof, stage left, the other, also aloof, stage right. The* Chorus *turns its attention to the Bacchus dancer)*

Voice 1:	Smile on us, turn your head, fair as a fair maiden's.
Voice 2:	Let your star-shining face shake off its veil of clouds, 410
Voice 3:	The grim menace of hell's forces and fate's rapacity.

(The Bacchus dancer is coaxed forward and reclines. Gently, two of the dancers approach to remove his [her] hood and offer a garland and a purple Phrygian cap)

Voice 1:	Your hair looks lovelier when crowned with springtime flowers.
Voice 2:	Your head, when capped in Tyrian purple,
Voice 1:	Your brow, when gently bound with ivy garlands, clustered in berries. 415
Voice 2:	Let your hair flow loose, scattered in disorder,
Voice 1:	*[in laughing disagreement]* Set in tight ringlets; it will still become you.

(The Bacchus dancer is now unhooded, hair garlanded and capped. Other members of the Chorus *move up to encourage the dancer to remove the gloomy and threatening robe)*

Leader:	Because you so feared your angry stepmother you grew up pretending your limbs were a woman's. With your blond tresses you passed for a young girl, 420 girdled your clothing with a sash of saffron.
Voice 3:	Since then you've always loved dressing in soft clothes, loosely sinuous, with lines long and flowing.
Leader:	So be it now! 425

(The Bacchus dancer now shakes off the robe, disclosing his androgynous, Dionysian costume)

Voice 4:	All vast boundaries of the lands of sunrise
	saw you thus, as you rode your golden chariot,
Voice 3:	Your harnessed lions draped in trailing mantles.
Voice 4:	Men who drink from the Ganges or break ice
	concealing the Araxes.
Leader:	*(resuming narrative)*
	The old Satyr Silenus tagged along on a rag-tag
	donkey,
	his aging, fat temples twined around with garlands
	of ivy.
	Your raunchy inner group takes the lead in your
	secret orgies.

430

Voice 1:	Then your followers	*Voice 2:*	women called Bassarids
Voice 3:	rhythmically dance	*Voice 4:*	Edonian dances
Voice 1:	on Mount Pangaeus	*Voice 2:*	on Pindus' pinnacles
Voice 3:	in Thracian country.		
Leader:			The scene's now Thebes.

435

(The Chorus *now removes the hood and robes from the second aloof dancer, who is dressed beneath as a soldier, and will mime the part of Pentheus, whose death is now described. Another member of the* Chorus *mimes the part of Agave, Pentheus' mother)*

Voice 4:	Among mothers	*Voice 3:*	amid Cadmus' daughters
Voice 4:	a maenad walks	*Voice 1:*	a companion of Bacchus
Voice 2:	an unholy killer.		
Voice 3:	Her skirt's a fawn skin	*Voice 4:*	sacred to the god
Voice 1:	A pine-cone tipped spear	*Voice 2:*	flexes in her hand
Voice 3:	stirring emotions	*Voice 4:*	deep in mothers' breasts.
Leader:	They unbind their hair...		

440

(The Chorus *mimes an attack on Pentheus while the Bacchus dancer looks on in satisfaction)*

Voice 2:	Once they've dismembered *Voice 3:* Pentheus her son,
Voice 1:	as the spell binding their limbs relaxes,
	they see their outrage *Voice 3:* but don't know
	it's theirs. 444
Voice 2:	Then, cursed Cithaeron first streamed with slaughter: 484⁶
Voice 4:	—dragon-blooded Pentheus. 485
Leader:	(*resuming narrative*)
	Ino, Cadmus' daughter, foster-mother to beautiful Bacchus, 445
	now has a realm in the sea. Shoals of Nereids are dancing
	around her.
	Amid the great sea's waves her own child—and blood-kin to
	Bacchus—
	though a newcomer, holds power. He is no minor god, her
	Palaemon!

(*The Bacchus dancer exchanges his pine spear for a lyre, steps forward, but is seized and bound by members of the* Chorus. *The Pentheus dancer gets up and rejoins the troupe*)

Leader:	When you were young, Bacchus, Etruscan pirates		
	made you their captive;		
Voice 3:	the sea-god, Nereus,	*Voice 4:*	thrust back
			swelling seas, 450
Voice 1:	changed blue waters into	*Voice 2:*	quiet meadows.
Voice 3:	Up sprang the plane tree	*Voice 4:*	green in spring
			foliage
Voice 3:	and the bay laurel,	*Voice 4:*	dear to Phoebus,
Voice 1:	in whose boughs chatter	*Voice 2:*	twittering songbirds.
Leader:	The pirate ship's oars snag fast in creepers. 455		
	Mast-head rigging, transforms into vine tendrils.		
Voice 1:	On the prow an Asian	*Voice 2:*	lion is roaring;
Voice 3:	sitting astern	*Voice 4:*	an Indian tiger.
Voice 1:	The pirates dive and swim,	*Voice 2:*	scared by this mirage.
Leader:	But their appearance shifts once they're in water. 460		
	Off fall their plundering arms, like clean-pruned branches.		
Voice 3:	Breasts slither into wombs	*Voice 4:*	and stick fast there.
Voice 2:	Dangling from their sides hang the tiniest hands.		

---

⁶ I have moved 484–485 here because they fit the theme more comfortably in this location.

Voice 1:	They arch their backs then plunge beneath waves,	
	cleaving salt sea with moon-crescent tails.	465
Leader:	*[indicating another change of scene]*	
	Pactolus: sluicing gold-rich water down in its torrents,	
	once carried you on its affluent streams near Lydian Sardis.	
	Massagetae, who drink in their cups milk mixed up with	
	fresh blood,	
	unstrung their bows for you and emptied their quivers of	
	arrows.	470
	Realms of Lycurgus, the axe-fighter, felt the full power of	
	Bacchus.	
Voice 1:	The barbarous homelands of the Dacians felt you,	
Voice 2:	And nomad herdsmen whom neighbor North wind	
	lashes with fury.	
Voice 1:	So did the tribes that icy Maeotis	
	laps with chill wave crests.	475
Voice 2:	So did the Arctic tribes seen from sky's summit	
	by the Arcadian	
	Bear Star and twinned Wain.	
Voice 1:	He tamed the scattered	
Voice 3:	and lonely	
Voice 1:	Geloni,	
Voice 2:	Disarmed the fighting girls they call Amazons	
	Whose clans inhabit wild lands near the Black Sea.	
Voice 4:	Fierce eyes downcast down to the ground they sank,	480
Voice 1:	All their light arrows finally discarded,	
Voice 4:	They became maenads.	
Leader:	Bacchus' cult reached his stepmother's own Argos	486
Voice 4:	—where Proetus' boastful girls ran wild in forests—	
Voice 2:	Aegean Naxos provided Ariadne	
Voice 3:	his bride: for Theseus	
Voice 1:	had jilted her, left her there	
Voice 4:	still virgin—	
Voice 2:	Her compensation was	
Voice 1:	a better husband.	490
Voice 3:	That night Naxos' lava spurted fresh wine	
	in celebration.	
Voice 4:	Brooks, keen to gossip, cut out through new grassland.	

Voice 3:	That night the deep earth sucked in precious liquids:
Voice 4:	gushed milk out snow-white
Voice 1:	—in purest fountains— 495
Voice 4:	and Lesbos' vintage perfumed with thyme's fragrance.
Leader:	When the new bride is introduced to heaven,
	Phoebus, hair loose on shoulders,
	honors her with a fine wedding song,
Voice 2:	On either side, a Cupid jiggles his 500
Voice 4:	flaming firebrand.
Voice 1:	But Jupiter lays down his own hot lightning shafts.
Voice 2:	He hates them when he sees
Voice 3:	Bacchus coming in.
Leader:	While glistening stars speed along on their course through
	the universe, age-old;
	and while Ocean envelops our sphere with its circling waters;
	while the moon still can regain lost fire and replenish her
	brilliance; 505
	And while the Great Bear, Callisto, avoids both the dark sea
	and Nereus;
	we'll show our awe for the sparkling face of the fair god
	who frees us.

ACT 3

Enter CREON, *slowly and uncertainly.* OEDIPUS *moves toward him
to greet him*

Oedipus:	I read in the expression of your face
	signs boding tears. But still, explain whose head
	must fall to make the gods calm once again. 510
Creon:	You ask me to voice the words my fear of you
	argues that I should silence and suppress.
Oedipus:	If Thebes' ruin does not move you enough,
	at least be moved by loss of royal power
	within a family of which you're part.
Creon:	What you so eagerly set out to learn
	you'll passionately wish you'd never known.
Oedipus:	Ignorance is an ineffective cure 515
	for ills and evil. Do you intend to hide
	the remedy prescribed for public health?
Creon:	When medicine has hideous side-effects,
	applying the cure could cause one some regret.
Oedipus:	State what you have heard, or you'll be crushed
	by torture's real evil. And then you'll know
	what force an angered king can bring to bear.
Creon:	Kings order men to speak, but hate what's said. 520
Oedipus:	You'll be dispatched as a cheap offering
	to Hell for all of us if you, with your own voice,
	do not reveal the secrets of your rites.
Creon:	Grant me the right to silence. Could I ask
	any more trivial freedom from a king?
Oedipus:	Freedom expressed by silence often becomes
	a greater obstacle to royal power
	and to a king than when it has a tongue. 525
Creon:	If we've no right to silence, have we any rights?
Oedipus:	And you destroy the basis of command
	when you stay silent, though ordered to speak.
Creon:	Since you force me to speak, stay calm, I beg,
	as you hear and digest the words I say.
Oedipus:	Has anyone ever been punished yet

for saying what he was compelled to say?
(*At this point* OEDIPUS *sits down on his throne.*)

Creon: At a good distance from the city, black   530
beneath the shading ilexes, a grove
encircles Dirce's hollow and her spring.
Over other trees the towering cypress
lifts its head. Its ever-vigorous trunk
branching with green, defines and marks the wood.
You'd also note an old oak, stretching out
gnarled branches, rotting where it stands, side gnawed   535
hollow by time, roots torn, its toppling mass,
its dead weight braced by the supporting beams
of other trees. And many kinds grow here:
slender lindens, Paphian myrtle trees,
sour-berried bays, alders that will, one day,
give driving force to oars powering through
the sea's immensity. You'd find a pine,   540
rising toward Phoebus' sunlight, baring
smooth trunk to stiff west winds.
                              And at its heart
stands a gigantic tree that dominates
the lesser growths with its oppressive shade.
It spreads its branches forth like tentacles,
Its grasp extends throughout the circling grove
warding intruders off all by itself.
Beneath it is a spring, slow-flowing, grim,
numbingly cold, always crusted with ice,
because it lacks all sense of what light is,
of what warmth is, or that Phoebus exists.   545
Around this lifeless font a marsh extends.

It's here the old priest comes. There's no delay
waiting for dark. The site provided night.
A trench is dug. Logs blazing, torn from pyres,   550
are tossed in it. The seer, his body now
shrouded in death robes, makes the ritual signs,
waving a full-leafed branch. Agèd and grim,
clothes dusted about in ash, he steps forward,

attired as a mourner. His funeral cloak
sweeps down across his feet; his hair, all white,
is tightly wreathed with deathly yew-tree leaves.   555
Black-fleeced sheep and black heifers are dragged
backwards, up to the trench, and hurled alive
into the death fires, where the vulture flames
feast on the livestock writhing in the blaze.
Next, he invokes souls of the dead and you,
who rule dead souls, and then the dog, guarding
the gateway to Oblivion's deep pools.   560
He spins a magic spell, and with a voice
menacing, madly possessed, chants out
formulas to conjure or calm ghosts,
solemnly offering blood on altar fires,
burning cattle alive, drenching the ditch
with bowls of blood, white milk, and Bacchus' wine   565
poured with his left hand. Louder still he chants,
head bowed toward the ground, voice ever
    more frenzied,
so as to waken the dead souls he has raised.
Hecate's hell hounds bay. The hollow vales
three times echo their eerie sound. The land   570
quakes, its topsoil pushed up from below.
"I'm heard," the seer murmurs, "I've offered words
approved and Death's blind singularity
is smashed, a pathway's made giving dead souls
access to those above." The woods cower
into the ground, leaves bristling up, oaks split,   575
as waves of horror shudder through the grove.
The earth caverns, subsides, groans from its depths.
Perhaps the hidden streams of Acheron
find thought, and think it wrong they
    are provoked,
perhaps it is the sound of earth herself
as she is breached to make way for her dead,
or Cerberus, his three heads stung to rage,   580
tugging the heavy chains that hold him down.

The land suddenly chasms from below
opening up a dizzying abyss.
With my own eyes I saw the stone cold pools
among the ghostly shadows, the pale gods,
what night really is. The flow of blood   585
chilled in my veins and froze. A fierce troop
of soldiers now leaps out and stands at arms,
the full, whole company of brothers born
from seed of dragon's teeth that Cadmus sowed.
The Demon of Blood-Feuds and blind Battle
shriek their rage and everything   590
endless darkness generates, then hides
from heaven, screams at once. Hair-rending Grief,
Sickness, struggling pathetically
to raise its wearied head, Old Age sinking
into itself, Anxiety choking
at rope's end, Plague, the greedy, evil force
devouring the populace of ancient Thebes.

Even Manto, so learnèd in the skills   595
and rituals her old father employs,
stood rooted, stricken dumb. Our spirits failed.
Teiresias himself is fearless, though,
bold in his blindness, summoning the hosts,
the bloodless multitudes of savage Dis,
the dead of Thebes. And they respond, flitting
like tiny puffs of cloud, sucking the breath
of freedom from sky's breezes. Their numbers?
More than falling leaves on Mount Eryx,   600
than flowers on Mount Hybla at spring's height,
when thick-swarming bees cluster, than waves
breaking in the Ionian Sea, than birds
cleaving the air in migratory flight
from ice forming on Strymon, who exchange   605
winter's arctic snows for Nile's warmth.
The trembling spirits eagerly seek out
places to hide inside the shady grove.

First from the soil sprang Zethus, wrestling   610
a wild bull by its horns, and Amphion,
his left hand clasping the lyre of tortoise shell
whose sweet sound charmed the stones to build
    Thebes' walls.
Then there's Niobe, child of Tantalus,
at last proudly united with her sons,
counting their ghosts, her heavy head held high,
her arrogant looks now safe. Agave too,   615
a mother more destructive yet, is here,
still dangerously insane, and following her,
her clutch of Maenad women whose bare hands
portioned their king's body. Following them
Pentheus himself, still threatening, comes,
still savage in his mutilated state.

Laius, called many times, at last lifts up
his head hunched down in shame.
    He moves away,
far from the rest, and hides. The seer persists,   620
doubling his prayers to the dead until
Laius reveals his face. How he appeared
I shudder to describe: he stood, limbs caked
with blood, his hair filthy, putrid with pus.
Words foamed forth insanely from his mouth: 625

(CREON *turns to the* CHORUS, *with altered voice and manner, as if
he were himself the voice of Laius*)

"Inspire your hands, brandish your Bacchic spears,
or sunder limb from limb, as I'd prefer,
the sons you've borne, you beasts of Cadmus' house,
always pleasuring in family blood!
Thebes' most particular and greatest crime
lies in a mother's love. Yes, human crime
it is, not gods' anger, that tears you now,   630
not the oppressive breath of southern winds,
that plagues you, not the soil too little fed

with heaven's rain that ruins you with dry
and radiant heat. It is your murderous king.
He, profiting by brutal butchery,
seized his father's throne and took his wife: 635
Ungodly incest! Here is a son to hate!
Yet he is worse as father than as son,
This loathsome offspring, again weighting the cursed
womb, thrusting his being back where he
        was born.
He spawned in his own mother live tissue
of incest, there begat himself brothers,   640
an act that has few precedents in beasts:
a freak of evil, a monstrosity
more convoluted than his vaunted Sphinx!

(CREON *now turns to* OEDIPUS)

"You hold my scepter in your bloodstained hands.
But I, your father, as yet unavenged,
will, with the whole world, hunt you down. With me
I'll drag the voice of Punishment itself,   645
the Fury of hell, screaming with lashing whips,
to chant her spell over your wedding bed,
destroy your nest of incest, and grind down
in civil war the gods who guard your house.

(CREON *turns again to the* CHORUS)

So drive this king beyond your boundaries
immediately, force him to banishment
anywhere to walk his path of death.
But he must leave our soil. Then it will bloom
again with springtime flowers, breezes will bring
life, and air that's good to breathe. The trees   650
will glow with blossoms. For when he departs,
Plague and Destruction, Toil, Death, Blight and Pain
will leave with him in worthy company.
He will himself yearn to escape our land

as fast as he can move. But I'll shackle,   655
I'll slow his feet. I'll hold him back.
He'll crawl along, unsure where the road is,
grimly probing with his staff, tapping
like an old man. You, part him from our earth.
His father, I, will purge him from heaven's sight."

(CREON *stops, eyes fixed on the* CHORUS, *who shift their gaze to*
OEDIPUS, *who remains seated, silent, and motionless for a while. As*
he begins to speak, his words are more for himself than for others on
stage)

Oedipus: Ice shivers through, seizes my limbs and bones:
             I am accused of having already done   660
             the things I feared I'd do. Yet Merope's still
             the wife of Polybus—proof absolute
             that I'm not sleeping in a bed of sin.
             And Polybus is still alive. That clears
             my hands of patricide. Thus both parents
             acquit me of both murder and incest.
             What charge I could be guilty of remains?
             Thebes mourned the loss of Laius long before   665
             I set foot in Boeotia.

(OEDIPUS *rises and moves slowly toward* CREON)

                          So then,
             is the old man a fraud? Is it the *god*
             who makes life hard for Thebes? It's a shrewd plot,
             and I've now caught the plotters. Our seer
             is telling lies, parading gods to mask
             his treachery. He's pledged my throne to you.   670
Creon: You think I'd want my sister thrown from power?
             Your family is part of my own blood.
             Even if sacred oaths of loyalty
             did not bind me to all this and define
             my status absolutely, such high stakes,
             such fortune with responsibilities

	and endless worries would scare me too much.	675
	Feel free and safe to set your burdens down.	
	They should not crush you as you step aside.	
	You'll be safer, in fact, if you select	
	another, humbler station for your life.	

Oedipus: Are you suggesting I, of my free will,
lay down my power and its responsibilities?

Creon: Such would be my advice to anyone
who has the freedom to make either choice.   680
You have no choice. You must. You must endure
the lot in life fortune assigns to you.

Oedipus: If you ache to be king, the path to power
that's guaranteed is gained by talk of ease,
of relaxation, by praising a life
of moderation. How often the mask
of restfulness is feigned by restless men!

Creon: Does then my long record of loyalty plead
so feebly to you now in my defense?   685

Oedipus: Loyalty is what gives disloyal men
the opportunity to inflict their harm.

Creon: I'm free of a king's burdens—yet enjoy
the good things a king's power brings. My house
bustles with crowds of citizens, there dawns
no day in time's ebb and flow when gifts,
offered because of my proximity
to power, fail to pour into my house.   690
Many owe their symbols of high rank,
their sumptuous feasts, even their very lives
to favors I bestow. Fortune has smiled
on me. What could I dream of that I lack?

Oedipus: Precisely what you *do* lack. For success
never knows how to stay within limits.

Creon: Am I to be found guilty, then, with no
investigation and no trial at all?   695

Oedipus: Did you and he give my life any thought?
Or did Teiresias hear my defense?
Oh no! But I'm assumed to be guilty.
You've set the precedent. I'm following it.

Creon:	And if I'm innocent?
Oedipus:	Where there is doubt
	it is quite usual for a king to fear
	the worst as proven.
Creon:	Anyone who fears 700
	groundless personal anxieties
	will get, and will deserve, real cause for fear.
Oedipus:	Let a criminal off, and he'll hate you.
	So when there's any doubt, strike down and kill.
Creon:	That's a prescription for hate.
Oedipus:	Hate?
	If you're unduly scared of others' hate 705
	you don't know how to be a king. It's fear
	that stands on guard, maintaining a king's power.
Creon:	But there's the catch. If he's a brutal king,
	who rules harshly, he fears those who fear him.
	Terror comes home to those who cause terror.
Oedipus:	(*to his attendants*)
	This man's a criminal. Keep him locked up
	inside a dungeon cell of solid rock.
	I'm going back to where I rule as king.

(CREON *is arrested and escorted off stage. The* CHORUS *turns to* OEDIPUS)

Leader:	You're not to blame for these, our great dangers.
	These aren't the fates hunting Labadacus' 710
	sons. No, it's gods and their ancient
	angers that dog us.

(OEDIPUS *gives the* CHORUS *center-stage and sits down, brooding, yet listening to their story*)

Voice 1:	Delphi's Castalian
	woods offered shade to a stranger from Sidon,
	Dirce's streams bathed Tyrian settlers.
Voice 2:	Yes, Cadmus, son of (and fearing) Great Agenor, 715
	first stopped beneath our trees' shade

	tired out by worldwide pursuit of Europa—	
Voice 1:	stolen by Jupiter—	
Voice 2:	to make his peace with her rapist.	
Voice 3:	Next, on Phoebus' advice,	

Voice 3: Next, on Phoebus' advice,
he went as bidden, herding a stray heifer   720
untrained for plowing,
unbent to the yoke of a lumbering wagon.

Voice 2: Thus he abandoned his quest for his sister
and, for that cursed heifer, called our country Oxland.

Voice 4: Ever since then this soil has sprouted monsters
never before known.   725

Voice 3: Up from a valley's depths there springs a hissing,
dragon.

Voice 1:   Round trunks of ancient oaks it spirals,
over the tall pines,

Voice 4: Over Chaonian forests even higher,
raising its dark blue head erect—

Voice 2: Still, though, the large part rests upon firm
ground.   730

Leader: <But Cadmus killed this dragon as instructed
by divine orders, sowed its teeth in furrows,
then waited, watching...>[7]
Our land, ungodly in what it gives birth to,
sprouted full-grown armies:
spiral horns blared loud, trumpet-calls through curved brass
shattered nerves with shrill blasts.
New men test new tongues, lips never before moved,   735
First in their war-cries: voices that they did not
know they had in them.

Voice 1: Armies of kinsmen filled the fields with battle.
But this crop's life-span, as befits its seeding,
measured in one day both planting and harvest.   740

Voice 2: Born: after morning's star had passed on.
Dead: before evening's star was born and rose up.

---

[7] Part of the story is missing in the text of this chorus. Scholars have proposed that there is a *lacuna,* a gap, usually between lines 734 and 735. I think the missing details fit better here, after line 730, and have inserted the bracketed words (mine, not Seneca's) to suggest a minimal supplement prefacing the LEADER's next line to make the text more intelligible.

Voice 4:	Cadmus, shocked by such monstrous horrors,
	fears he must fight with this people freshly born
	Until the brute youths <fall in mutual slaughter>.[8] 745
Voice 2:	Mother Earth sees sons she has just brought to birth
	plunged back in her womb where they were nurtured.
Voice 1:	May cursed civil war thus have passed forever!
	May Hercules' Thebes have just this one taste
	of brothers fighting. 750
Leader:	What of the doom of Cadmus' grandson,
	transformed, horned with a live stag's antlers
	branching, strangely shading his forehead:
	hounded by his own dogs—
Voice 3:	he, once their master?
Voice 1:	Down from forests, down from the mountains
	swiftly Actaeon flees, his feet now quicker,
Voice 2:	past rock and clearing, *Voice 3:* no home to go to,
Voice 4:	spooked by bright feathers fluttering in spring winds,
	he guards his life from deer traps he once set,
	till he sees his horns *Voice 3:* mirrored, and
	his beast's face 760
Voice 4:	there in that still pool where he'd watched Diana
	bathing her virgin limbs, *Voice 3:* and grasps the
	god's price
	for outraging *Voice 4:* her ruthless sense
	of honor.

---

[8] The text does not specify, as my version does, that the warriors born from the dragon's teeth were killed by one another. Hence the brackets.

ACT 4

Oedipus: My mind doubles back to its anxiety,
and finds its way to personal fears again.
The powers of heaven and hell declare
that Laius' death resulted from my crime.   765
Yet, in defense, my mind, in innocence,
known better to its own self than to gods,
denies the charge. The memory comes back
along a narrow track: a man had blocked
my path. I struck him with my thick cane, dispatched
him to the dead. He was old, I young. He rode   770
a chariot, got there first, and arrogantly
pushed me aside. We were far from Thebes; at a place
in Phocis where one road splits into three.

(*Enter* JOCASTA)

Dear wife, my soulmate. Untangle, I beg,
my jumbled thoughts. What age was Laius when
he died ? Strong, in life's prime, or broken and old?   775

Jocasta: Between youth and old age. But nearer to age.
Oedipus: Was there a large troop escorting the king?
Jocasta: Most were confused about which fork to take:
it was not clear. They wandered off. A few
toiled faithfully to stay with the chariots' pace.
Oedipus: Did anyone, then, die at the king's side?   780
Jocasta: Just one. His loyalty and valor kept him there.

(JOCASTA *starts to leave the stage, but is recalled when* OEDIPUS *calls for a last detail*)

Oedipus: (*inwardly*)
I've caught the guilty man. They fit: the place,
the number. But the time...
(*then, aloud, to the departing* JOCASTA)
                When did it happen?

(JOCASTA *stops. As she stops, enter a* CORINTHIAN, *admitted by the* GUARDS *after a brief (and silent) interchange from the opposite side of the stage. He stands and waits until* JOCASTA *has finished speaking*)

Jocasta: It's now the tenth harvest: nine years ago.

(OEDIPUS *sinks down on his throne, stunned.* ATTENDANT SLAVES *escort the* CORINTHIAN *toward* OEDIPUS. *The* CORINTHIAN *announces his message abruptly, but cautiously*)

Corinthian: The people of Corinth call you to the throne
your father held. For Polybus has found   785
eternal peace.
Oedipus: How savagely Fortune strikes
at me from every side! Come, tell me the stroke
of destiny by which my parent fell.
Corinthian: Old age. A gentle coma freed his soul.
Oedipus: There was no killing, then! But my father
lies dead. Now I can raise my hands to heaven   790
without sin. Witness! They are clean. They need
fear no crime now. Yet there remains that part
of destiny that I must fear still more.
Corinthian: Power in your father's realm will quell all fear.
Oedipus: Would I go home and take my father's realm?
Thoughts of my mother make me shudder though.
Corinthian: You fear a parent who so anxiously   795
waits in suspense for your return?
Oedipus: I do.
My love and my respect keep me away.
Corinthian: You'll leave her all alone now she's widowed?
Oedipus: Widowed—the word with which you touch my fears!
Corinthian: What deep-set terror presses on your mind?
Tell me, I'm used to offering loyalty
to kings. I'm used to keeping my mouth shut.
Oedipus: Delphi warned I'd marry my mother.   800
That's why I tremble.

Corinthian: Stop worrying pointlessly!
Shrug off disgraceful fears. For Merope
was not your real mother.
Oedipus: (*pausing to reflect before he answers*)
If she was not,
what did she hope to gain by bringing up
the child of someone else?
Corinthian: Children make kings
proud and faithful to their wives.
Oedipus: Explain exactly how you could pick up
the secrets of the royal bedchamber.
Corinthian: Because these hands gave you to your parent
when you were just a baby.
Oedipus: You gave me
to my parent? But who gave me to you?
Corinthian: A herdsman on snow-covered Cithaeron.
Oedipus: What brought you to Cithaeron? Just pure chance?
Corinthian: I followed my horned flocks up to that peak.

(OEDIPUS *again pauses before continuing his interrogation*)

Oedipus: I have marks on my body. What are they?
Corinthian: Insteps pierced through with iron. Your swollen,
piteously injured feet gave you your name.
Oedipus: But who gave you my person as a gift?
I ask you, who?
Corinthian: A man responsible
for feeding a king's flocks. He supervised
a junior mob of herdsmen at the time.
Oedipus: What was his name?
Corinthian: In old men, memory
is the first thing to go. It sits for years
unused, it tires and rots and quietly slips away.
Oedipus: Would you know his face—the way he looks?
Corinthian: Maybe I'd know him. I have often found
that some slight mark recalls a memory
overlaid by time's expanse, erased.

Oedipus:	Then every flock must be brought to
	the shrines
	and altars, with its drovers following.[9]
	Summon those who are in general charge
	of flocks. Set to it, slaves. And hurry now.
Jocasta:[10]	(*motioning the slaves to stay, and moving closer to*
	OEDIPUS' *throne*)

It could be there's a reason it's concealed.　　　　825
It could be Fortune's way, just circumstance.
(*assuming an oracular tone*)
Show patience with what has lurked latent so long.
Let it stay concealed. Often the truth,
made patent, brings out evil for the man
who digs it out.

Oedipus:　　　　　　　　　　Can any evil, then,
be more fearful than what I have now described?

(OEDIPUS *motions the* SLAVES *to leave*)

Jocasta:	You know that what is sought with great effort
	is also great itself.
Corinthian:	And there exist
	conflicting interests on either side:
	the people's welfare, and that of the king.　　　830
Jocasta:	Keep your hands neutral. Don't disturb a thing.
	Let destiny unravel this itself.
Oedipus:	There's no practical reason to shake up
	a prosperous state. But, when a crisis comes,
	you can move anything you like safely.
Jocasta:	You yearn for something even nobler than　　　835
	a royal pedigree? Look carefully!
	You may regret the parentage you find.
Oedipus:	I'll seek proof of my blood-line, even if
	it's something I'll regret. I am resolved to know it.

---

[9] I follow the manuscripts' jussive subjunctive *sequantur* here not the indicative *sequuntur* preferred by some editors.

[10] The manuscripts assign these lines to the Corinthian Old Man. Some editors (Weil and Fitch) assign them and 829–32 and 835–36 to Jocasta as I do, with slight modification.

(*Enter* PHORBAS, *dressed as a poor shepherd, accompanied by* GUARDS *one of whom is dressed as a jailer and holds a blazing torch.* PHORBAS *approaches slowly*)

                Look now, here he is: Phorbas,
an old man, well-advanced in years, who once
was overseer of the royal flock.
Do you recall this old man's name or face?   840

Corinthian: His general appearance stirs my thoughts.
The face—I just don't know it well enough.
Yet then again, it's not unknown to me.

Oedipus: (*turning to address* PHORBAS, *in a calculated manner*)
When Laius ruled, were you the slave who ran   845
large, well-fed flocks on lands near Cithaeron?

Phorbas: Cithaeron, always rich in grass to graze
provides the summer pasture for our flocks.

Corinthian: (*looking at* PHORBAS *carefully, and positioning himself so* PHORBAS
      can get a clear view of him)
Do you know me?

Phorbas: The memory's unclear.
I can't decide.

Oedipus: Was some child given by you
to this man here? Speak up! You can't decide?
What's happened to the color in your cheeks?
Why do you grope for words? Truth hates delay.   850

Phorbas: You're stirring things shrouded by many years.

Oedipus: (*giving a sign for one of the* GUARDS [*but not the one holding the*
      torch] *to approach and seize* PHORBAS)
Say what you know. Then pain won't force the truth.

Phorbas: I did give him a child—a useless gift.
It lacked the strength to bask in light, to live.

Corinthian: Heaven forbid this omen of ill luck!   855
He is alive. Long may he live, I pray!

Oedipus: What makes you claim this child you gave him died?

Phorbas: An iron wire was threaded through both feet,
tying his limbs together. So the wound
produced a swelling; gross infection spread
racking the child's body with fevered pain.

Oedipus: (*inwardly*)
What more do you search for? Now destiny is near.
(*aloud*)
Inform me who this baby was.   860

Phorbas: I cannot break my oath.

Oedipus: (*to the* GUARDS)
                                        Then, one of you:
bring fire to help us temper, hammer away
the shackles of his oath of loyalty.

(*The* GUARD *with the torch approaches. The others pin* PHORBAS'
arms behind his back)

Phorbas: Will paths of blood lead to the truth?

(*The torch-bearing* GUARD *brandishes the flame close to* PHORBAS'
body)

                                        I beg,
spare me the fire!

(*The torch-bearing* GUARD *looks toward* OEDIPUS, *but* OEDIPUS
signals him to keep the flame where it is. OEDIPUS *moves closer to*
PHORBAS, *looks him in the eye*)

Oedipus: You think I am a brute,
that I abuse power. Well, here's your revenge!   865
It's in your grasp. It's set to go. Just speak
the truth! Who was he? Who was its father?

(PHORBAS *still maintains silence.* OEDIPUS *prompts the torch-bearing* GUARD *to apply the flame to* PHORBAS' *body*)

His mother, then?

Phorbas: (*in pain*) His mother was your wife.

(OEDIPUS *falls back.* JOCASTA *rushes off. The* GUARDS *release* PHOR-
BAS, *who slumps to the ground and is comforted by the* CORINTHIAN.

OEDIPUS *moves downstage, then turns so he can address both the*
audience and PHORBAS *and the* CORINTHIAN)

Oedipus: Earth, open up! And you, ruler of ghosts
whose power controls the darkness's tight grip,
hurl me to the depths of Tartarus!
I, who once fathered life where I was born!   870
Hurl stones at my accursed head! Kill me,
citizens, with spears, if you're a father.
Or, if you're a son, strike with your swords.
Husbands, wives, brothers, arm yourselves!
Plague-stricken people, pull out blazing logs
from your cremating fires, hurl them at me.
I range at liberty, a blight of crime
upon the times in which I live, hated   875
by gods, a force deadly to sanctity
of laws, deserving death the day I drew
my first crude breaths!
(*inwardly and with bitter sarcasm*)
                              Get back your courage now,
achieve some deed that lives up to your crimes.
Come on, step smartly into your domain.   880
Congratulate your mother. For her house
now has more children than it had before.

(*Exit* OEDIPUS, *leaving the* CORINTHIAN *and* PHORBAS *staring*
at one another. They exit separately, followed by the GUARDS *and*
SLAVES, *leaving the* CHORUS *alone on stage*)

Leader: Were I the master of my destiny,
could I but mould its shape
the way I wanted it,
I'd set my sails when
gentle west winds blow,
so that the yards would not   885
be strained and shudder
under heavy gales.

	I'd like a moderate, mild	
	and steady breeze,	
	not broadside gusts,	
	to guide my vessel,	
	winds that rouse no fear.	
Voice 3:	I'd like my life to run its course	
	carrying me along the middle road.	890
Voice 2:	Fear of Knossos' king	
	drove a young boy to trust	
	a revolutionary art	
	and fly toward the stars,	
	trying to outreach	
	the real birds.	895
Voice 1:	He asked too much	
	of imitation wings,	
	and stole the name	
	of what is now his sea.	
Voice 2:	But Daedalus, old and worldly-wise,	
	balanced his path of flight,	900
	stayed resolute,	
	below the median of	
	confining clouds,	
	watching, awaiting	
	his own winged son	
Voice 4:	as if he were a bird	
	fleeing a menacing hawk,	
	gathering her fledglings	905
	scattered in fear	
Voice 3:	until the boy	
	flails upon the sea	
	arms pinioned,	
	entangled in the wing-straps	
	of bold air flight.	
Leader:	Anything surging beyond	
	moderation	
	hangs in suspense above a spot	
	where nobody can stand.	910

ACT 5

Enter a Messenger *from Oedipus' palace, holding* Oedipus' *sword in his hands*

Leader:	What is it now?
Voice 1:	The sound of doors opening.
Voice 2:	See—one of the king's slaves
	strikes head with hand in grief.

(*to the* Messenger)

Leader:	Tell us what news you bring.	
Messenger:	Once Oedipus grasped that his destiny	915
	was as foretold, and that his family	
	was cursed by incest, he declared himself	
	guilty of criminal acts, sentenced himself,	
	and, striding quickly, resolutely grim,	
	headed for the palace. He thrust deep	
	into the rooms he so hated to see,	
	mad as a Libyan lion raging across	
	plowed fields, tossing his tawny mane, scowling	920
	with menace. His face expressed ferocity	
	his eyes flashed angrily, he groaned and roared	
	a stifled roar. Cold sweat bathed all his limbs.	
	Foam flecked his mouth, he poured out threats.	
	From the vast lake of pain suppressed within	
	waves crested and broke out. In savage mood	
	he plans some formidable act to match	925
	his destiny. Then "Why do I put off	
	my punishment?" he asks. "Why can't someone	
	pierce this wicked heart of mine with steel,	
	burn it with blazing fire, crush it with rocks?	
	Would any tigress, any bird of prey	
	fly up to feed on innards such as mine?	
	Cithaeron, mountain holy and accursed,	
	you have a great capacity for crime,	930

send out your wild beasts, or send rabid dogs
against me, or bring back Agave now.
Spirit of mine, what do you fear in death?
For death alone can tear the innocent
from the ambiguous grip of Fortune's whims."
With these determined words,[11] he claps the hand   935
that killed his father to sword-hilt, unsheathes
his blade. "Is this how it's to be? Are you,"
he wonders, "to atone for such huge crimes
with such a short sentence? You'll compensate
for all that you have done with just one blow?
Your death—this does enough for your father.
But what about your mother, what about
your children, born into the light of day
so sinfully? And what about this land,
your pitiable homeland, which now pays   940
for your crimes with such great catastrophe?
You cannot pay your debts. Nature, giver
of life, you overturn the laws you make
only for Oedipus, invent new ways
of birth. Invent, then, some new penalties
for me.
          So you must live again, die   945
yet again, ever reborn, so you
can pay new penalties, again, again!
Poor wretch, use your capacity to think!
Death comes to us not often: only once.
It should then be prolonged. Select a death
that lingers, hunt a path of violence
which you can roam not in the company
of those buried and dead, yet nonetheless
abandoned, shunned by all who are alive.   950
Die, but stay *this* side of your father's grave.
Spirit of mine, are you still holding back?"
Look! A rain of tears wells up, spurts forth,

---

[11] The Latin here is *fatus*, "having spoken," from the same root as *fatum*, "(the spoken word of) fate."

sombering his countenance, flooding his cheeks.
"Is it enough to weep? Clear, sparkling tears,
that's all the liquid that my eyes should spill?
The eyes must follow the tears they shed, forced out   955
from their fixed homes. You gods who bless marriage,
will *this* suffice? That I gouge out my eyes?"
He spoke, quivered with fury, and his cheeks
blazed and threatened with defiant fire.
His eyes themselves strain from their own sockets.
His expression screamed ferocity,   960
anger, the rashness of violence,
flushed with madness. A deep groan rumbled forth,
and then a hideous roar as he twisted
his own fingers into his eyes. And they
stood out, fiercely and willingly,
stretching to meet, and following the hands
they knew so well, rushing to greet the wounds
that blinded them. Hands talon-hooked, he probes   965
in search of his perception of the light.
At once he tears both eyeballs from their nerves
and roots, and sends them spinning to the ground.
His hands stay trapped inside the emptiness,
and far within rip with their fingernails
in useless savagery the empty folds
of flesh, the deeply hollowed recesses
of sight. His fury does its work, and more.   970
The threat of light is quenched. He lifts his head,
surveys sky's bounds with hollow sightlessness,
and finds pitch dark. His eyes, crudely gouged out,
left nerves and veins dangling. He severed these.
His battle won, he calls on all the gods:
"Behold, I pray you! Spare my native land!   975
I've done what's right, endured the penalty
deserved. At last I've found the kind of night
that is appropriate for my wedding."
A loathsome, driving rain dampens his face.
His mutilated head spews streams of blood
pulsing from veins that he has torn apart.

(*The* MESSENGER *sets* OEDIPUS' *sword down on the stage and exits.
The* CHORUS *watches him leave and then turns to meditate*)

Leader: Destiny herds us on.
            Do not fight destiny.   980
            Anxiety and fretfulness
            cannot alter the spun threads
            by which we hang.
            All we endure,
            we humans marked for death,
            all that we do
            comes from above.   985
Voice 1:   Lachesis keeps guard
            on her spindle's
            downward spinning law
            which no hand can rewind.
Voice 2:   Everything moves down
            a preset path:
            the last day is determined
            by the first.
Leader: Our individual thread
            runs its straight path
            woven in its causal tapestry.   990
            No god can make it swerve,
            no prayer can shift
            what has been planned
            for each of us.
Voice 4:   Many, indeed, are ruined
            by their fear.
Voice 3:   Many achieve their destiny
            while and because
            they fear
            what destiny may have in store.

(*The palace doors open, and* OEDIPUS, *now blinded, enters*)

Leader: The sound of doors.
            Orphaned of sight,

244

	with no one guiding him,	995
	he labors his way out
	alone.

Oedipus: All's well. It's over now. I have paid all
I owed my father, as was right and just.
The darkness closes me in such relief!
What god, at last, is soothed and pours a veil
of total liquid blackness on my head   1000
and not punished my crimes? I have escaped
daylight and its awareness.
(*inwardly*)
                              You owe no debt
to your good hand. You killed your own father.
Daylight fled from you. This is the way
the face of Oedipus should display itself.

Leader: Jocasta, mad with grief and pain: 1005

Voice 1:   Look, watch!

Leader: Like a wild beast, feet flashing, pouncing,
dazed, raging, like the Theban mother who
tore off her son's head, only realizing
too late what she had done.

(*Enter* JOCASTA, *running, searching for* OEDIPUS. *When she sees him,
she stops, wants to embrace him, but checks herself. She approaches
him slowly*)

Leader: (*almost in a whisper*)
                              She hesitates
to speak to him in his deep suffering.
She wants to, fears to. Now embarrassment
and shame, faced with catastrophe, crumple.
But, as she starts to speak, her tongue won't move.

(JOCASTA *looks in silence at* OEDIPUS, *and finally finds words to
say to him*)

Jocasta: What should I call you? Child? How can you doubt:
Child you were born! Are you ashamed that you

were born my child? You would prefer silence,   1010
I know, but speak, my child.

(OEDIPUS *desperately turns his head away from the sound of her voice*)

                                                    It's so useless
to turn your head away. Your hollow face
cannot react.

Oedipus: Who tells me I must not
enjoy the blessings of my darkness now?
Who gives me back my sight? My mother's voice:
I see her sound. I've wasted all my work.
(*to* JOCASTA)
We have no right to come together now.
Vast seas should keep us, the accursèd ones,   1015
unseen miles apart, the hidden earth's
recesses, let them chasm between us now.
And if, beneath our planet, there extends
a counterworld facing an alien sky,
a sun, both distant and remote, let it be home
to one of us and carry one away.

Jocasta: For what is destined no man bears the guilt.

(OEDIPUS *approaches* JOCASTA *in a softer, more tender way*)

Oedipus: Go gently. Spare your words and spare my ears,   1020
I beg you, mother, by the relics of
my maimed body, by the accursed offspring
of my blood, and by each unholy name,
or holy name that could describe our bond.

(JOCASTA, *shamed, stops her attempt to minimize her own and*
OEDIPUS' *responsibility and tries to confront her own sense of*
guilt)

Jocasta: What slows you down, my soul? You partnered him
in crime. Why fight against your punishment?   1025
You shared incest. Through you, all decency,

all bounds of human law were blurred and lost.
So die. Force out your sinful breath with steel.
Even if the father of the gods
should shake this tidy universe and toss
shimmering bolts of fire with ruthless hand
I never could be penalized enough,
sentenced to bear what I should have to bear.   1030
Unholy mother, death is what you wish.
But how? What kind of death?

(*picking up* OEDIPUS' *sword from the stage and placing it in* OEDI-
PUS' *hands*)

                           Come, if you killed
your father, then let that same hand now help
your mother. The last chapter of your work.

(OEDIPUS *lets the sword slip from his grasp.* JOCASTA *stoops down and
picks it up*)

No. *I* must use this sword. This blade once killed
my husband—oh, give him his proper name,   1035
my bridegroom's father. So then: should I plunge
the weapon in my heart or bare my throat
and cut it to the spine? You don't know how
to choose where you should strike. Then I suggest
you thrust it here, into this ample womb
where both your husband and your sons were born.

(JOCASTA *drives the sword between her legs and upward, and then
collapses on the stage. The* CHORUS *swiftly moves to surround her
and raise her head. They look up toward* OEDIPUS, *who is unaware
of exactly what has happened*)

Leader: She lies, taken by death. And now her hand
dies as it makes the wound. Torrents of blood   1040
have pushed the blade out with their gushing flow.

(OEDIPUS *raises his hands and head to the heavens and prays*)

Oedipus: Voice of destiny, who sits as god
and arbiter of truth, I challenge you!
My father's death alone settled my debt
to destiny. Yet now I've also killed
my mother. I am twice a parricide,   1045
more lethal and more guilty than I feared.
My crime destroyed her.
                              Phoebus, how you lied!
I have surpassed the immorality
of destiny itself.

(He attempts to move forward and unwittingly begins to approach Jocasta's *body. His thoughts are now turned in upon himself)*

                              Now you must fear,
avoid, stumble through life, take roads faded
from sight, feel for footsteps, master night's
blindness with your groping hands. Hurry!

(His feet slip a little as he nears Jocasta's *corpse which is surrounded by blood from her wound)*

To exile! Stride! Your feet are slipping. Move!   1050

(His feet now come into contact with Jocasta's *corpse. He halts immediately)*

Take care, stop here! Don't fall on your mother.

*(*Oedipus *breaks from his preoccupations and turns to the audience)*

All you with bodies tired, slowed by disease,
who hardly breathe, whose hearts have almost stopped,
Look now: I go, I leave for exile. Look!
No more bowed heads. The sky, the air will turn
and stay gentler and healthier when I leave.   1055
If you lie sick, fighting for breath, clinging
to a soul struggling to flee from you,

let your being draw deep into itself
the liquid drafts, the force of life.
Hurry to help those readied for the grave,
for, as I leave, I exorcise the live
corruption that brings death. Come with me now,
brutal destiny, disease fevered
and shuddering, shriveled, wasted gauntness,
blackness of plague, insanity of pain.   1060
My pleasure now is using you as guides.

Curtain

Indexed Glossary

The indexed glossary lists most ancient names and terms mentioned in the introductory essay, all names mentioned in the texts of the two tragedies, and gives brief comments on those not discussed in the introduction. Reference is by page number; references to Sophocles' *Oedipus Tyrannus* are marked "Soph."; those to Seneca's *Oedipus,* "Sen."; and those to the introductory essay, "Two Faces of Oedipus," "Essay." Names that do not occur in the original texts but are present only as allusions, or in the essay or footnotes, are written in italics. An asterisk (*) by a word indicates that it has its own separate entry in the glossary.

Pronunciation guide. Translators of Greek tragedy want their products to be performable, so they generally (and wisely) use the traditionally familiar forms of Greek names, which are often, but not always, the Latinized versions which fall easily into the rhythms of English. English-speakers usually accent Greek words as if they were Latin and pronounce both Latin and Greek names as if they were English. So I have not followed the fashionable practice (immensely confusing to students) of giving Greek names a kind of restored Greek look (Oedipus as Oidípous, for example, Socrates as Sokrátes, or Achilles as Akhilleús), but still putting the accent on the wrong syllable and/or pronouncing them as English words. Occasionally, however, I have used, in both Seneca and Sophocles, the Greek spelling for places which tourism has made so familiar over the last fifty years that the Latinized versions now seem eccentric.

All words listed are stressed on the first syllable unless marked with an acute accent (´) to indicate that the (conventional) stress falls on some other syllable. Final "e" and "es" are *always* pronounced, as "ee" and "eez" respectively. "Ae" and "oe" are usually pronounced "ee"; but, when italicized as "*ae*" and "*oe*," they are pronounced "eye" and "oy" respectively. Both "c" and "ch" are pronounced "k" except before "e," "i," or "y," a diphthong pronounced like an "e" or "i," when "c" is traditionally pronounced "s." When "c" = "s" the "*c*" is italicized. In those instances where "c" is pronounced "sh" it is written as "ç"). "G" is pronounced as in English (like "g" in *goal* before an "a," "o," or "u," but (when italicized) as "*g*" in *general* (before "e," "i," and "y" and any diphthong that is pronounced like an "e" or "i").

Most Americans pronounce Oedipus "Edipus" (as I do). But the British pronunciation "Eedipus" is gaining ground in scholarly circles.

Ab*ae*, in Phocis★ (Greece), site of a temple of Apollo★ that had been sacked by the Persians in 480 BC and was in ruins (but still consulted by the Thebans★) in Sophocles'★ day: Soph. 169

Acheron, a river in the underworld; the underworld itself: Sen. 224

Actaéon, cousin of Pentheus,★ killed by his own hounds on Mt. Cithaeron★ either because he tried to rob Zeus★ of Semele's★ love or because he had seen the goddess Artemis★ bathing naked: Sen. 232

Adrástus, king of Argos,★ only survivor of the "Seven against Thebes"★: Essay 85

Aegéan, the sea between Greece and Asia Minor: Essay 96; Sen. 220

Aegýptus, father of fifty sons who were married to the fifty daughters of Danaus.★ All but one were killed on their wedding night by their wives: Essay 75

Aenéas, Trojan prince, cousin of Hector, son of Venus and Anchises, who fled Troy as that city fell to the Greeks; hero of Virgil's★ *Aeneid:* Essay 31, 117, 120–121, 216n

Aeschylus, first Greek tragedian any of whose works survive: Essay 7–8, 17n, 18, 20, 38, 40–41, 49, 55, 60–61, 63–70, 72–73, 76–77, 79–80, 83, 91–92, 103, 125

Agamémnon, king of Mycenae★ (and in later Greek tradition, Argos★), who commanded the Greek forces at Troy in the Trojan War; title of tragedies by Seneca and Aeschylus★: Essay 14–15, 35, 40, 49, 61, 72, 93, 124

Agáve, daughter of Cadmus★ and mother of Pentheus,★ whom she kills while under the control of Dionysus★: Essay 21; Sen. 226, 242

Agenor, founder of the kingdom of Phoenicia,★ ancestor of Cadmus,★ the founder of Thebes★ in Greece: Soph. 146, 230

Agríppa, Marcus Vipsanius Agrippa, Octavian's★ admiral during the civil wars at Rome between 36 and 31 BC, who defeated Octavian's major enemies (Sextus Pompey,★ Cleopatra queen of Egypt, and Mark Antony). Agrippa was for many years the heir-presumptive to Octavian's power: Essay 129–130

Agrippína (the Younger), the emperor Nero's★ mother; murdered on Nero's orders: Essay 13

Ajax, second-ranked Greek warrior in the *Iliad*, who, robbed of his senses by Athena, butchers livestock instead of the major Greek officers he planned to kill (for the Greeks had failed to award him the armor of the dead Achilles, to which he believed himself entitled); on realizing what he has done, he kills himself in shame; Sophocles' tragedy of that name: Essay 9, 39, 41

Alexander the Great, king of Macedon 336–323 BC and conqueror of the Persian Empire: Essay 96; Soph. 143n; Sen. 220n

Amazons, mythical female warriors who lived in the vicinity of the Black Sea: Sen. 220

Amphion, founder (along with Zethus★) of Greek Thebes★ in some traditions: Essay 76n; Sen. 206, 226

Andrómache, widow of Hector★; her son Astyanax was sacrificed by the Greeks after the fall of Troy (a major theme in Seneca's *Trojan Women*, and a lesser theme in Euripides' *Trojan Women*); she was given as a concubine to Pyrrhus (son of Achilles) after Troy's fall, and had a child by him (Euripides' *Andromache*; Virgil, *Aeneid* 3). When Pyrrhus was killed by Orestes, his rival for the love of Hermione, Helen's daughter, he willed Andromache and part of his kingdom to Helenus, Hector's brother, who had saved Pyrrhus' life by advising him how to return to Greece safely: Essay 93, 99, 117, 124

Antígone, daughter of Oedipus★ and either Euryganeia★ or Epicaste★ in some early traditions; in Sophocles★ and Seneca,★ Jocasta★ is her mother; name of a tragedy by Sophocles: Essay 9, 39, 41, 45–46, 63, 70–72, 93, 113; Soph. 135n, 191n, 193n

Antíphanes, Greek comic poet of the fourth century BC, whose works survive only in fragments: Essay 60, 63, 73

Apóllo, a god associated with prophecy, music, the bow, plagues, and often with the Sun (Gk. Helios, Latin Sol), also called upon as Phoebus★: Essay 29, 38, 40, 44, 51, 54, 62, 64, 85, 97–98, 107; Soph. 137, 139, 141, 150–151, 155, 163, 167, 169–170, 172, 186; Sen. 200

Arabs, a Semitic people that, in Sophocles'★ and Seneca's★ day, lived mostly in Yemen and adjacent areas: Sen. 204

Aráxes, a river running through Armenia which was, more or less, the eastern boundary of Roman power, dividing Armenia from Parthia (Persia): Sen. 218

Artemidórus of Daldi, second-century AD Greek author of a book about dreams: Essay 89

Arctic: Sen. 220, 225

Arctúrus, a bright star whose setting and, more particularly, whose rising in the autumn bring bad weather: Essay 65; Soph. 178

Ares (usually pronounced "air-ease"), god linked with war and with what were in antiquity the wild areas of northeastern Greece, Thrace★; roughly the equivalent of the Roman war god Mars: Soph. 143

253

Argos/Argive, city in the Peloponnesus,★ successor to the power of Mycenae★;
 sacred to Hera★ (Roman Juno★). In myth Argos is symbolic of Greece
 and Greek power; "the Argives" often = the Greeks in general: Essay 68,
 72, 76, 85; Sen. 220

Ariádne, daughter of Minos★ king of Knossos,★ sister of Phaedra,★ and half-sister of
 the Minotaur (see Theseus★). She helped Theseus kill the Minotaur and
 escape from the maze where it was kept, and fled with him. But he abandoned her on the island of Naxos,★ where she was found by, and became
 the bride of, Dionysus★: Sen. 220

Aristóphanes, younger contemporary of Sophocles,★ whose comedies satirized many
 of his contemporaries, including Aeschylus★ (in his *Frogs*), Sophocles★
 (*Birds*), Euripides★ (*Thesmophoriazusae, Frogs*), Socrates★ (*Clouds*), Cleon★
 (*Knights*): Essay 5n, 7–8, 42–43, 61, 64, 66, 68, 82, 92–93, 101–103

Aristotle, philosopher of the fourth century BC and tutor to Alexander the Great★;
 his *Poetics* is the first surviving work in which anyone tries to prescribe in
 detail what tragedy ought to be: Essay 9, 31, 52–53, 83, 93, 101, 124

Asclépius, son of Apollo★ and famous as a healer; killed by Zeus,★ but brought back
 from the dead by Apollo★; god of medicine: Essay 8–10, 126

Artemis, virgin goddess, presiding over hunting, night-time dark (and thus linked
 with the moon); twin sister of Apollo★ (she was born on the sixth day of
 the month, Apollo on the seventh, though traditions are inconsistent as to
 which month); she also is the goddess invoked at childbirth: her Roman
 counterpart is Diana★: Essay 35, 96; Soph. 141, 143

Asia, generally means Asia Minor (the Middle East) in Greek and Roman writers:
 Essay 127; Sen. 220

Athéna, virgin goddess both of war (she is often represented in armor) and of civilized arts (particularly spinning and weaving); patron goddess of Athens;
 also known as Pallas (Athena) and as Minerva (by the Romans): Essay 36,
 38–39, 83, 97; Soph. 137, 141

Athenaéus, learned Greek of the second century AD, author of a work called *Deipnosophists* (= Learned Men at Dinner): Essay 60, 79n

Athens, main city in the Greek region of Attica; Athens became a powerful imperial
 democracy in the fifth century BC and home to tragedy, comedy, philosophy, medicine, and the arts: Essay 2, 5–11, 15, 20, 31, 36, 40, 42, 43,
 59–62, 64, 71–72, 76, 80, 83–87, 90, 95, 97–103, 113–115, 118, 121–122,
 126–127; Soph. 145n

Augústus, "the August One," the title assumed by Caius Iulius Caesar Octavianus
 (Octavian★) when he had consolidated his control of the Roman world in
 27 BC. He is the second "Caesar" (and was son, by adoption, of the first
 "Caesar," Caius Iulius Caesar): Essay 12, 15, 34, 116, 120, 129–131

Bacchanals, revels and revellers associated with the god Bacchus★ (Dionysus★): Sen.
 177

Bacchae, title of a tragedy by Euripides: Essay 21, 108, 178

Bacchus, also known as Dionysus,★ honored as the god protecting the vine at springtime festivals in Athens and other cities. He also represents the power of

254

wine and the violent passions and behavior it induces: Essay 84; Soph. 143; Sen. 197–198, 204–205, 210, 213, 216–221, 224

Bassarids, followers of the god Bacchus★ (Dionysus★), so named because they wore fox-skins (*bassara* = fox, fox-skin); Bacchus himself was sometimes called Bassareus: Sen. 218

Bear Constellations, Ursa Major and Ursa Minor, the Greater and Lesser Bear: Sen. 220–221

Black Sea, called the Euxine Sea in antiquity, bordered by modern Turkey, Bulgaria, Ukraine, Russia, and the Republic of Georgia; the eastern limit of Greek maritime travel from the 8th century BC until the days of Alexander the Great★

Boeótia, "Oxland," the region of central Greece in which Thebes★ is situated: Essay 57, 78–79; Sen. 228

Briáreus, a hundred-armed giant who in some traditions guarded the Titans★ (enemies of the Olympian gods) in the underworld: in passage from the *Aeneid* facing p. 1.

Cadmus, son of Agenor★ of Phoenicia,★ founder of Thebes★ and ancestor of Laius★ (son of Labdacus, son of Polydorus, son of Cadmus): Essay 21, 62, 76, 78; Soph. 136–137, 146; Sen. 204, 206, 218–219, 225–226, 230–232

Calígula, nickname of the Roman emperor Caius Caesar Augustus Germanicus, the fourth "Caesar": Essay 12, 13, 15

Callísto, a nymph in the service of Artemis★; she was raped by Zeus,★ metamorphosed into a bear by Artemis, and, in some traditions, made one of the stars in the Bear Constellation★: Sen. 221

Carthage, Phoenician colony established in North Africa (Tunis), traditionally in 814 BC (the more likely date is 673–663 BC); major power in western Mediterranean until destroyed by Rome in 146 BC: Essay 31

Castálian Springs, at Delphi,★ linked with the oracle (prophetic shrine) of Apollo★: Sen. 208, 210, 230

Cerberus, mythical three-headed dog guarding the entrance to the underworld: Sen. 224

Ceres, goddess who watches over grain (hence "cereals") and agriculture, the Roman equivalent of Greek Demeter; mother of Proserpina (Gk. Persephone) who was abducted by Pluto, god of the dead: Sen. 201

Cithaeron, a mountain range bordering Thebes★: Essay 49–50, 65–66, 74; Soph. 152, 174, 176, 178, 188, 191; Sen. 219, 235, 237, 241

Chance, Greek *tyche,* Latin *casus* or *fortuna:* Essay 10, 13, 19, 26–27, 47–51, 55, 61, 64–65, 67–68, 123, 125; Soph. 139, 146, 153, 157, 164, 171–172, 174, 176–177, 191, 194; Sen. 236

Chaónia, a region in Epirus, named for Chaon, brother of the Trojan prince Helenus; home to Dodona,★ a city famous for its oracle of Jupiter: Sen. 231

Chimaéra, a monster in Lycia★ (Asia Minor): a goat with a lion's head and a dragon's tail: in passage from the *Aeneid* facing p. 1

Chorus, the singing dancers who were originally the dominant presence in a Greek tragedy (or comedy), but whose role is progressively diminished by the addition of a second actor (by Aeschylus) and of a third actor (by Sophocles): Essay 18–21, 25–26, 28–30, 32–33, 37–38, 44, 46, 48, 53, 61, 82, 84, 90–91, 94–95, 104, 106–107, 110, 124–125; Soph. 135, 141, 146–147, 150–151, 153–156, 158–162, 166–170, 175–177, 180–182, 185–187, 189, 194; Sen. 197, 204, 209, 211, 216–219, 226–228, 230–231, 239, 244, 248

Christianity, Essay 4, 12, 23–24, 30, 34–35, 38, 60, 122

Claudius, Tiberius Claudius Nero, the fifth "Caesar": Essay 13, 15, 114, 122

Cleisthenes of Athens, descendant of Cleisthenes of Sicyon★ and founder of democracy in Athens (510 BC): Essay 85, 87

Cleisthenes of Sicyon, tyrant of Sicyon,★ a city near Corinth,★ who reorganized that city's tribes and poetic festivals: Essay 84–85, 87

Cleitias, Athenian painter whose signature is on the François vase (which gives a different list of participants in the chariot race at Patroclus' funeral from that given by Homer in *Iliad* 23): Essay 37

Clytemnéstra, wife of Agamemnon,★ mother of Iphigeneia,★ Electra,★ and Orestes★; she killed Agamemnon when he returned from Troy (according to the version in the tragedians) and was herself killed by Orestes (abetted by Electra): Essay 38, 61

Cleon, popular leader at Athens, whose influence was at its height between 428 and 422 BC, around the time that Sophocles probably wrote *Oedipus:* Essay 6, 10–11, 95, 99–103

Corinth, city on the narrow strip of land connecting the Peloponnesus★ to the rest of Greece, with ports on the seashores of both sides; city where Oedipus was raised, and of which he was a citizen. Corinth was a major military and trading city in Greece until it was sacked by the Romans in 146 BC: Essay 5–6, 9, 19–21, 36, 41, 44–49, 52, 65, 73, 75, 78–80, 84–85, 95, 97, 104–105; Soph. 165, 170–173, 177, 188; Sen. 210n, 234

The Corínthian, also marked in texts and some translations as "messenger (from Corinth)": Essay 9, 19–21, 36, 41, 44–49, 51–52, 54–55, 65–67, 74, 85–86, 91, 95, 105, 108, 110–111, 125; Soph. 135, 164–165, 169–175, 177–180, 183n; Sen. 197, 234–239

Cordoba, city in Spain, birthplace of both Senecas★ and of Lucan★: Essay 11–12

Courtier: Essay 91; Soph. 135, 182–183, 185

Cratylus, dialogue of Plato★ in which Socrates★ discusses the nature of language with the learned Cratylus: Essay 79n, 105, 108–111

Creon, "Ruler," son of Menoeceus, brother of Jocasta★; in some mythic versions, father of another Menoeceus who gives his life for Thebes; in yet others (Sophocles' *Antigone*) father of Haemon who is pledged to Antigone,★ daughter of Oedipus. He usually becomes tyrant of Thebes after the death of Oedipus' sons; in Sophocles, uniquely, he becomes tyrant before their deaths: Essay 2–3, 6, 10, 17–22, 29, 32–33, 39, 41, 43, 46, 49, 56–59, 62–63, 69–72, 76, 78, 80–82, 91, 93, 94, 97, 100–104, 110–113, 121, 125–127; Soph. 135, 138

Critias, a student of Socrates★ who overthrew Athenian democracy in a coup d'état in 404 BC; he instituted the reign of the so-called thirty tyrants, but was defeated by democratic forces a few months later: Essay 5, 7–8

Cupid, son of Venus,★ in later Greek myth; also known as Eros by the Greeks and Amor by the Romans. In art from the third century BC onward he is often represented as a very young child armed with a bow that causes people to fall in love, and is frequently pluralized in paintings and sculptures: Sen. 221

Cyclops, name of a satyr play written by Euripides: Essay 61, 102, 107. See also Polyphemus★

Cylléne, mountain in Arcadia (Greece), birthplace of Hermes★ (Latin Mercury) who is often called the "Cyllenian" god: Soph. 177

Dacia, a Roman province including modern Romania: Sen. 220

Daedalus, mythic Athenian artist who designs the labyrinth maze in Knossos★ for Minos,★ its king, and who, when imprisoned there, escapes with his son Icarus by inventing wings; Icarus rashly flies too high and is killed. In Roman literature he is sometimes symbolic of the artist who is obliged to work on commissions from the emperor: Sen. 240

Danaus, king of Argos who married his fifty daughters to the fifty sons of Aegyptus★: Essay 75–76. See also Aegyptus★

Danube, the great European river that flows into the Black Sea: Soph. 182

Daulis, a city in Phocis; site, in some versions, of the mythical banquet of Tereus; after Tereus raped Philomela, sister of his wife Procne, his wife, in revenge, fed him his own child, Itys, for dinner: Soph. 163

Delos, Aegean island near Mykonos★ and a cult center of Apollo among the Ionian★ Greeks: Essay 98, Soph. 141

Delphi, city in the mountains north of the Gulf of Corinth and famous for its cult and oracle of Apollo★; during the Peloponnesian War★ it was largely under the control of Athens'★ foes, the Spartans★: Essay 2–3, 20, 41–42, 54, 78, 80–81, 86, 96–99, 102, 104, 106, 121–122; Soph. 138, 145, 154, 163; Sen. 207, 210, 230, 234

Demos (= "People"), allegorical character in Aristophanes'★ comedy *Knights,* symbolizing the gullible populace of Athens★: Essay 89, 102

Demósthenes, famous Greek orator, politician, and law-court advocate in fourth-century Athens: Essay 53

Destiny, the course of events seen as predetermined by divine or mechanistic forces: Essay 13, 16, 23–29, 39–40, 69, 111, 124; Sen. 202, 234, 236, 238–239, 241, 244, 246, 248–249. See also Fate★

Diána, Roman equivalent of Artemis★: Sen. 232

Dido, mythical founder of Carthage★: Essay 31, 117

Diógenes, philosopher of the fourth century BC, who rejected (and satirized) human preoccupation with possessions and with themselves: Essay 1

Dionysus, the more official name for the god evoked as Bacchus★; the presiding deity of drama; commonly represented as born in Thebes★ as the son of Zeus★

(Jupiter) and Semele★ (daughter of Cadmus★); represented as a foppish character on stage in Aristophanes'★ *Frogs* and as a much more menacing figure in Euripides'★ tragedy *Bacchae*, where he causes his aunt (Agave,★ Semele's★ sister) to tear her own son Pentheus★ to pieces: Essay 7–8, 2, 38, 64, 83–84, 90, 92, 108, 122

Dirce, wife of a ruler named Lycus and aunt of the twins Amphion★ and Zethus.★ She was jealous of, and imprisoned and mistreated, the twins' mother Antiope; the twins took vengeance on her by harnessing her to a bull and having her torn to pieces: Sen. 201, 206, 208, 223, 230

Dis, one of several Roman names for the god of the underworld (also Orcus,★ Pluto,★ "Stygian Jupiter") = Greek Hades,★ Pluto★: Essay 57; Sen. 216, 225

Domitian, Titus Flavius Domitianus, the twelfth Caesar: Essay 117, 119, 128

Dorian, a term used generally to indicate Greeks (as opposed to non-Greeks), and also to distinguish Greeks from the Peloponnesus (and parts of central Greece) from the Ionian★ Greeks of Athens, the Aegean, and Asia Minor: Soph. 164

Edónia, another name for parts of northeastern Greece, particularly Thrace★: Sen. 218

Electra, sister of Orestes★ who aided him in killing their mother; title of two tragedies, one by Sophocles,★ one by Euripides★; see also *Clytemnestra★* and *Orestes★:* Essay 9, 38, 61. 93, 99

Epicáste, name of Oedipus' first wife in the Greek epic tradition: Essay 62, 78–79

Epicuréan, school of philosophy founded by Epicurus in the fourth century BC: Essay 13, 20, 124

Eryx: (1) a Sicilian mountain and town; (2) a son of Venus and king of Sicily who founded that town: Sen. 225

Etéocles, one of two sons of Oedipus★ (the other was Polyneices★); after Oedipus blinded himself, they fought a bitter war over the throne. It culminated in their deaths at each other's hands: Essay 62–63, 68, 70–72, 74, 85, 121, 125

Eurygáneia, (second) wife of Oedipus in the epic tradition: Essay 62, 68, 73. See also Epicaste★ and Jocasta★

Eurípides, Athenian tragedian, author of eighteen surviving tragedies and one satyr play; younger contemporary of Sophocles: Essay 7–8, 10, 18, 21, 35, 38–41, 51, 55, 60–61, 62–64, 67–68, 72–75, 81–83, 90–92, 95, 99–100, 103, 107, 122

Evénus, river in Aetolia (north-central Greece): Sen. 211

Fate, "the pronouncement of Jupiter," destiny: Essay 13–14, 24–28, 33, 35, 39, 55, 57, 123, 125; Sen. 200, 202, 204, 207, 208, 211–212, 217, 230, 242

Forked Road (Greek *Schistè Hodós*), the place where, traditionally, Laius★ was killed: Essay 78–80; Soph. 163; Sen. 209–210

Flavian dynasty, the tenth through twelfth Caesars (Vespasian, Titus, Domitian): Essay 128

Four emperors, Year of, AD 69 when Galba, Otho, Vitellius, and Vespasian★ seized power in turn in a series of vicious civil wars: Essay 128

François vase: Essay 37

Freud, Sigmund Freud, modern founder of psychology and framer of "the Oedipus complex": Essay 16, 18, 22, 24–28, 30, 43, 53, 88, 105

Furies, spirits of vengeance symbolizing the wrath of a dead person that afflicts his or her killer; more generally, demons of destructive madness: Essay 38; Sen. 205, 227

Gallio, Lucius Iunius Novatus Gallio, brother of the Younger Seneca★: Essay 12

Ganges, the great river of India: Sen. 218

Gelóni, a people of the northern Black Sea area: Sen. 220

Hades, thought by many Greeks, most notably Plato, to come from the negation of the root "id-", "to see"; hence the Unseen One, or the Unseeing, the Dead; another name for Pluto,★ god of the underworld and also a name for the underworld itself. See also Dis★ and Orcus★: Essay 62; Soph. 172, 187

Hector, the most important Trojan warrior in the Trojan War; killed and mutilated by Achilles★: Essay 31, 117, 124

Heracles, son of Zeus★ and Alcmena, born in Thebes★; the most powerful of all Greek mythic heroes: Essay 39, 79, 101

Hercules, Roman equivalent of Heracles★: Essay 15, 39, 114; Sen. 232

Hermes, Roman Mercury, the god most commonly used as a messenger by Zeus; he is linked with the rough pastoral world of Arcadia (north central Peloponnesus★): Soph. 177

Heródotus, contemporary of Sophocles and the earliest surviving writer of Greek prose and Greek history: Essay 17–18, 36, 76, 85–86, 127

Hippias, the last of the family of the Athenian tyrant Peisistratus,★ who hoped to be restored to power when Xerxes of Persia invaded Greece in 480 BC: Essay 86, 90, 129

Hippócrates, contemporary of Sophocles, Greek philosopher and scientist who founded the first school of medicine in Athens★ in the fifth century BC: Essay 8–9, 42

Hybla, a mountain (and city) in Sicily, famous for bees and honey: Sen. 225

India: Essay 21; Sen. 204, 219

Ino, daughter of Cadmus★ and sister to Agave★ and Semele★; in some traditions, she raises the infant Dionysus★ after he is rescued from the womb of Semele★ when the latter is destroyed by Zeus' thunderbolt. Ino and her husband are punished for this act of charity by Hera,★ who drives them both so mad that they kill their own children. On realizing what she has done, Ino leaps into the sea with the body of her son Melicertes. She is transformed into the nymph Leucothea (the "White goddess" of the foam) and her son into a sea-god, Palaemon. Both aid sailors at sea (Ino saves Odysseus in *Odyssey* 5): Essay 21; Sen. 219

Ion, king of Athens and founder of the Ionian★ people; title of a tragedy by Euripides: Essay 51, 95, 99

Iónia, Iónians, the Greek cities (and their inhabitants) on what is now the coast of Turkey; also most of the Aegean islands and their inhabitants; Athens also considered itself an Ionian city. There was a myth that Ion, son of Apollo,★ became king of Athens and thus established the roots of the Ionian peoples (Euripides' tragedy *Ion* gives a version of the tale): Essay 36, 95, 98; Sen. 225

Iphigeneía, first-born daughter of Agamemnon★ and Clytemnestra,★ sacrificed by Agamemnon to secure passage of the Greek fleet to Troy at the beginning of the Trojan War; title character in two tragedies by Euripides (*Iphigeneia in Aulis; Iphigeneia among the Taurians*): Essay 35, 39, 91

Isméne, daughter of Oedipus, sister of Antigone★: Essay 23, 135, 191, 193

Ismenus, a river in Boeotia, near Thebes★: Soph. 137

Jocásta, wife of Oedipus (in writers of the fifth century BC and later): Essay 19, 41–42, 44–49, 51, 54, 57–60, 62–63, 66, 68, 70–74, 79–8, 86, 89, 91, 94, 102, 105, 110–111, 113, 118, 131; Soph. 135, 160–164, 166–167, 169–172, 175–176, 182–183; Sen. 197, 199–200, 202–204, 233–234, 236, 245–248. See also Epicaste★ and Euryganeia★

Julio-Claudian, the family ruling Rome from, in effect, 48 BC to AD 68 (Julius Caesar, Octavian [Augustus], Tiberius, Caligula, Claudius, Nero): Essay 12

Julius Caesar, Caius Iulius Caesar, conquered Gaul (59–49 BC), established himself as perpetual dictator of Rome after a civil war (49–45 BC); murdered in 44 BC: Essay 22, 86, 103, 120, 129–130

Jupiter, Roman equivalent of Zeus★: Essay 27; Sen. 209, 221, 231

Knossos, principal city of Crete in the days of king Minos★: Sen. 240

Labdacism, a speech impediment (and aristocratic affectation) causing the substitution of "l" (Greek la(m)bda) for "r": Essay 101–102

Labdacus, ruler of Thebes, father of Laius★: Essay 29, 102; Soph. 144, 146, 155, 182

Lachesis, one of three divine sisters who are represented as spinning (Clotho), measuring (Lachesis), and cutting (Atropos) the threads of individual human lives: Essay 25; Sen. 244

Laius,★ son of Labdacus,★ first husband of Jocasta★: Essay 2–3, 18–19, 28, 32, 41, 54, 56–60, 63, 66, 68, 70, 72–74, 78–82, 102, 106, 120–121, 130–131; Soph. 139–140, 144, 147, 157–158, 162–164, 166, 167, 169, 174, 177–180, 182–183, 188; Sen. 207, 209, 215, 226, 228, 233, 237

Lesbos, Aegean island, famous for its poets (notably Sappho, Alcaeus, and the mythic Arion); one of its main cities is Mytilene,★ which the Athenians came close to exterminating in 427 BC: Sen. 221

Leto (Roman form is usually Latona), mother of Apollo and Artemis (Roman Diana): Sen. 208

Libation Bearers, tragedy by Aeschylus: Essay 61. See also ★Electra:

Livy, Titus Livius, contemporary of Virgil and Octavian, who wrote a huge history of Rome of which some parts survive: Essay 126–127

Loxias, an epithet for Apollo,★ said to be derived from a word meaning "obscure": Soph. 167, 172, 177

Lucan, Marcus Annaeus Lucanus, nephew of the Younger Seneca, Roman senator, author of *Pharsalia* (also called *The Civil War*), who spearheaded a conspiracy to murder the emperor Nero: Essay 11–12, 117, 121, 127

Lucretius, Titus Lucretius Carus, Roman epic poet and Epicurean philosopher of the early first century BC; author of *De Rerum Natura (On the Nature of Things):* Essay 20, 124

Lycaéan, associated with Mount Lycaeus (Greek Lykaios) in Arcadia (in the Peloponnesus); used of Zeus and Pan as well as of Apollo (as it is in Sophocles' *Oedipus,* where perhaps the reference is to Apollo's temple at Bassae): Essay 44, 87; Soph. 143, 170

Lycia, a mountainous country with high peaks along its coastline, in what is now the southeast of Turkey; Apollo had a shrine there at the town of Patara: Soph. 143

Lycúrgus, mythical king of Edonia★ (Thrace), who banned the worship of Bacchus★ and the cultivation of the vine in his lands and was punished by the god for doing so: Sen. 220

Lydia, a country in Asia Minor, which enjoyed its most glorious days in the first half of the sixth century BC; held by many Romans to be the original home of the Etruscans, who are often called Lydians by Roman poets: Essay 36, 127; Sen. 220

Maenad, a woman frenzied by the influence of Bacchus★: Soph. 144; Sen. 197, 218, 220, 226

Maeótis, area round the Sea of Azov, home to the nomadic Maeotians: Sen. 220

Manto, daughter of Teiresias★ in Seneca' *Oedipus:* Essay 21, 122; Sen. 197, 211–214, 216, 225

Massagétae, a people living to the east of the Caspian Sea (Mongolia): Sen. 220

Medéa, daughter of Aeétes, king of Colchis,★ who was made to fall in love with Jason, leader of the Argonauts, helped him gain the golden fleece, and returned with him to Greece: Essay 14–15, 93, 112, 114, 116–120, 124

Mela, Lucius Annaeus Mela, son of the Elder Seneca★ and brother of the Younger; father of Lucan★: Essay 11–12

Melaníppus, a Theban warrior fighting for Eteocles★ against the foreign forces led by his brother Polyneices★; famous for killing Tydeus (father of Homer's Diomedes): Essay 85

Meletus, fifth-century BC intellectual and poet, author of a tragedy *Oedipus;* most famous for being one of Socrates' accusers: Essay 18, 64, 104

Melos, island in the Aegean whose male population was exterminated and whose women and children were sold into slavery by the Athenians in 416 BC: Essay 6

Menoéçeus, father of Creon★; also the name of a son of Creon's in some authors: Essay 127; Soph. 138–139, 193

Merope = "human," mother (or in most traditions, stepmother) of Oedipus: Essay 41, 74; Soph. 164, 172; Sen. 210, 228, 235

Messalína, first wife of the emperor Claudius: Essay 13

Mytiléne, city in Lesbos threatened with annihilation by the Athenians, under Cleon's influence, in 427 BC: Essay 6

Naxos, Aegean island where Theseus★ abandoned Ariadne★ and Dionysus★ found her: Sen. 220

Neptune, Roman sea-god (Gk. Poseidon): Sen. 209–210

Nereid, a sea-nymph, "daughter" of Nereus★: Sen. 219

Nereus, a lesser sea-god: Sen. 219, 221

Nero, Nero Claudius Caesar Drusus Germanicus, the fifth Caesar (born Lucius Domitius Ahenobarbus), tutored by Seneca★ the Younger; forced the deaths of the Younger Seneca and many others in the aftermath of a botched coup d'état (AD 65) in which Lucan★ was a leading figure: Essay 12–15, 114, 117, 121, 128

Nióbe, daughter of Tantalus and wife of Amphion,★ king of Thebes★; she boasted that her seven sons and daughters far outdid the twins of Leda, Apollo★ and Artemis★; in retaliation, the two gods killed all her children. Niobe herself was metamorphosed into stone that forever streamed with water: Sen. 226

Nile, the famous river of Egypt: Sen. 225

Oblivion: Essay 4, 106; Soph. 168; Sen. 224

Ocean: Sen. 199, 204, 209, 221

Odýsseus, hero of the *Odyssey*★; usually a villainous character in tragedy: Essay 36, 39, 61–63, 105–108

Ódyssey, the Homeric epic telling of Odysseus'★ return home: Essay 36–37, 59, 61–62, 67, 75, 105–108, 121

Oedipus: Essay, Sen., and Soph. throughout

Oedipus at Colonus, last tragedy of Sophocles: Essay 9, 63, 71–73

Olenus, town in Aetolia, north-central Greece (there is another town of the same name in the Peloponnesus), famous as the home of Tydeus★: Sen. 211

Olýmpia, town in the Peloponnesus famous for its Temple of Zeus: Soph. 169

Olýmpus, Olympians, (1) mountain in northern Greece; (2) the heights (and inhabitants) of heaven: Essay 40; Soph. 167–168n, 177

Orcus, Roman god of the underworld, Death; also, the underworld itself: in passage from the *Aeneid* facing p. 1

Oréstes, son of Agamemnon★ and Clytemnestra★; he killed his mother and was driven mad by the Furies★; title of a tragedy by Euripides: Essay 38–40, 61, 90–92, 99–100, 117. See also *Electra*★

Ovid, older contemporary of the Elder Seneca★ and one of Rome's greatest poets; author of *Metamorphoses*: Essay 11, 23, 31, 41n, 116, 130

Oxland = Boeotia: Sen. 231

Paches, commander of the Athenian force sent to destroy Mytilene: Essay 6

Pactolus, river near Sardis★ famous for yielding gold-dust and nuggets: Sen. 220

Palaémon, name of Ino's★ son after he becomes a sea-god; see Ino★: Sen. 219

Pan, lecherous rural deity, often represented as a goat: Soph. 176

Pangaéus, a mountain on the border between Thrace★ and Macedonia: Sen. 218

Parnássus, mountain with double peaks at Delphi: Soph. 154; Sen. 208, 210

Patróclus, friend of Achilles★ who took Achilles' place in battle and wore his armor, but was killed by Hector: Essay 37

Paul, the apostle, traditionally executed in Rome in Nero's★ reign: Essay 12

Pausánias, second-century AD Greek traveler, geographer, and commentator on ancient sites; author of *The Description of Greece:* Essay 62, 77, 79–80, 82, 86, 98

Peisístratus, tyrant of Athens in the sixth century BC; collector and editor of Homer's epics, and credited with the establishment of tragic performances at the festivals of Dionysus★: Essay 36–38, 59, 83–86, 90

Pelopónnesus, Greece south of the Isthmus of Corinth★ (literally = the Island of Pelops★); dominated by Sparta★ in Sophocles' day. Sparta and the major cities of the eastern Peloponnesus (except Argos), together with Thebes★ in central Greece, constituted the main body of the Peloponnesian League which waged what the Athenians called the Peloponnesian War on Athens, on and off, between 431 and 404 BC: Essay 5, 71, 97–99, 120

Pelops, son of Tantalus, killed and served to the gods by his father Tantalus,★ but restored to life by Zeus★; ancestor of the royal house of Mycenae★: Essay 35

Pentheus, son of Agave★ (Cadmus'★ daughter), and killed by her when he tried to observe the women's revels honoring Dionysus★: Essay 21, 108, 117; Sen. 218–219, 226

Pericles, leading politician in Athens in the mid fifth century BC: Essay 5n, 10–11, 87, 92, 95–97, 99–100, 103–104

Phaedra, sister of Ariadne★ and wife of Theseus★ who fell in love with her stepson Hippolytus; Seneca's tragedy of that name: Essay 12, 15, 39, 95, 114, 118–119, 124

Phasis, river in what is now the Republic of Georgia, flowing into the Black Sea at Colchis★; home of Medea★: Soph. 182

Philoctétes, heir to the famous bow of Heracles whose aid was needed to accomplish the fall of Troy; title of a tragedy by Sophocles: Essay 9, 39, 102

Phoebe, sister of Phoebus★; Artemis★ (Roman Diana): Sen. 209

Phoebus, Apollo as "the one who illuminates": Essay 39–40, 99: Soph. 138–141, 146–147, 162, 165, 173, 176; Sen. 200–201, 203–204, 207–211, 219, 221, 223, 231, 248

Phoenícia, Phoenícians, the inhabitants of what is now, roughly, modern Lebanon: Essay 36, 76, 79

Phoeniçian Women, title of tragedies by Euripides★ and Seneca★: Essay 15, 21, 58, 63, 72–74, 83, 114

Phocis, the province of Greece in which Delphi★ is situated: Essay 57; Soph. 163; Sen. 210, 233

Phorbas, Greek word for a herdsman used as a name: Essay 66; Sen. 197, 237–239

Phrygia, an area of Asia Minor east of Troy; "Phrygian" often = Trojan, though usually with overtones suggesting effeminacy: Sen. 217

Pindus, a high mountain (range) in northwest Greece; one of the homes of the Muses: Sen. 218

Plato, Athenian philosopher, poet, and critic of the fourth century BC: Essay 1, 8, 16, 38, 40–41, 43, 64, 79, 87–88, 90, 93, 98–99, 104, 106, 108

Socrates, philosopher of the fifth century BC, contemporary of Sophocles: Essay 1, 5, 7–8, 18, 38, 40, 42–43, 64, 87–88, 92, 97–98, 101, 104, 106, 110

Sophilos, sixth-century BC Greek potter and painter: Essay 37

Sophillos, father of Sophocles: Essay 5, 37

Sophocles, son of Sophillos, the poet: Essay 1–24, 26–28, 30–33, 37–46, 48–56, 58–61, 63, 65–74, 76, 78–85, 88–93, 95–97, 99–115, 117–118, 120–122, 125–126, 131–132; Soph. 134

Sophocles, son of Sostratides, the general: Essay 5

Sparta, Spartans, militarized city-state in the Peloponnesus; Athens'★ leading opponent in the Peloponnesian War★: Essay 5–8, 76, 86, 96–100; Sen. 205

Sphinx: Essay 1–2, 19, 56, 53, 74–79, 82, 89, 96, 106, 109–111, 120, 129–131; Soph. 140; Sen. 203, 209, 227; symbol on Augustus' signet-ring: Essay 130–31; title of satyr play by Aeschylus: Essay 79

Statius, Publius Papinius Statius, Roman epic poet of the late first century AD; author of the *Thebaid:* Essay 62, 70, 74, 76, 121, 127–128

Stesíchorus, Greek poet of the seventh century BC: Essay 37

Stoicism, school of philosophy founded in the fourth century BC: Essay 13–16, 23, 26–27, 30, 123–25

Strymon, a river in Thrace★: Sen. 225

Styx, Stygian, the most famous underworld river and the adjective used to evoke its deathly associations: Sen. 205, 216

Tantalus, punished by the gods for killing his son Pelops★ and serving him to the gods at a banquet: Essay 35; Sen. 226

Teirésias, master of prodigies, the most famous prophet of Thebes★: Essay 1–2, 21, 29, 39, 41, 43, 46, 48, 49, 70, 91, 94, 97, 100, 104, 106–107, 110–112, 121–122, 125, 130; Soph. 135, 146–153; Sen. 197–198, 211–216, 225, 229

Suppliants, title of tragedies by Aeschylus★ and Euripides★: Essay 62–63, 76

Tertúllian, Christian writer of the second century AD: Essay 12

Thebes, Theban: Essay 1–2, 5–6, 9, 17–21, 40, 43–44, 46–47, 49–50, 55, 57–8, 61–63, 65, 68–74, 76, 78–81, 85–86, 94–95, 97, 101, 103, 108, 109, 113, 121, 125–128; Soph. 135–136, 140–141, 148, 153, 181, 188, 194; Sen. 197, 199, 203–205, 208, 216, 218, 222, 225–226, 228, 232–233, 245

Tiberius, Tiberius Claudius Nero, the third Caesar: Essay 12

Titus, Titus Flavius Vespasianus, the eleventh Caesar, son of Vespasian★ and brother of Domitian★: Essay 128

Therámenes, Athenian intellectual and statesman, contemporary with Sophocles; he favored a more limited democracy: Essay 5, 7–8

Theseus, king of Athens,★ killer of the Minotaur (a hybrid creature, part man, part bull) and, perhaps unintentionally, of his own father, Aigeus, who commits suicide when he sees the black sails on the Athenian ship returning from Crete; Theseus was supposed to use white sails to indicate that he was still alive: Essay 36, 62, 71, 96; Sen. 220

Thrace, Thracians, area and people of northern Greece famous for their ferocity: Sen. 218

Thucýdides, Greek historian, contemporary of Sophocles: Essay 3, 6, 10, 87, 97–98, 100